LOW FAT & Loving It

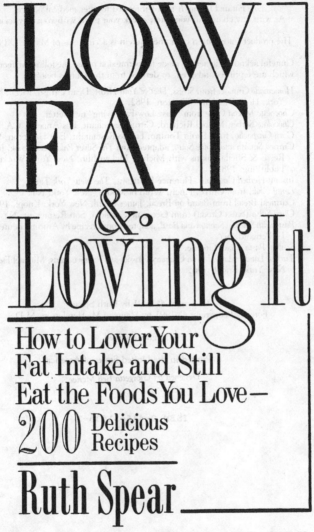

LOW FAT & Loving It

How to Lower Your Fat Intake and Still Eat the Foods You Love — 200 Delicious Recipes

Ruth Spear

Introduction by Maureen Henderson, M.D., D.P.H.

WARNER BOOKS

A Time Warner Company

The product information contained herein is accurate as of March 1, 1990.

Grateful acknowledgment is made for permission to use the following recipes, which are reprinted, adapted, or derived from the sources below.

Homemade Granola from *Stress, Diet & Your Heart*, Dean Ornish, M.D., New York: Holt, Rinehart, Winston, 1982.
Chocolate Mocha Cake from "Easy Low-Fat Living" newsletter.
Chocolate Sorbet, Michel Richard, Citrus Restaurant, Los Angeles, CA.
Corn Gazpacho, from Paolo Tonino, Fresno Restaurant, East Hampton, NY.
Curried Squash and Apple Soup, adapted from *The Silver Palate Cookbook*, Julee Rosso & Sheila Lukins with Michael McLaughlin, New York: Workman Publishing, 1982.
Instant Herbed Couscous, Florence Fabricant, *The New York Times*.
Lentil Chili, from Christi Finch, Word of Mouth, New York, NY.
Oatmeal Bread from *Beard on Bread*, James Beard, New York: Knopf, 1973.
Olive Salsa (Salsa Cruda) from Georgine Cavaiola, Sofi Restaurant, NY.
Pasta with Smoked Salmon and Basil, adapted from a recipe by Antoine Bouterin, Le Perigord, NY.
Scallop Pasta, Gael Greene.
Turkish Lamb, adapted from *Culinary Classics and Improvisations*, Michael Fields, New York: Knopf, 1965.

Printed in the United States of America

Designed by Giorgetta Bell McRee

ISBN 0-446-51535-3

To my mother and father

CONTENTS

Part III / APPENDIXES

FOREWORD

by Maureen M. Henderson, M.D.

My specialty is preventive medicine. After research on diet and the prevention of premature births, and on diet and the prevention of heart disease, I find myself deeply involved in research on diet and the prevention of cancer. My most recent study has made nutritional history. Two thousand healthy women volunteered to participate in a dietary prevention trial and proved that middle-aged American women *will* change their patterns from high- to low-fat cuisine and *will* maintain the low-fat pattern for at least four years. Why is diet so important in maintaining so many aspects of health?

We are what we eat! The amount and type of fat we eat today affects how our bodies look and feel tomorrow. For example, the fat we eat coats our red blood cells for the three months they are around. It also influences our fat tissue cells during the next one or two years. Luckily as we get older and wiser, we can improve our fat-eating habits and modify the effect of fat on our bodies.

Why does it take us so long to change our eating patterns? It may be due to an even better translation of the link between diet and good health, namely, "we are what we like to eat." This is something that we all know but rarely put into words. My parents realized this when their children, on their annual French vacations, would refuse to eat any dish not known and liked in their Scottish home. Even highly motivated volunteers in our dietary intervention studies to prevent breast cancer were reluctant to try new recipes unless they had tasted them first.

It's wonderful that Ruth Spear can show us how to continue to eat what we like while we make healthy changes in the fat we eat each day. She calls it "Low Fat and Loving It," but it actually is much more than that. She is telling us that with a little effort we can have healthy recipes for virtually every dish we like, and the low-fat version won't harm the taste.

If only I had had this book 25 years ago when my father had his first episode of coronary heart disease. He was the eldest of six brothers raised as healthy athletes in the Scottish lowlands. His parents worked hard to feed them three solid meals a day. Porridge, bacon and eggs for breakfast, soup, meat, potatoes and vegetables and dessert for lunch and again for dinner—not to mention whipping cream poured over both porridge and dessert at the table. Only one of those six brothers is still alive in his late seventies, and he spent his early professional years in India where he became addicted to vegetable dishes and physical fitness.

Once my father had his coronary heart disease warnings, the whole household adopted a restrained eating plan to cut down on saturated fat, cholesterol and calories. My father loved food, and although our regimen kept him alive and active for another twelve years, he would have enjoyed those years a lot more if he could have continued to eat the dishes he enjoyed so much. He was on a permanent fast as well as a pretty tasteless routine.

Today, it's relatively easy to change from whole-fat to low- or non-fat dairy products—there is a good range of choices in virtually every grocery store, and low-fat choices are easy to recognize. It's also becoming easier to identify lower fat cuts of meat and to find well-trimmed selections. It's much harder to sort out the cooking oils and salad dressings and select those that are low fat and not just low cholesterol. The same is true of breakfast cereals and cookies. Talking about breakfast cereals —watch the salt. The same is true of low-fat frozen foods—there seems to be serious competition among manufacturers to put more salt into their lower fat versions.

This book is appearing on the shelves at a time when we are pretty sure that a diet that provides no more than 30 percent of daily calories from fat is heart healthy. This is particularly true if the fat eaten is more or less equally balanced among the three common types of fat: saturated, which we get mostly from meat and dairy products; polyunsaturated, which come mostly from vegetables, grains and cooking and salad oils; and monounsaturated, found mostly in peanuts and salad dressings, as well as meat and poultry.

What we don't know yet is whether a diet with 30 percent of calories from fat is low enough to protect us against some of the common cancers that appear to be influenced by diet. Nor do we know exactly how the three different types of fat should be balanced to give maximum protection against these cancers. In other words, this book takes the average family as far as it can confidently go today. But it also lays the foundation for any further reductions that may be advantageous.

The only thing both heart and cancer specialists can agree upon without reservation is that total fat consumption should be cut to somewhere between 20 and 30 percent of calories. For most of us 25 percent is a reasonable goal, and make sure that you don't let up on fresh fruits and vegetables.

One of the most dramatic demonstrations of successful dietary prevention in our lifetime was the virtual disappearance of stomach cancer. This cancer was one of the most common, and it became one of the rarest in a matter of 30 years. Almost everyone agrees that it was prevented by cold storage and all its consequences. In one fell swoop we abandoned other chemical and physical means of preserving food, we stopped eating moldy fruits and vegetables, and we started eating fresh produce all year round.

There is, in fact, strong evidence suggesting that a year-round, well-balanced diet protects against a number of cancers. This has been supported by recent studies of the specific preventive influence of vitamins and minerals on the risk of getting cancer. These include cancers of the lung and esophagus, and probably bladder. But there is some likelihood that protection works best if the vitamins and minerals are part of a well-balanced, mixed diet rather than eaten as supplements. And when you reduce dietary fat, there may be some additional benefit from vitamins and minerals found in the foods used to replace fat calories. As yet, we don't know to what extent their addition will add further protection over and above that given by the reduction of dietary fat alone. If we are lucky, there will be a double bonus and we will be even healthier. This is not an unreasonable hope because most of the studies indicating that low-fat diets protect against cancer have made comparisons between countries with well-balanced high-fat diets and poorly balanced low-fat diets. Low-fat diets with a good balance of proteins, vitamins, and minerals have seldom been eaten on the scale we hope to eventually see— so we wait with anticipation to see how beneficial they can be.

As I read this book, I was constantly delighted and surprised by the breadth of the author's understanding of the successful strategies for fat reduction and her sympathetic handling of the barriers and frustrations met by committed low-fat eaters. She makes it clear that, in the long run, healthy low-fat eating depends upon successful shopping, cooking and meal planning. No amount of self-discipline at the table will make up for appropriate adaptation of these basic food use behaviors. Personally, I was delighted by the way she dealt with my own particular harassments: packed lunches and the need for quick, unplanned dinners. Professionally, I was impressed by the way she makes it seductively easy to begin to replace fat calories with calories from grains and other complex carbohydrates. This was the hardest part of the transformation from high-fat to low-fat healthy eating for most of our volunteers.

ACKNOWLEDGMENTS

A book like this can come about only through a great deal of input from others. Deepest thanks are due to Professor Paul Saltman, of the biology department of the University of California, San Diego, for valuable time spent in Aspen tutorials, sharing ideas, sharpening perspectives, and reading text; to my agent, Susan Lescher, for being always available to read text and recipes and make thoughtful suggestions; and to Lynne Hill of Nutrition Associates, Inc., who provided all the nutritional information and answered countless questions with patience and good cheer. Frances Rappa's kitchen expertise was invaluable in testing recipes.

I am grateful to Brooke Kroeger Goren for her editorial suggestions; to Arthur Adler for his meat expertise, and to all those who contributed recipes and ideas, especially Christi Finch and Gael Greene.

Particular thanks go to my editor, Liv Blumer, who shepherded this book through several drafts and whose personal dedication to this book inspired me and cheered me on, to Dr. Maureen Henderson for her diligent and expert eye and the enthusiasm with which she embraced this project, and to my husband, Harvey Spear, who read each draft with a keen and sensitive eye and kept his patience when mine was long gone. I also want to thank Dr. Ernst Wynder of the American Health Foundation, whose views on prevention first defined for me the role of dietary fat in disease and the responsibility food writers have to pass the word along.

INTRODUCTION

As far back as I can remember I have been interested in and excited by food. It is an important part of my family life, not in the sense that we eat fancy or elaborate things, but food is taken seriously and seriously enjoyed. Whenever I travel, food shops are the first windows I look into—I feel that if I understand what people eat, I will know them better. I've always been an enthusiastic cook so that, as a writer, specializing in food writing was a logical choice.

My first interest in the relationship between food and health had to do with my husband, who, when we married 25 years ago, was forever trying to lose weight and was committed to eating only steak and salad, which I found unbelievably dull. It didn't seem to work, because he kept gaining and losing what seemed to be the same six pounds. He also had an astronomical blood cholesterol level of 340 and his father had died of coronary heart disease. (Later, his brother required a quintuple bypass.)

But it was his weight problem and the boring steak dinners that made me first take a long look at meat. I knew it was fatty; you could *see* it, for God's sake, and I got the idea that what made you fat was—fat. It seemed to me that the easiest way to lower his intake of fat was to reduce the quantity of meat we ate by adding other, different foods to our meals. So I began cooking dinners built around vegetables, rice, beans, interesting breads—the things I liked to eat.

The potatoes I served practically gave him a heart attack from fear. "THIS IS A STARCH!" he would bellow. "STARCHES MAKE YOU FAT!" He said the same thing about rice and bread. But to please me, he ate them. It was one baby step in the direction we all know today is the healthful way to eat. Of course, we still had a long way to go. Like most people 20 years ago, our idea of good nutrition was mainly avoiding junk food. We still buttered our bread in restaurants, ate Eggs Benedict, bacon, quiche, pâté, cheese with our salad, whipped cream or the new discovery, *crème fraiche*, with our desserts, and ice cream whenever we felt like it.

Anyway, even with such forays into fat as would be unthinkable for us today, our way of eating changed bit by bit. My husband, who had also begun to exercise moderately but regularly, found himself losing weight—five or six pounds a year at first, later on a little less—which, over a ten-year period, resulted in a new, svelte person who was interested in staying that way. What's more, his cholesterol level dropped steadily. By the time articles began to appear in the newspapers about the dangerous relationship between high-fat diets and cardiovascular disease, he was already ahead of the game.

Around this time, the late 1970s, I was hard at work on my second cookbook, on fish and shellfish. With 600 recipes to make and test (and eat) there wasn't much time to eat anything else. My husband dropped more weight and I went from a size 10 to a size 8. His cholesterol level kept on dropping. By this time we were crazy about the rice pilafs, the main-course salads, and the pastas, not to mention all that fish and shellfish, and we loved the way we looked and felt. But it didn't all come together until later, not even when I was diagnosed with an early breast cancer in 1981. I had a lumpectomy and radiation and after a couple of years regarded myself as cured. In 1984, a new tumor turned up in the other breast, smaller than the first, but unfortunately it had begun to spread to the underarm lymph nodes. It was only after I recovered somewhat from the shock of learning that I would have to undergo chemotherapy that I began to scutinize what *I* ate.

I wanted to do whatever wasn't crazy to maximize my chances to live, to get through the ordeal and have as normal a life as possible. My oncologist gave me a list of suggestions, which included cutting down animal fat consumption and replacing many of the foods containing them with complex carbohydrates—starchy foods, grains, fruits, and vegetables. If this could help me avoid gaining the weight often associated with a chemotherapy regime, I thought, why not. There was also talk, then, about a fat–breast cancer link, but my reason was more immediate: if I was going to lose my hair and feel awful, at least I didn't need to be huge to further depress myself.

By this time I was writing a vegetable cookbook, so it really wasn't hard to concentrate on eating vegetables, legumes, and grains. I still ate poultry, fish, and meat, but in small amounts and no more than three times a week. Whether the way I ate affected the way my body handled the toxic chemicals cannot be proven. Although there were times I felt rotten, I neither threw up nor gained weight. When the chemo was over, the way we ate seemed perfectly normal; we had adopted a food lifestyle I truly liked. I didn't feel deprived—I felt only joy that I'd come through and a conviction that our low-fat diet had something to do with it. I can truly say that since then, we have never eaten better or enjoyed our food more. It hasn't seemed hard or unpleasant to do, and though devising a low-fat eating plan requires some education and attention at first, it soon becomes second nature.

What This Book Is and Isn't About

And that is what this book is about; a low-fat plan for eating well and staying healthy as a lifelong pursuit. It isn't about a crazy diet or deprivation. It relies on your good sense and love of life to maximize your chances for longevity by limiting certain foods while eating more of others. There are only a few no-nos, strictly speaking, but a good number of suggestions, which aim to lower your over-all intake of health-damaging fatty foods.

Although dieting in order to lose weight is not the primary aim of my low-fat plan, it is a pleasant bonus. I can virtually guarantee that if you gradually phase in some of the modifications and changes I suggest, so that no more than 25 percent of your calories come from fat, you will lose weight. Combine the plan with any moderate but regular exercise (even walking briskly for 45 minutes 3 times a week) and the weight will stay off.

How You Do It

The simple key is to monitor the amount of fat you eat and watch portion size. This becomes a way of life as opposed to being on a "diet," because you do it in the most natural, pleasurable way possible *for you.* Of course, it would be a cinch to lower your fat consumption by eating little or no meat and naked salads, avoiding dairy products and desserts, and leaving the butter and oil out of everything. I can tell you, however, that if you were to follow such a stringent plan, you would probably get a serious case of gustatory *ennui* or downright depression, and sooner or later you'd go back to your old unhealthy habits. Once I show you which foods contain a lot of fat, either limit them or save them for the occasional treat and concentrate on the good, tasty ones that are at the lower end of the fat spectrum. Believe it or not, over time your taste for some of the fatty foods you now enjoy will fade, as you gradually substitute less fatty alternatives. I promise you fun, too. The strategies you develop as you tailor your new eating repertoire will give you a high sense of food adventure. You'll love eating healthily, while loving what you eat. I do, and I can honestly say that I never have a sense that I'm making a sacrifice. There are so many good low-fat foods to eat and so many ways to reach your goal.

The eating plan I would like to see you develop and use for the rest of your life is founded on two principles: recognizing the foods you like that are not high in fat calories and learning to trade off, or compensate, when you do indulge in some high-fat eating. While you are discovering and adding some wonderful low-fat foods to your life, you'll be phasing out some of the higher-fat ones you've been used to eating. To do this easily you have to learn: (1) the fat content of the foods you commonly eat; (2) a sense of what constitutes a portion (because a triple portion of chicken may add up to more fat grams than a smaller portion of steak); and (3) after determining *your* ideal daily fat allowance, the way to keep track of fat so you'll know the amount of fat grams you have to "spend" in a day. You'll also learn which foods are so disproportionately high in fat that they become too "expensive" in terms of fat grams, although no food is forbidden as long as you count it in and compensate for it with low-fat foods at the next meal. It's all in knowing how to trade off.

I'll help you shape this new lifestyle by providing enough information to give you a sound basis for making healthful changes, sharing with you what's worked for me and my family and guiding you to some foods that should play a significant role in your revamped diet. I've included over 200 delicious recipes you can draw on, so you can taste what a joyful eating experience the low-fat way of life can be. Don't coerce yourself or get the guilts—this experience is for you and for your life, and it should be a joy.

RUTH SPEAR
East Hampton, New York

Part I
UNDERSTANDING FAT

1

THE GOOD LIFE AND WHY IT'S BAD FOR US

If you are an average American, nearly 40 out of every 100 calories you consume daily are taken in the form of pure fat, whether the fat is visible (as in oil, margarine, and butter) or invisible (meat, dairy products, nuts, etc.). This makes the American diet one of the fattiest in the world, and you a candidate for one or more of the major killer diseases our society has to offer.

Diet and Heart Disease

Our high-fat diet first drew medical attention because of an increasing awareness of the relation between serum cholesterol levels and heart disease, the leading cause of death in this country. In the long-term Framingham Heart Study, men with an average serum cholesterol level of 260 milligrams had a subsequent heart attack rate three times greater than those men with an average cholesterol level below 195 milligrams.

In 1984 a study by the National Heart, Lung and Blood Institute (NHLB) called the Coronary Primary Prevention Trial (CPPT) further demonstrated, for the first time, that lowering cholesterol levels can *lower* men's risk. Participants in the study all followed diets designed to lower cholesterol; a majority were also given a cholesterol-lowering drug. The study showed that every 1 percent reduction in serum cholesterol equated with a 2 percent reduction in the incidence of coronary heart disease.

While evidence showing the benefit of dietary intervention unassisted by drugs remained sketchy (the CPPT sample only included middle-aged men with high serum cholesterol levels to start with), these studies did serve to focus media attention on the value of limiting dietary cholesterol and ways to do it. The suggestion was there.

Early in 1989, federal health officials recommended for the first time that all Americans, not just those with high cholesterol levels, reduce the fat content of their diets to lower heart disease. The new report was resoundingly endorsed by a coalition of no less than 38 federal agencies, organizations of health professionals, and health organizations. The panel members said that the information that has been accumulating for years indicates that everyone over the age of two would benefit from a low-fat, low-cholesterol diet. In particular, people are advised to keep the fat content of foods firmly in mind as they select them at grocery stores and in restaurants.

Diet and Other Diseases

Evidence has been mounting that strongly implicates dietary fats not only in heart and circulatory system diseases but also in late-onset diabetes and several types of cancer. Data collected in 36 countries show that where fat consumption is high (with one exception—Finland) so is the incidence of breast cancer. And where the breast cancer rate is high, the colon cancer rate is usually high too. Here in the United States, Seventh Day Adventists, roughly half of whom are vegetarians (the other half eat meat sparingly), have less breast and colon cancer than the rest of the population.

Although many other lifestyle factors besides diet may play a role in evidence of this sort, it was persuasive enough that in the early 1980s virtually every major organization devoted to improving the health of the American public officially recommended that we change the way we eat, with special emphasis on cutting down fat intake.

In 1982, the Committee on Diet, Nutrition and Cancer of the highly respected National Research Council (the research arm of the National Academy of Sciences, a federally chartered but independent organization of scientists that studies technical issues for the government) issued interim dietary guidelines based on the fat–cancer link, recommending that the then-current 40 percent fat intake level be reduced to 30 percent of calories or less.

Soon after, The American Heart Association and the American Cancer Society issued similar diet plans aimed at reducing the consumption of animal fats and increasing the consumption of fiber.

In 1988, Surgeon General of the United States C. Everett Koop issued the Surgeon General's Report on Nutrition and Health, reviewing the ways certain dietary factors influence specific diseases. Concluded Koop: Reduction of fat intake is the nation's *first* dietary priority.

Then, in February 1989, the National Research Council issued another study, drawing on earlier findings but going well beyond them, in recommending that Americans eat less salt, fat, and dietary cholesterol to avoid a wide range of chronic diseases. The report addressed the role diet plays in cardiovascular disease, cancer, diabetes, obesity, osteoporosis, chronic liver and kidney diseases, and even tooth decay.

The advice included cutting total fat intake to 30 percent or less of total calories and saturated fat (see page 53–59) to less than 10 percent, with a daily cholesterol intake of 300 milligrams or less. The report also cited evidence that reducing total fat to even less than 30 percent "may confer even greater health benefits" in terms of cardiovascular disease and certain kinds of cancer.

The significant recommendation was to increase consumption of complex carbohydrates (vegetables, fruits, legumes, and whole grains) to 55 percent of total calories.

Regarding protein, which Americans are thought to consume to excess, it was recommended that it be cut to no more than twice the RDA—or about what you get in one hamburger.

Clearly the connection between what we eat and how well we are—and remain—was at last being taken very seriously.

The Diet–Cancer Link

One of the most encouraging facts to emerge from cancer research in this decade is the accumulating evidence that nutrition may be a factor in the development of certain cancers. Why encouraging? Because one of the few things we can control and change is what we put in our mouths. Based on hundreds of studies, the National Cancer Institute estimates that *about one third of all cancers are in some way linked to what we eat.* One group of researchers estimated the proportion of cancer deaths attributable to diet to be a staggering 40 percent for men and 60 percent for women. Yet many Americans remain either unaware of the diet–disease connection or unsure of what action to take.

Diet and Breast Cancer

American women have one of the highest rates of breast cancer in the world; about one in nine develop this potentially deadly disease. It is second only to lung cancer as the leading cause of cancer deaths in women. Aside from known risk factors like having a family history of breast cancer, the role of diet in the development of this disease is of particular concern.

Animal experiments have provided abundant evidence that fat, protein, and calorie intake influence the promotion of mammary, or breast, tumors. Over 40 years ago, a series of experiments carried out by researcher Dr. Albert Tannenbaum at the Michael Reese hospital in Chicago showed that animals treated with carcinogens and given high levels of fat in their diet developed more breast cancers than those fed a lowfat diet. Results of these experiments were published in the 1940s and 1950s, to which not much attention was paid, until the U.N. Food and Agriculture Organization published a report on worldwide food intake in 1975. Comparing fat consumption of different countries, Canadian biochemist Kenneth Carroll noted that low breast cancer mortality seemed to prevail in countries with low fat intake (see graph below) while the opposite was true of high fat intake. Could there be a link between a population's fat consumption and its breast cancer rate?

The Japanese diet is one of the lowest in fat in the world. Among Japanese farmers and fishermen, it hovers around 11 percent of calories from fat versus 40 percent in the U.S. Sumo wrestlers notwithstanding, obesity, until recently, was virtually unknown. (In fact, the Japanese have the highest life expectancy in the world, which many experts credit to their low-meat, high-fiber, heavily fish-based diet.) The Japanese are

DIETARY FAT INTAKE IN RELATION TO BREAST CANCER–RELATED DEATH RATE.

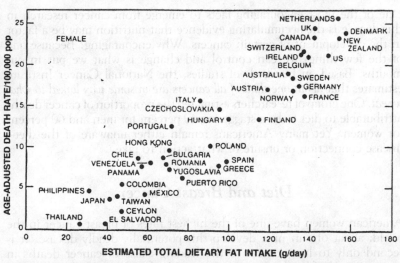

SOURCE: Carroll, K.K., and Khor, H.T., 1975. Dietary Fat in Relation to Tumorigenosis.

exposed to as much pollution as we are; our educational and health patterns are similar. Yet Japan's breast cancer rate is only one fifth that of the United States, up from one tenth due to greater post-war contact with the U.S. Furthermore, when the Japanese migrate to Hawaii and California, the next generation's breast cancer death rate rises to approximate that of Americans, narrowing the possibility of causes other than diet.

More evidence of the relationship between a high-fat diet and an increased risk of breast cancer appeared in a 1989 study of 250 Italian breast cancer patients, living in a region with very diverse ingrained eating patterns, which concluded: "A diet rich in fat, saturated fat or animal proteins may be associated with a two-fold to three-fold increase in a woman's risk of breast cancer." Although the women with breast cancer did consume moderately higher amounts of calories than the healthy controls, the significant factor appeared to be their higher consumption of high-fat cheese, whole milk, and other fat-rich dairy products.

How can women ignore such dramatic evidence? Even if all the studies turn out to be flawed, lowering consumption of fatty foods is usually accompanied by weight loss—and there are certainly worse fates than being svelte!

More research is needed to determine just how valid the association is between fat intake and breast cancer. While almost no one suggests that all American women should adopt a 20 percent fat diet (considered the average level needed to cut breast cancer rates in half) the consensus is the recommendation to lower current fat intake to, *at most*, 30 percent of one's daily calories.

Diet and Other Cancers

In the United States cancer of the colon and rectum is the second most common cancer in men and third most common in women. Evidence is accumulating that diet is almost surely a causal factor; both animals and people who eat high-fat, low-fiber diets get colon cancer more often. Relatively high-fat diets are thought to release large amounts of bile acids into the colon, which may be converted by colonic bacteria into cancer-causing byproducts. (Here is where fiber is hypothesized to come in: It may reduce the concentration of these byproducts by moving waste matter—and any carcinogens—out of the intestines more rapidly.)

Researchers have always been puzzled as to why those who dwell in rich countries have different kinds of cancers from those who live at or near the poverty level. Besides cancers of the breast, colon, and rectum, cancers of the prostate, ovary and endometrium (the lining of the uterus) seem to afflict the affluent. Though unproven, dietary fat is one hypothesis, which new studies are making ever more compelling. Early findings from a study of the eating habits of 6,500 Chinese, the most comprehensive study ever mounted to assess the relationship between diet and the risk of developing disease, suggests strongly that an eating plan based on plant rather than animal food is more likely to promote health. For example, serum cholesterol levels in China range from 88 to 165 milligrams per 100 milliliters of blood plasma, making their high our low. Beyond cholesterol, the data from the Chinese study offers us much food for thought:

• Protein consumption, especially from animal sources, is linked to rates of chronic disease. Americans consume a third more protein than the Chinese. Only 7 percent of the protein eaten by Chinese comes from animals, compared with 70 percent for Americans. The highest rate of heart disease, diabetes, and cancer—the Western diseases of affluence —are found in areas of China where the people eat the most protein and the most animal protein.

• A diet rich in calories, protein, calcium, and fat promotes rapid growth early in life and may also increase a woman's risk of developing cancer of the reproductive organs, including the breast. Along with accelerated growth, diets like ours promote early menarche, which is associated with high breast cancer rates. Chinese women, who rarely have these cancers, start menstruating three to six years later than Americans.

• Osteoporosis is uncommon among the Chinese, though they do not consume dairy products and obtain their calcium instead from vegetables.

• Obesity seems to be related more to *what* people eat than the quantity. Adjusted for height, the Chinese consume 20 percent more calories than Americans, yet Americans are fatter by 25 percent. While this may relate, at least in part, to greater physical activity on the part of the Chinese, researchers note that the Chinese eat only about a third of the fat Americans consume and twice as much starch. It is thought that the body may store fat easily but expends as heat a larger proportion of carbohydrates consumed.

The Chinese data leads some experts to think that reducing dietary fat to less than 30 percent, the current recommendation in this country, may not be enough and that 20 percent of calories from fat would significantly lower heart disease and cancer risks.

Diet and Diabetes

About 11 million Americans are estimated to suffer from the spectrum of conditions called diabetes, characterized by elevated concentrations of glucose in the blood and severe, long-term physical complications. In our country, this disease is directly responsible for nearly 36,000 deaths each year, and is a contributing cause in thousands of other deaths.

There are two major forms of diabetes: Type I, or insulin dependent (formerly known as juvenile-onset diabetes), which usually appears before age 40, begins abruptly, and accounts for about 4 percent of all cases; and Type II, which usually comes on gradually in mid-life, most commonly among people who are overweight or obese. The type associated with obesity is far and away the most common.

Throughout history, physicians and researchers have rarely agreed on the best approach to diabetes, although most do agree that nutrition plays a pivotal role. Current research suggests that diets relatively low in fat, cholesterol, salt, and protein can reduce the risk of the cardiovascular, hypertensive, and renal complications of the disease. Since obesity greatly increases the risk of developing Type II diabetes, the expert recommendations, which by now should have a familiar ring, are: reduce fat intake; increase foods containing complex carbohydrates and soluble fibers; and combine these with appropriate levels of physical activity.

If fat is the villain in so many diseases, why are we eating so much of it? Let's take a look at where it comes from.

2

FOCUSING ON FAT

If you are like a lot of people you may find it hard at first to accept the basic premise that almost half the food you have been eating is composed of pure fat. Here's how it breaks down, according to a government survey: the meats we eat supply roughly one fourth of our total fat intake; the next big chunk comes from dairy products—milk, cheese, and ice cream. Cooking fats and several of the super-fatty foods that Americans adore, like bacon, peanut butter, and cream cheese, provide the rest.

All the foods you love most, right? So must you then turn your back on all your favorite foods for a longer, healthier life? Not really. Changes do have to be made, and one way to start is by making the small, easy ones at first. Begin by replacing two meat dinners each week with a pasta-and-vegetable dish or a seafood dish that can be eaten with a filling, nourishing grain, like a seafood stew with rice. When you do eat meat, choose leaner cuts of beef, like top round or eye of round, leg of lamb or pork tenderloin. Trim all exterior fat before cooking. Pour off what accumulates in the pan. Check your supermarket for beef from cattle especially bred for leanness.

Plan dinners to include terrific vegetables and more starchy foods like beans, rice, potatoes. See if you can use less butter and oil in cooking. Reduce the oil in your salad dressing and compensate with a mellow vinegar or herbs. Dress salads sparingly. Find a bread that is so good you won't need to butter it, and eat it with your dinner or with the salad. The next time you have chicken, try a tasty recipe that doesn't include the skin, since it contains most of the chicken's fat, which doubles the fat calories.

You don't have to say goodbye forever to any food, unless you really lose interest in it. You will see, by the time you finish these chapters, that what I'm proposing is this: Eat less fat, not less food. Less meat, more starchy foods. More rice, more beans, more vegetables, more fruit. More good bread, less processed stuff. You won't go hungry: Simply *eat less fat.* This means not only saturated fat like the fat in beef, but *fat from all sources.*

Your next aim is to replace those fatty foods with foods selected from the categories mentioned above that *you,* personally, find delicious. Don't eat anything you don't like. Don't eliminate your favorites for the moment, just eat them less frequently and in smaller amounts. Changing the way you eat permanently is a lot easier when it's done in stages. Try reworking your pet recipes after looking at the recipe substitution suggestions on page 35. Then *you* can decide where, when, and how you want to cut back and even what you might eventually want to cut out. Give yourself a daily fat allowance (Chapter 4 tells you how) and have fun deciding how to spend it. You may find, as I did eventually, that the foods you crave become the ones that are best for you.

Fat: What It Is and Where It Comes From

When people ask me for advice on lowering their fat intake, it seems that they are most confused about fat and cholesterol and what foods are high in fat, aside from the obvious sources like butter and meat. This is further complicated by the erroneous perception that lowering intake of foods with cholesterol is what is meant by a "low-fat diet." (Actually, cholesterol is just one of eight or nine kinds of fat present in the food we eat.) Knowing about fats and how they work may help you get on more intimate terms with the food you put in your body.

Dietary fat is composed of three fatty acids called saturated, monounsaturated, and polyunsaturated. Foods are classified by the fatty acid that predominates. The second two fatty acids are less saturated than the first. The less saturated fatty acids are, the softer or more liquid they are.

SATURATED FATS

Highly *saturated* fats are easily recognizable because they are hard at room temperature, like butter, lard, or the fat marbled in steaks. Consuming saturated fats tends to raise cholesterol levels in the blood (known as *serum cholesterol*) even though most serum cholesterol is produced by the body itself. This raises your risk of heart disease.

Sources of saturated fat include most fat from animal sources—such as beef, pork, lamb, veal, poultry—plus certain fish, margarine, and hydrogenated or partially hydrogenated vegetable oil. Coconut oil, along with palm oil, is one of the few vegetable oils consisting almost entirely of saturated fatty acids (86 percent). It is found in processed foods, non-dairy creamers and the solid white vegetable shortening used in deep-frying.

Because saturated fats are linked not only to cardiovascular disease but also to cancers of the colon, breast, and prostate, and to diabetes, experts believe we should restrict them to not more than 10 percent—or roughly one third—of your *total daily fat intake*. If you follow current guidelines, daily fat intake should be no more than 30 percent of your *total daily calories*, a good interim fat consumption goal.

You'll learn how to determine your ideal total daily fat intake in Chapter 4.

MONOUNSATURATES

Primarily monounsaturated fats are liquid at room temperature and be-come viscous or hard when refrigerated. Food sources are olives, olive oil, peanuts, peanut oil, avocados and Canola oil, which is made from rapeseed. Recent research indicates monounsaturates may lower blood cholesterol in a way that improves the balance of the more protective high-density to the more harmful low-density lipoprotein compounds which transport fat throughout the body.

Can you go hog-wild eating these? No, because until we know a lot more than we do now, we're trying to reduce fat intake across the board. So your total fat intake should be capped at 30 percent of all the calories you eat and monounsaturated fat ideally should represent about one third your fat or 10 percent of your total calories.

POLYUNSATURATES

These are fats found primarily in vegetables and vegetable oils such as soybean, safflower, sunflower, sesame, cottonseed, and Canola oils. They are liquid at room temperature and remain that way when refrigerated. In the early days of raising fat consciousness, it was thought that switching to them was a guarantee against heart disease. But while some studies indicate polyunsaturates can lower cholesterol in the blood, they have also been directly linked to cancer in laboratory animals and indirectly to cancer in humans. Thus, polyunsaturates should not be increased beyond the necessary amount, currently thought to represent another (10 percent) of your daily calorie intake.

OMEGA-3S

Different fats function differently in the body. Recent research has identified a special type of polyunsaturated fatty acid—the omega-3s—found in deep-water fatty fishes such as salmon, sardines, and mackerel. Two of the main omegas, EPA and DHA, seem to have specific cardiovascular benefits—namely, lowered blood pressure, less clumping of blood platelets, and fewer blood clots. The inhibition of arterial inflammation and the lowering of triglycerides are other benefits and some studies indicate these fatty acids may retard the spread of malignant growths as well.

HYDROGENATED FATS

It would seem, on quick inspection, that any fat from a vegetable source would be more desirable than those from animal sources because they are more unsaturated and contain no cholesterol. When vegetable oils are exposed to a commercial process called hydrogenation, however, they change from a liquid to a semi-solid state, and therefore are more saturated and less healthy. A stick of margarine that is as firm as butter at room temperature has gone through the hydrogenation process and therefore part of its polyunsaturated fatty acids have been turned into saturated ones. Soybean oil, in the same low-saturated range (15 percent) as corn and safflower oil, is frequently hydrogenated to make products like Crisco, and ends up being closer to 25 percent.

Cholesterol

Cholesterol is a waxy, fatty substance, one of a number of substances called lipids, found only in animals and foods deriving from animal sources. Most of the cholesterol in your blood is manufactured by your body, primarily by the liver. Varying amounts, usually about 1,000 milligrams a day, are produced from the fat, protein, and carbohydrates you eat. In addition, the average American consumes, on the average, 400 to 500 milligrams of what can be considered another type of cholesterol (although there is no metabolic difference between the two) in foods eaten daily. This is the cholesterol we take in from our food, called *dietary* or *preformed* cholesterol.

Dietary cholesterol is found only in foods derived from animals (meat, poultry, fish, eggs, and dairy products); it is not present in plants. The fat in one's diet, however (not only how much, but what kind), also contributes to serum cholesterol, the cholesterol level in the bloodstream.

Ironically, we need cholesterol. Our bodies use it to make bile, which allows us to digest fats, and to form cell membranes, sex hormones, and other substances vital to the body. Since cholesterol is both synthesized in the body and obtained from the diet, however, we don't have to eat large amounts of cholesterol-rich foods to make sure we're amply supplied. In fact, when too much cholesterol is present, it can accumulate in the walls of blood vessels, resulting in a condition known as atherosclerosis. Nodules, called plaques, are formed, which impede the flow of blood and favor the formation of blood clots. The resultant blockage may ultimately cut off blood flow to a vital organ; in the coronary arteries blockage leads to a heart attack, and in the cerebral arteries, it can cause a stroke.

It's important to understand that your cholesterol can be raised in two ways—by consuming any and all foods *containing cholesterol*; and/or by eating a food *containing saturated fat*, which raises your serum cholesterol (the cholesterol in your blood). Remember that a food can contain saturated fat even though it contains no cholesterol, like stick margarine and coconut oil or any of the partially hydrogenated fats.

WHAT ARE WE DOING ABOUT CHOLESTEROL?

Although more people have a heightened awareness of the dangers of excess cholesterol than a decade ago, they still represent only about 20 percent of the population. One recent poll determined that 79 percent of us don't even know what our cholesterol levels *are*, let alone what they *should* be. Another study shows that more than one third of Americans 20 years old and above, or 36 percent of adults, need to lower their blood cholesterol because they are at increased risk for coronary heart disease.

WHAT LEVEL IS DANGEROUS?

In 1987, health experts established a "dangerously high" risk level of 240 milligrams of cholesterol per 100 milliliters of blood. At that time it was estimated that 40 million Americans would be in the danger zone and should take steps to correctly assess and reduce their risk. But this alert level did not take into account the balance of good (HDL) and bad (LDL) components of total cholesterol. Nor did it give weight to the presence or absence in individuals of *other* coronary risk factors like cigarette smoking and high blood pressure. Thus, by newly establishing high-risk categories as shown in the chart below, many more people fell into the net than were previously thought to exist.

The latest recommendation for all adults by the National Cholesterol Education Program (NCEP) organized by the National Institutes of Health and other major health organizations is:

TOTAL CHOLESTEROL	LDL
(mg/dl)	*(mg/dl)*

	TOTAL CHOLESTEROL *(mg/dl)*	LDL *(mg/dl)*
Desirable	under 200	under 130
Borderline high	200–239	130–159
High	240 or more	160 or more

Your total, or serum, cholesterol level refers to the amount of cholesterol, measured in milligrams, per 100 milliliters (1 deciliter) of blood. Thus a cholesterol level of 200 means 200 milligrams of cholesterol per 100 milliliters of blood. An LDL reading of, say, 140, would put you in the "borderline high," even if your cholesterol reading was "desirable."

Physicians are particularly concerned about patients who show a high level of LDL, the artery-clogger, and a low amount of HDL, which is thought to confer some protection against heart disease.

Ideally, LDL ought to be no higher than 100, and HDL above 40. Anyone with an LDL count over 160 ought to be on a low-fat, low-cholesterol diet regardless of what the HDL is. The same holds true for anyone with an LDL count of 140 and an HDL of less than 40.

"GOOD" CHOLESTEROL AND "BAD" CHOLESTEROL

To adequately gauge the risk of heart disease, it's important to know not only how much cholesterol is in the bloodstream, but also how it's being transported. Here's where the HDLs and LDLs come in. What's called "good" cholesterol is a complex particle assembled in the liver called high-density lipoprotein, or HDL. As it circulates in the bloodstream, the sturdy HDL seems to have the ability to pick up cholesterol and haul it back to the liver for reprocessing or excretion.

The LDL, or low-density lipoprotein, on the other hand, is a delivery system, carrying cholesterol through the circulatory system and dropping it off where needed for cell building. Seemingly unable to make it back to the liver with any excess, it deposits unused residues in arterial walls.

If you have trouble remembering which is which, think of HDLs as pick-ups or garbage trucks, collecting and carrying fat out of the blood, and LDL as delivery vans, delivering fat where needed and also depositing excess amounts. Or think "H" for "helpful, "L" for "lousy."

The proportion of LDLs to HDLs in the bloodstream now is thought to affect the development of atherosclerosis as well as and perhaps even *more* than the overall serum cholesterol level. The higher the relative amount of the HDLs, the lower the risk of heart disease. Women, for example, usually have relatively higher levels than men; non-smokers more than smokers. Those who exercise also have high HDL levels, as do those who drink alcohol in moderation. Obesity correlates with low levels. But HDLs come in various forms and the protective strength of each one of them has not yet been defined.

Knowing the terms is helpful in reading about cholesterol and understanding and discussing your blood profile with your physician.

Some of the measures you can take to lower total blood cholesterol that can improve the *ratio* between HDLs and LDLs are:

• Cut down on dietary cholesterol (aim for no more than 300 mg daily).
• Cut saturated fats to less than 10 percent of daily caloric intake.
• Consume more soluble fiber (see Chapter 5).
• Consume more fish, especially those rich in omega-3 fatty acids.
• Exercise more.
• Don't smoke.

As far as cholesterol-lowering drug therapy is concerned, it is generally considered only as a last resort, when dietary and lifestyle changes haven't worked.

THE CHOLESTEROL CONTROVERSY

The role of cholesterol in cardiovascular health is not a fad that is going to go away, despite a 1989 book by Thomas J. Moore, *Heart Failure*, which makes the case that the role of cholesterol in heart disease is not proven. To those not familiar with the reams of scientific research on the subject, Moore's conclusions might make sense. My view, shared by many in the scientific community, is that Moore is wrong, and that cholesterol is clearly a matter of concern.

Among other things, Moore charges that there is no evidence, after ten years of research, that lowering your cholesterol will lengthen your life. But the studies Moore cites were not designed to show this; rather they sought to show that lowering cholesterol would *prevent fatal and non-fatal heart attacks*. We do not know whether reducing the total amount of fat in the diet (hence, lowering cholesterol) has the potential of reducing total mortality as well.

Isn't it better to be safe than sorry?

3
GETTING TO KNOW YOUR FOOD

It's easier to keep track of the fats you consume if you understand which foods are naturally high in fat. It's also easier to figure out pleasant and acceptable changes in eating habits when you know something about how fats function in the foods you like.

Why We Like Fat

Fat is present in both animal and vegetable products. While people will confess a weakness for chocolate or sweets, few will acknowledge they are hooked on fat. That is because fat is not, strictly speaking, a taste; it is, rather, a taste hidden by other flavors. It is not the frying grease we adore in French fries even though it is the fat that makes the potatoes taste so good. We do not crave the taste of butterfat in ice cream and cheese, although this is what makes them good as well. Fat dissolves the aromatic compounds of foods so they get to the taste buds more easily. And because fat coats the taste buds, fat is what you experience as a *taste*. It also adds a texture that you experience as pleasurable. The experts call it "mouthfeel." Giving up fat-laden foods (or eating them only occasionally) amounts to a re-education of your taste buds, as well as a revamping of the way you buy and prepare food or order it in a restaurant.

Here is some background information that will help you in planning meals and adapting your favorite recipes so they have a lower fat content. (You'll find more tips on eliminating fat throughout this book.) Your ultimate aim is to balance your intake of higher-fat foods with those that are lower in fat. Creamy soups, meat, and desserts can still be part of your life. You'll just learn how to trade off a high-fat food for a low-fat one.

Fats in Cooking

Fats give food flavor and texture and are especially important in baked products. Eating would be dreary without fats, but they can be reduced; it just takes some experimentation. Start by reducing the amount called for in a recipe by one third; if that works, you might want to consider cutting down further and see if the result is still acceptable, and so on. Use non-stick pans wherever possible.

Meats

Where fat is concerned, meat has gotten a very bad press. There's no doubt that Americans eat too much of it, and they favor fatty cuts. Even after all visible fat is trimmed from the meat we eat, a substantial portion of fat still remains, running through the flesh. These tiny streaks of fat interlaced with lean muscle tissue are called "marbling." The more marbled the meat, the more tender and delicious it is—and, alas, the more fat it contains. Thus, a 4-ounce serving of well-trimmed beef, ground, can still draw as much as 31 percent of its calories from fat. You can expect 3 ounces of well-trimmed T-bone or Porterhouse to contain 11 and 15 grams of fat respectively per serving. And most people eat more than 3 ounces.

If you crave beef, consider some of the leanest cuts like "select" grade eye of round, top round, top loin, tenderloin and sirloin. A well-trimmed 3-ounce serving (after cooking) of any of these cuts has fewer than 180 calories and less than 8 grams of fat.

Veal is the meat generally lowest in fat, followed by lean ham. By trimming portions well, you can decrease the fat content considerably. Remember, however, that even closely trimmed meat is a high-fat item. And if it's not well trimmed and you eat it three or four times a week, you simply cannot manage a low-fat diet! It is manageable if you eat meat once or twice a week and you change the nature of the meat you eat.

CHOOSING THE LEANER MEATS

Meat (3 ounces cooked)	Calories	Fat (grams)	Cholesterol
Eye of round, roasted	143	4	59
Round tip, roasted	157	6	69
Top round, broiled	153	4	71
Top sirloin, broiled	166	6	76
Tenderloin, broiled	179	9	71
Chuck or round, ground, 17% fat	218	14	71
Veal chop, loin cut, broiled	149	6	90
Veal cutlet or roast, round cut, leg	128	24	88
Veal ground, lean, broiled	146	16	88
leg of lamb, whole, roasted	162	7	76
Lamb chop, loin cut, broiled	184	8	81
Pork tenderloin, roasted	141	4	79
Ham, fresh, whole, roasted	187	9	82
Ham, canned, extra lean	102	4	33

Beef figures are averages of the 3 grades.

SOURCE: USDA Agriculture Handbooks No. 8–10, 8–13, 8–17. Values are for meats trimmed and cooked without added fat.

Should I Give Meat Up?

I do not suggest that anyone give up meat unless he or she really wants to. Meat contains a number of valuable nutrients, among them iron, copper, zinc, manganese, B6 (piridoxine), B12, folic acid, and niacin. You can get these nutrients in other foods, but it's not as easy. Even though meats deliver the greatest amount of dietary fat, they are relatively easy to work with in your new eating scheme. You simply plan fewer meals around them, increase your use of fish and chicken and exercise strict control over portion size. These are the key elements in lowering fat intake while still eating many of the foods you like.

The 16-ounce steakhouse steaks and half-pound chopped meat burgers we are accustomed to have no place in a low-fat lifestyle. Even a relatively lean meat like leg of lamb can become a high-fat item if you eat three-quarters of a pound at a sitting. Beef cuts like round and flank steaks can be used to good advantage, as long as you keep the ground rules in mind. The figures in the table on page 19, Choosing the Leaner Meats, are based on a 3-ounce cooked portion, and this is, except where stated, the amount recommended by most experts. It is probably less than you're used to eating. If you feel that amount will leave you or your family members hungry, add to the meal a tasty, filling rice and bean dish, the Oven "Fried" Potatoes on page 237, a soup for starters, or a crisp salad following the main course. Or all of the above!

In cutting back on meat over the years, I have largely lost my taste for it. I rarely think of it when planning meals, as there are so many other delicious foods I really crave. But whenever my children remind me they haven't had meat for a *really* long time, or I just get a yen—I turn to London Broil (page 207). Made with flank steak, one of the "lesser" cuts, with a fabulous flavor from marinating, it is a family favorite. The chewiness gives you a high sense of satisfaction; the thin slices help control portions. Trimmed flank steak has only 9 grams of fat per 3-ounce serving. Leg of lamb, trimmed to within an inch of its life, is our other favorite lower-fat meat.

When shopping, choose USDA "select" or "choice" grades of top round, top sirloin, or sirloin tip. The lower the grade of beef the less fat. The "prime" or top grade is heavily marbled with fat. The next grade, "choice" has less fat, and "select," the lowest grade, the least fat. Ground beef should be as lean as possible; even the beef packaged as lean can be fattier than is healthy. Instead of picking up pre-packaged ground beef, ask the butcher to grind a sirloin steak for you, with all the visible fat trimmed off first. In addition, my butcher always cleans the machine, too, to remove any fat from earlier grindings.

Rather than having ground meat as a hamburger, think about using it in dishes like Beef Squash Pot (page 210) or pasta with Quick Meat Sauce for Pasta (page 159). When cooking ground beef to add to a dish or sauce, use a non-stick skillet and let the fat drain off in a paper towel-lined colander before proceeding with the recipe.

If you find extra-lean hamburger meat drier and perhaps not as tasty as you're used to, try adding moisture and flavor with a bit of catsup, Worcestershire, grated onion, and the like. Cook in a very hot, non-stick skillet with a spray of PAM.

Finally, keep an open mind about venison, which is quite lean (about 4 grams of fat in 4 ounces). The steaks can be exquisitely tasty when tenderized by marinating and then broiled. Ground venison can also be used for burgers and to replace beef in Stroganoff.

Processed meats: Bologna, salami, sausages, and hot dogs are high-fat foods; generally 70 to 80 percent of their calories derive from fat. Eat them infrequently and look for lower-fat versions being marketed. Keep in mind, however, that even these have about 3 grams of fat in just an ounce.

Poultry

Poultry, along with fish, is the lowest in fat of our usual main-course foods. Chicken, though relatively high in cholesterol (about 85 mg in only a 3½ ounce serving, again less than most people, especially men, would be happy with), is relatively low in the amount of fat calories it contains—18 to 20 percent in a skinless breast, 47 percent in dark meat. The skin *doubles* the fat content, because most of the fat is in and just under the skin. It shouldn't be eaten, and some people even remove it *before* cooking, since a good deal of the fat is absorbed through the flesh as it cooks.

Turkey belongs in your low-fat repertoire, much more often than just at Thanksgiving. Not only is it extremely economical, but it is also an excellent substitute for beef and veal, ground, in a "meat" loaf, or as cutlets. Note that ground turkey, the current low-fat diet darling for those who want to eat meat and feel virtuous, may not be as low as you'd think. The label on one popular brand says it's only 10 percent fat, but this is by weight. It still means 30 percent of the package's calorie content derives from fat.* That's because packaged ground turkey is not all lean breast meat; the dark meat, which is included, has over twice as much fat—not as high as beef, but not exactly a low-fat food either. Buying turkey breast and having the butcher grind it for you (or doing it yourself) will ensure you lower-fat turkey.

Turkey leftovers can be used in all sorts of interesting ways, and turkey breast, either homemade or as a deli item, makes good sandwiches with lettuce, tomatoes, pickles, or whatever you like to add moisture.

Game birds, such as pheasant and quail, are also lean, and can be prepared in many delightful ways. Rabbit, while not a member of the poultry family, is also a good low-fat, low-cholesterol source of protein, and many people feel it tastes like chicken. In almost every country except the United States, rabbit is a highly desirable food.

Duck and goose make admittedly delicious eating, but these two birds contain twice as much fat as a comparable amount of chicken. In terms of cholesterol content, however, the three birds are all very close, so you can see that if you are vigilant *only* about cholesterol intake you can still end up eating a lot of fat. Of course you may want to eat duck and goose on special occasions; just don't eat the skin, watch the portions, and enjoy them thoroughly!

*More on this in Chapter 6, Buyer Beware.

Fish and Shellfish

Most fish and shellfish are relatively low in both fat and cholesterol, in comparison with meat. Yet the most confusing controversy surrounds this food group. Early on, nutritionists told us to limit certain seafoods —salmon and mackerel because they were relatively fatty; shrimp because they were high in cholesterol. This was a misconception arising from traditional methods of food analysis, which identified certain fats in shellfish *similar* to cholesterol as true cholesterol. Actually, the cholesterol content of most shellfish is lower than that of canned tuna or broiled chicken breast. While you should monitor quantities of fatty fin food like mackerel and swordfish, you should also make a concerted effort to include them in your diet because of the protective omega-3s they supply. This polyunsaturated acid, also known as EPA and common to most cold-water fish, reduces both triglyceride and cholesterol levels. While some fish have more EPA than others, all cold water fish supply some EPA. Don't be put off by the notion of "fatty" fish—all fish, while matching beef for protein, contain much less *saturated* fat. Canned tuna in water and canned salmon are two easy ways to get omega-3 oils regularly. Other omega-3-rich fish are anchovies, herring, sablefish, pink salmon (with the skin), coho salmon, sardines, shad and red salmon eggs. Try to plan at least two fish or shellfish meals a week. Shrimp, especially, lends itself to delightful low-fat preparation methods, like Pan-Grilled Shrimp (page 183) and my favorite, Steamed Shrimp with Garlic and Scallions (page 184). Watch amounts and keep track of the cholesterol content; 300 milligrams daily is the recommended limit.

Eggs

Eggs are second only to meat as a cholesterol source, and most dietary guidelines limit them to two or three a week. When I began writing this book, one whole large egg had 5.6 fat grams and 274 milligrams of cholesterol, both all in the yolk. Then a study came out suggesting that the cholesterol content of an egg might actually be about 24 percent lower than previously thought—200 to 220 milligrams of cholesterol.

These claims, now considered valid by the USDA, may be attributed to two factors—changes in the way chickens are fed and changes in the way cholesterol is analyzed. Nevertheless, since your ideal *total* daily cholesterol intake is between 250 and 300 milligrams *daily from all sources*, lower-cholesterol eggs still use up most of your daily allotment. Keep in mind that this change in cholesterol content does not mean a change in the *fat content*. Eggs still need to be limited and traded off, especially since they are such a necessary ingredient in cooking; more of them are hidden in foods than we realize. Egg yolks work to stabilize, bind, and moisturize, and in certain recipes it is hard to cook without them. Certainly cutting out egg yolks can make some baked goods and other dishes dry and tasteless. In recipes calling for more than one egg, try using one whole egg and two whites for two eggs. I've had great success making some favorite recipes with egg substitutes.

Dairy Products

Dairy products and cheese are another major source of fat in our diet. Since they are considered an important source of calcium, however, when cutting down, you will still want to use them in low-fat versions.

Milk: Whole milk gets 49 percent of its calories from fat, which translates to 9 grams of fat in an 8-ounce serving. It also contains a fair amount of cholesterol. Even 2-percent low-fat milk gets a high 35 percent of its total calories from fat. If you use milk, get the 1 percent or skim. To ease the transition, go first to 2 percent, then 1 percent, and then nonfat. I bet that after a while whole milk will taste "wrong" to you—too heavy, too thick, and not thirst-quenching enough.

Cream, light or heavy, with its high butterfat content, and whipped cream, which is made from heavy cream, should both be on your "strictly limit" or "avoid" list. Though non-dairy creamers don't contain cholesterol, they are not artery-friendly, because their fat content is as high as cream, and it's saturated fat besides. A number of replacements for cream can be found on the Substitutions List (page 35).

Butter is high both in cholesterol and saturated fat, and must be strictly limited. When nothing but butter will do, try to limit its use to a couple of teaspoons. (You'll see that I've done this in a number of recipes.) Butter Buds, a commercial non-fat butter substitute, properly used, can be great on hot, moist foods, such as a baked potato or vegetables. If its flavor can fool my teenaged mashed potato junkie, you know it's good!

If you must have butter as a spread, use whipped butter (it has less fat because of the water beaten into it) and let it come to room temperature before using so it can be spread very thinly. Try not to use more than a teaspoon. Use olive oil wherever possible to replace butter as a cooking medium, or use a non-stick pan lightly coated with PAM. Or use your own olive oil in a spray bottle. (The propellant in olive oil PAM adds a strange taste.)

Margarine: A butter substitute made from vegetable oil, margarine has no cholesterol but the same number of fat grams. Use sparingly as recommended above for butter. Varying amounts of the vegetable oil may be saturated. Use one of the soft tub margarines that has a ratio of at least twice as much polyunsaturated fat to saturated. Those listing a hydrogenated oil (see page 13) as the first ingredient are usually higher in saturated fat. Diet margarine would be roughly comparable to whipped butter; it contains more water and so has half the calories and fat.

Cheeses present a real problem, delicious as they are, because they tend to be high in fats and calories. Look at some of the frequently consumed cheeses:

	% calories from fat	Fat g 1 oz	Calories per 1 oz
American, Brie, Muenster, Monterey Jack, Swiss (1 slice)	72	8 (average)	103
Parmesan (pre-grated)	60	8.5	129
Mozzarella, whole-milk	69	6.1	80
Mozzarella, part-skim	72	4.5	72
Cream cheese (2 Tbs.)	89	9.9	98

Look into Sapsago cheese and other low-fat cheeses with a eye to substituting them for your favorites. Although it is high in sodium, Borden's Lite Line at 2.0 is nice when a grilled cheese sandwich hunger strikes. Parmesan, although it draws 63 percent of its calories from fat, is a good cheese to go with because it is primarily used in grated form; a little goes a long way, and a small amount yields a lot of great flavor.

Cream cheese: Of the 99 calories in 2 tablespoons of cream cheese, 89 come from fat, most of it saturated. Cream cheese is also lower in protein and calcium than comparable cheeses. Think of it as you do butter or margarine—to be used sparingly. See the Substitutions List (page 35).

Cottage cheese: Surprisingly, this is not a great calcium source; you'd have to eat 2½ cups and 500 calories (less in the low-fat version) to get the same amount of a nutrient you could get in only 6 ounces of low-fat milk. It's high in sodium, too. In my opinion, it is a boring and highly overrated food, a holdover from the days when it was the dieter's delight because of its high protein content. Now we know that as adults we get much more protein than we need anyway, so I see little reason to eat it unless you love it. Creamed cottage cheese has 9.5 grams of fat in a cup; the 1 percent kind has only 1.6 grams.

Yogurt: This is an important food in your low-fat diet. Not only is yogurt a good substitute for sour cream, but it is also a snap to turn non-fat yogurt into a luscious, double-thick version (see page 275) that you can use in all sorts of interesting ways.

Check the label when buying yogurt; the fat content ranges from 7.7 grams for an 8-ounce container of whole-milk yogurt and 3.4 grams in the low-fat version to only 0.4 grams for the non-fat kind, which tastes just as good. This is a real fat savings. Watch out, though, for those premium yogurts made with cream!

Fats and Oils

All fats and oils used in cooking, *regardless of source*, contain the same number of fat grams. Thus a tablespoon of butter has exactly the same number of fat grams as one of margarine. The differences are in the degree of saturation. All fats, saturated or not, provide 9 calories per gram of fat. Every time you use 1 tablespoon of any oil you use 13.6 grams of fat, the equivalent of 120 calories.

OILS AND SPREADS: HOW THE FATS STACK UP

Generally, any fat that's solid at room temperature is more likely to raise blood cholesterol than one that's liquid, regardless of whether it came from an animal (butter) or a vegetable (stick margarine). The lower the number (percent saturated) the better.

	% saturated
Canola	6
Safflower	9
Corn	13
Olive	14
Soybean	14
Liquid and soft tub margarines*	14
Peanut	17
Stick margarines*	25
Vegetable shortening	25
Cottonseed	26
Chicken fat	30
Lard	39
Palm oil	49
Butter	50
Palm kernel oil	81
Coconut oil	87

*Averages of several brands.
SOURCE: USDA Handbook 8–4.

Vegetable oils, being non-animal in origin, contain no cholesterol, but vary widely from one to the other in the ratio of the saturated to unsaturated fat they contain. Peanut oil, for example, is 18 percent saturated; olive oil is 14 percent; and bottom-of-the-line safflower is 9 percent saturated. Coconut oil, on the other hand, is 92 percent saturated, more highly saturated than lard (41 percent) and butterfat (66 percent)! While saturated fats are linked to heart disease, fats with a high polyunsaturated content like safflower and corn oil are linked to cancers of the reproductive system in both men and women. The point is, simply being able to say that an oil (or a food) has "no cholesterol" can be meaningless, huckster's hype.

Olive oil, because it is lowest in polyunsaturates as well as being acceptably low in saturated fat, is one of the two best oils to use for cooking and salads. Of course there are times when you do not want the olive oil flavor (such as in baking) and there I would recommend canola oil or "lite" olive oil. Bear in mind that "lite" means light in olive flavor; the fat grams, as usual, are the same.

Peanut oil has a somewhat higher saturated fat level, but it can be used in small amounts for stir-frying where its higher smoking point and flavor are desirable.

Keep in mind that adding or subtracting one food element does not "fix" all the problems inherent in high-fat intake and, in fact, often disguises the problem by giving you the illusion of "doing something healthy." It is far better to make a fat gram allowance for yourself and "spend" it in a healthful way that satisfies you. The next chapter will tell you how.

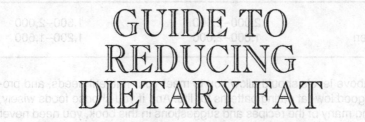

4

GUIDE TO
REDUCING
DIETARY FAT

I have tried to show you that you can protect your health by cutting down on fat consumption and to tell you where the fat is in the food you eat. Now I'll show you how to cut down the fat.

Lowering the fat you consume and keeping it lowered for life does not mean you have to cut out any particular food or group of foods in order to maintain a 30 percent fat gram goal—although you may decide to do this later on. You can still use oils in moderation and even some butter for flavor. What you're going to do is try to prune from your diet those high-fat foods that will use up your fat gram allowance *unwisely*. You can still eat meat, dairy products in moderation, snacks, and desserts, and, because you choose wisely, really lower your fat intake. Just remember, there will always be something good to eat!!!

Two changes are going to take place here: You are changing the *way* you eat and *what* you eat. But you are in charge; you are going to make changes that suit you. Otherwise, you'll never keep it up.

The First Step

First, let's identify the high-fat foods you now eat that can be replaced with lower-fat foods *you like*.

Begin by keeping a food diary for four or five days (including a weekend). Start by recalling the two days *prior* to the start of your real record to avoid unconscious changes. Write down everything you eat. List the calories of each food and, in a separate column, the fat grams contained. This information is in Appendix A, The Fat, Cholesterol,

TYPICAL CALORIC LEVELS*

	Daily calories for weight maintenance	Daily calories for losing weight
Men	2,000–2,500	1,600–2,000
Women	1,600–2,000	1,200–1,600

The above levels should allow you to meet your nutrient needs, and promote good low-fat eating patterns for life. And if you choose foods wisely, tapping many of the recipes and suggestions in this book, you need never be hungry.

If you are seriously overweight your physician or dietician should recommend the appropriate calorie plan for you.

*The degree to which you are sedentary or active is a factor in selecting the lower or higher number.

and Calorie Contents of Common Foods (pages 281–96). This will give you an idea of how many calories you consume daily and how many of them derive from fat. Once you determine the sources of your dietary fat, you can then decide where you might begin to cut back. The first group to scrutinize is meats and meat byproducts. Get some idea of which are highest in fat, like well-marbled steaks, regular hamburger meat, bacon, and pork sausages. You might even want to list them in descending order of fat content. Then consider replacing items at the top with those from the lower end. Similarly, examine the dairy products and desserts on your list, to see what changes you're comfortable with.

Establishing Your Daily Fat Allowance

Let's compute the number of grams of fat in a day that would keep you at or under the 30 percent limit. Think of these fat grams as a *per diem allowance*—daily spending money, except the currency is fat. You'll make your food selections so that the grams of fat and particularly saturated fats are within *your* allowance. The calorie level you choose is based on what you now eat and, whether you wish to maintain, lose, or gain weight and how physically active you are.

Here's how I arrived at mine: I know I can happily maintain a 30 percent fat diet. However, because of my personal health risk, 20 percent would be the ideal. That's hard, however, so I've compromised at 25 percent. I don't need to lose weight. I eat about 1600 to 1800 calories a day.

Your Daily Fat Gram Allowance table (page 30) tells me my fat allowance is 50 grams daily. (I even try to streamline this a bit by making 45 grams my aim, but this is a little game I enjoy playing, just to see if I can do it; you don't have to.)

Because saturated fats are linked to breast cancer, and because my husband is genetically at risk for heart disease, we've chosen a daily saturated fat allowance of 7 percent of daily calories. (The current recommendation is 10 percent or less.)

So my diet plan looks like this:

Daily calories: 1,800
Percentage calories from fat: 25 percent
Daily fat gram allowance: 50 grams
Daily saturated fat allowance: 7 grams

My general strategy is to spend about half of my allowance on breakfast, lunch, and a snack combined, and save the other half of my allowance to spend on a nice dinner (and maybe a piece of chocolate!). If I happen to have a bigger midday meal than usual, because I've been out to lunch, I'll trade off that "expensive" meal with a cheaper (in fat grams) one at dinner.

The following figures are based on a 30 percent daily fat allowance. I recommend aiming for this figure; later on you may find you want to and can go lower, but small changes now can make the next stage easier. If you want to know how these figures are arrived at, it's explained in Appendix B, page 297.

Trading Off

By consulting the food tables in Appendix A, you can see which foods are low in fat per portion and can be eaten frequently and which are high and need to be limited or avoided if possible. If you want to indulge occasionally in a high-fat item, you can—if you make up for those spent grams of fat by being prudent with the rest of the food you eat that day. This is known as trading off.

The trading off concept has larger implications, too. You must be comfortable with your choices. Your plan must be one *you* can live with. I can't give up whole milk in my morning coffee or olive oil in my salad dressing. I can, on the other hand, give up steak, butter on my baked

(continued on page 31)

YOUR DAILY FAT GRAM ALLOWANCE

(1 fat gram = 9 calories)

Daily calorie intake	Daily fat grams *(% of total cals)*			Saturated fat grams for a 30% diet *(% of total cals)*
	30%	**25%**	**20%**	**10%**
1,200	40	33	27	13
1,500	50	42	33	17
1,800	60	50	40	20
2,000	67	56	44	22
2,200	73	61	49	24
2,500	83	69	56	28
3,000	100	83	67	33

How to use this chart: Find the figure that represents your current or desired average daily caloric intake. Choose the percentage of daily fat you would like to aim for. The figure is your daily allowance. Thirty percent is recommended for the general population. You can start with that and go lower later on, if you feel like it or if your physician suggests it.

The food table (Appendix A) will tell you how many fat grams are in commonly consumed foods. If you eat larger portions than the amount specified, do your math accordingly. Food labels can tell you how many fat grams are in a portion of packaged foods.

The ideal ratio of *types* of fat you should consume is one-third saturated, one-third polyunsaturated, one-third monounsaturated. Thus, on a 30 percent fat diet, saturated fats should be no more than 10 percent (one third) of your total daily caloric intake. Those whose cholesterol levels have not shown a significant reduction on a 30 percent fat diet or who have other health considerations might wish to reduce their fat consumption to 25 or 20 percent of calories, which will also reduce saturated fats proportionately. To know how many saturated fat grams you should eat on lower fat diets, simply divide the fat gram figure of your goal by one third.

The simple mathematical formula for these figures is explained in Appendix B.

potato, and ice cream because they don't mean that much to me. My choices are made with this in mind. I'm comfortable with my plan, and I'm confident that after some experimenting you'll find one you are comfortable with.

You'll be surprised at how quickly you get to know the high-fat foods and how much is in a portion. You will not have to consult Appendix A or get involved in higher math before every bite!

Look at Hints for Lowering Fat (page 33), at the end of this chapter. I'm sure you'll find at least a dozen ways to start cutting back that will not be too onerous. See which ones work for you. The recipes will give you still more ideas. At first, do not worry about every last fat gram, but concentrate on the larger picture—which is cutting back. You can fine-tune later, in what might be termed the second phase of the low-fat lifestyle, after you're thoroughly familiar with where the fat is, have decided what you can cut out, and are happy with the replacements you've chosen.

While you should learn which foods are so disproportionately high in fat that they constitute a "bad investment," you're not stuck to any hard and fast rules; you just have to know how to trade off. If you just had an overwhelming craving for a juicy hamburger at lunch . . . you'll make a conscious choice to have pasta with a low-fat sauce for dinner. Or, if you must have the hamburger, have only a 4-ounce one, and forgo the fries for a bean salad (which isn't just low fat, but filling and high in fiber, besides). You get the idea. The flexibility of trading off, by the way, is enhanced by starting the day with a fat-deficit breakfast (little or no fat). This is the easiest meal at which to fill up with nutritious, low-fat food, leaving you that much more to "spend" during the rest of the day.

Portion Control

Be really strict about portion control. People often tell me proudly that they "almost never eat red meat, and eat lots of fish and chicken." If I ask, "How much chicken at a sitting?" they shrug their shoulders and look puzzled. "Chicken's okay, isn't it?" they say. Of course it is, along with a lot of other animal protein foods. An "okay" food, however, doesn't come with a license to eat as much as you want. Especially where animal protein foods are concerned, an important consideration is "portion control." I know the phrase sounds like a cafeteria business term, but it is really important to know what a portion is when keeping an eye on fat grams.

A 4-ounce portion of chicken (3 ounces, cooked) with only 6 fat grams? Terrific. But if you eat a triple portion you have to own up to 18 fat grams, which, depending on what else you eat, can be high for one food at a meal. Either cut back on the chicken, or cut back somewhere else. Remember, only you know what you put in your mouth, so you have to be in charge.

A 3-ounce portion of cooked chicken or roasted meat is about the size of the palm of your hand or a deck of cards. Remember that meat and chicken lose 25 percent of their weight when cooked. A portion of breakfast cereal is usually a cup. Fill up a metal 1-cup measure with your favorite cereal and pour it in a bowl. Look at it. That's a portion. Of course, you don't measure every day unless you're a fanatic—it's to give you an idea.

Certain foods we are very used to eating are high in fat, even though they contain no cholesterol, and they must be factored into your daily allowance. A half cup of peanuts, for example, has 33 grams of fat. Avocado, with 19 grams of fat in just a half, is also high, as is a 4-ounce chocolate bar, with 40 grams of fat. All fats and oils used in cooking, regardless of source, contain the same number of fat grams. Every time you use 1 tablespoon of oil you spend 13.6 grams of fat.

A fast-food double-meat cheeseburger with condiments, with 35 grams of fat, and a large order of French fries, with 19 grams, add up to 54 *grams of fat.* For someone like me, whose fat per diem is 50 grams, that is more than my whole fat allowance for the day! (Furthermore, a high percentage of that fat is saturated, because of the meat.) Even for a person with a fat allowance of 60 or 65 grams, this would mean two unsatisfyingly small other meals that day, not to mention no dessert or snacks. Maybe you can find other pleasing ways to "spend" your fat allowance in a wiser way.

Once your over-all fat consumption is low, an occasional splurge on a fat-intense food like a hotdog will have a negligible effect. Just keep track of splurges, as you do the rest of your food.

A special exception to this middle-of-the-road approach would be people who have congenitally high cholesterol levels even while being on a low-fat diet. These people should have their cholesterol monitored at frequent intervals by a doctor and should do everything possible dietetically to bring their levels below 200, since they are at greater risk than the rest of the population to die prematurely of heart disease.

HINTS FOR LOWERING FAT

General Planning

• Avoid the following or eat in small amounts: butter, margarine, cooking oil, chicken skin, bacon, well-marbled meat, hotdogs, most salad dressings, mayonnaise.

• Have at least two non-meat dinners weekly, using a pasta with vegetables or a hearty dish or soup featuring grains, like Lentil Chili (page 147) or Minestrone alla Milanese (page 104)

• Measure or weigh meat, fish, or poultry servings until your eye becomes familiar with the amounts recommended.

• Broil, bake, poach, steam, or braise fish, poultry, and meat instead of frying or sautéing. Use a non-stick pan and PAM whenever possible.

• Non-stick pans greatly reduce the amount of fat required for cooking.

• To sauté onions and garlic, start them in a tablespoon of olive oil in a non-stick pan, and then add broth or water so they steam/sauté. Or eliminate the fat entirely and just use the liquid.

• Instead of buying pre-packaged ground beef, which can be quite fatty, find a market with a butcher and have him grind a sirloin steak for you, with all the visible fat removed first.

• Cook soups, stews, and gravies ahead of time and chill so that hardened fat can be easily removed; then reheat.

• Get to know your microwave. This cooking method requires no additional fat. There is additional microwave information on page 51.

• Use reduced-calorie mayonnaise instead of regular.

• Don't put butter on the table.

• Include salads with every meal.

Breakfast

• Don't eat eggs more than two or three times a week, and poach or boil rather than fry them. Since the protein is in the white, try an omelet made with one yolk, two whites in a non-stick pan using PAM.

• Serve breakfast cereal with skim milk, raisins, and bananas or grated apple; the fruit both sweetens and adds fiber.

• Use low-fat milk for your coffee.

• If you are going to butter toast or English muffins, use whipped butter and take it out of the refrigerator so it can come to room temperature; that way it will spread more thinly.

• Make pancakes with skim milk and substitute an egg white for one egg. Boost nutrition by using whole-wheat or buckwheat flour.

• Save croissants for an occasional treat; they are made with lots of butter.

• Sourdough bread is made without fat and makes fabulous toast.

Lunch

• Stay away from hotdogs and processed luncheon meats. Go for turkey breast, small amounts of lean roast beef, or sliced chicken breast.

• Use water-packed tuna, instead of the kind in oil.

• Avoid buttering sandwich bread or slathering with mayonnaise; moisten filling by adding tomatoes, lettuce, cucumbers, mustard instead.

• If you eat cottage cheese, make it low-fat.

Dinner

• Trim as much fat as possible from meat.

• Don't eat the skin of poultry, which doubles the fat content. Ideally, remove it *before* cooking.

• Plan dinners to include more vegetables and more starchy foods like rice, pasta, and potatoes.

• In place of sour cream as a topping for baked potatoes use a couple of tablespoons of non-fat yogurt with chopped scallions or blenderized low-fat cottage cheese with chives.

• If you don't like low-fat salad dressing, try extending your regular dressing with lemon juice or water. Or extend with half low-fat buttermilk and lots of flavorful herbs.

Snacks

• Avoid high-fat nibbles like potato chips and corn chips and commercial baked goods. Try Graham crackers, flatbread, rye or whole-wheat crackers, bread sticks, or matzoh. Also chunky hard pretzels without salt.

• Air-popped popcorn (just 46 calories and 1 fat gram in 2 cups) with a glass of tomato or V-8 juice is a splendid mid-afternoon snack.

• Make "rabbit food"—like celery, carrot, and cucumber sticks, radishes, or green and red pepper strips—more satisfying by keeping a low-fat dip on hand, such as Chickpea Spread (page 81) or Curry Dip for Crudités (page 82).

• Keep favorite berries and squares of ripe cantaloupe and honeydew, already speared on toothpicks, in the fridge.

Desserts

- Make fruit cobblers and crisps instead of a two-crust pie.
- Another pie ploy: a Graham-cracker crust using only 2 tablespoons melted butter or margarine.
- In cake baking, use 2 egg whites instead of 1 whole egg. (This will result in a slightly more crumbly, but still quite acceptable, cake.)
- Use half the amount of nuts called for in cake recipes, since nuts are high in fat.
- Use raisins and chopped dried fruit in baking as an alternative to chocolate chips, which are high in fat.
- Grease baking pans with a non-stick spray instead of butter.
- Be on the lookout for tasty, low-fat recipes (ones that contain less than ½ cup butter or margarine and only 1 egg) that you can add to your dessert repertoire.
- Angel food cake has virtually no fat; serve it with your favorite berries for dessert.
- Don't stock your freezer with any dairy dessert other than low-fat frozen yogurt, ice milk, sherbets, or sorbets.

RECIPE SUBSTITUTIONS

I am against changing recipes in ways that take the heart and flavor out of them. I'd rather eat a higher fat food less frequently or give up something else, rather than eat something I love in an unacceptably altered form. Most of the substitutions below, however, have been used in this book with good results and I urge you to try them; any time you can cut back on fat and not notice it, you're ahead of the game. You probably have many recipes of your own that you can tinker with and create lower fat versions by using some of these ideas.

When the recipe calls for:	**Use**
Whole milk	Skim or non-fat milk
Eggs	Egg substitutes, like Egg Beaters
In baking	
1 whole large egg	2 egg whites
2 whole large eggs	3 egg whites or 1 egg plus one white

When the recipe calls for:	**Use**
Unsweetened baking chocolate	¼ cup cocoa plus 2 tsp. butter or margarine for each 1 oz.
Butter 　on hot vegetables, popcorn 　for sautéing 　for sautéing onions and garlic	 Butter Buds olive oil chicken broth
Sour cream	Mock Sour Cream (recipe, page 276) or Double-Thick Yogurt (page 275) or plain low-fat yogurt or 1 cup low-fat cottage cheese blended with 2 Tbs. skim milk, 1 Tb. lemon juice
Crème fraiche	Double-Thick low-fat yogurt (page 275)
Heavy cream	for ½ cup cream: 1 Tb. Butter Buds mixed into ⅓ cup skim milk
Roux (mixture of butter and flour for thickening soups)	Remove some vegetables from the pot, purée and return purée to pot or 1 Tb. Butter Buds mixed into ⅓ skim milk

5

FIBER

As you cut down on high-fat foods you'll be filling up by eating more complex carbohydrates, like starchy foods, vegetables, and fruits. Because many of these foods are naturally high in fiber, you get another built-in bonus of the low-fat lifestyle. Just about every authority on nutrition and health has stated unequivocally that Americans need to increase their intake of not only complex carbohydrates but also fiber.

What Is Fiber?

Fiber is a non-absorbable carbohydrate. It comes from the cell walls of plants, the part that humans cannot digest. While it is not an essential nutrient, you live much better with it and it helps your body to run smoothly. Foods high in fiber are usually those in their natural state, which have been processed minimally or not at all—for example, whole-grain bread, bran and oat cereals, brown rice, kasha, cornmeal, barley, nuts and seeds, and those legumes and dried beans I'm always selling. Fresh fruits and vegetables, especially raw ones, are excellent fiber sources.

Insoluble and Soluble Fiber

There are two basic forms of fibers: the kind that is soluble in water and the kind that isn't. These two kinds of fiber function differently; the fiber in bananas and beans has a different effect on the body than the fiber in wheat bran does. An insoluble fiber, wheat bran acts as a natural laxative, keeping things moving in the intestines. As it does not dissolve in water, it passes through the body more quickly than the soluble kind. The theory is that this shortened transit time lowers the risk of colon cancer, because potential carcinogens ingested with food are ushered out of the system more quickly. Insoluble fiber is also thought to be effective in preventing other related problems like diverticulosis and hemorrhoids.

Soluble fiber plays another role. It acts like a sponge, absorbing water and nutrients in the stomach and slowing food absorption; the bulk helps you feel satisfied sooner from the food you eat. Consequently, you may eat less, which is a nifty added benefit. The great interest in soluble fiber has been generated by studies, notably those by James W. Anderson of the University of Kentucky, that show that foods containing soluble fiber are also a relatively cheap and effective way to lower both cholesterol and triglyceride levels that are associated with heart disease. The blood carries fats to the organs of the body in the form of triglycerides which are therefore a crude measure of recent fat consumption.

Enter Oat Bran

Because it contains such a high concentration of soluble fiber, the spotlight so far has focused primarily on oat bran. One study showed that eating one to one and a half cups of oat bran a day as part of a very lowcalorie diet can cause a 13 to 19 percent reduction in cholesterol levels. And therein lies the rub. Almost no one can eat that much oat bran; consequently, few people experience a meaningful cholesterol reduction. Participants in another study showed lowered cholesterol levels by eating a half pound of specially prepared bread made of rolled oats *every* day; in another, 2 oat bran muffins eaten for 28 *straight days* did the trick. One recent study confirmed that oat bran does indeed reduce cholesterol, but primarily by making people too full to eat fatty foods. The study concluded that the same effect could be achieved by eating linguine!

There is nothing magical about oat bran *per se*. It is not the only source of cholesterol-lowering soluble fiber available, just a source with a higher concentration than some other foods. If, on the other hand, you start adding tasty, soluble fiber-rich foods to your repertoire, like bean side dishes and salads, savory bean dips for crudités, lentil and pea soup and such, you can just relax, knowing your cholesterol level *plus* your general state of health are bound to be the beneficiaries, because of all the fat-laden foods you're *not* eating.

To keep my husband's formerly high cholesterol in check, I am always exploring ever tastier ways to get soluble fiber in our diet, satisfying foods we are delighted to stick with. And since soluble fiber has to be ingested on a regular basis for the effects to last, an interesting variety of foods is what keeps our interest up, especially since there are so many foods that qualify to choose from.

The average American consumes about 10 grams of fiber a day. The National Cancer Institute recommends increasing this to 20 to 35 grams a day and suggests 5 servings of fruit and vegetables per day as a way of getting enough fiber.

Following are some easily available foods that you can add to one day's meals to boost your fiber intake. Of course, you don't have to eat them all, nor is this *all* you'll be eating! It's just to give you an idea.

Food Sources of Fiber (page 41), will suggest plenty of other sources. Don't go crazy worrying about whether you're getting enough fiber, or feel you have to count up every fiber gram. Just plan to work more of the appropriate foods into your menus and remember that variety is the name of the game. Think of all the agreeable ways to eat legumes, peas, beans, lentils, corn, sweet potatoes. Consider asparagus, carrots, and okra, a particular favorite of mine. (If you think you don't like okra, try

FOODS THAT BOOST FIBER

Food and serving size	Fiber (g)
Breakfast 1 whole orange, peeled	3.6
Oatmeal, ⅔ cup cooked	2.9
(⅓ cup, 1oz, uncooked)	
with ¼ cup raisins	1.9
Lunch 2 slices rye bread in sandwich	3.1
½ cup grated cabbage in cole slaw	.8
Afternoon snack 2 fig bars	1.3
Dinner ½ cup cooked broccoli	2.0
1 medium potato with skin, baked	4.2
2 slices whole-grain bread	3.4
1 grated raw carrot in salad	2.3
1 cup strawberries	4.0
Late snack 1 sliced apple, skin on	3.0
TOTAL FIBER	32.5

Okra–Corn Stew on page 231; it may change your mind!) And remember that grains and legumes eaten in combination give you fat-free protein besides!

There is valuable soluble fiber in most fruits, too, especially citrus fruits, and vegetables (which also provide valuable vitamins and minerals as well). Would you guess that strawberries, raspberries, and bananas are good fiber sources?

Fiber Labeling

Many new products are taking a ride on the oat bran craze, even if they contain an insignificant amount, or other undesirable ingredients that cancel out the benefits. Now the term fiber crops up frequently on packaged foods and nutrition labels and may even be broken down further into soluble and insoluble fiber. There are no regulations, however, that specify how fiber must be listed or the amount that must be contained to call a product "high fiber," one of the reasons why it is more sensible not to regard any one food like oat bran as a fiber panacea, but rather to make sure your diet contains a steady variety of many fiber-rich foods.

I was amused when a friend with congenitally high cholesterol (who really watches what she eats) told me excitedly that a terrific gourmet market near her home was featuring oat bran doughnuts. This is a perfect example of how food hype works. You hear the buzz word, and you stop thinking. Doughnuts, with all the oil from frying, are something she wouldn't touch normally. Add oat bran—to a not particularly healthful food—and suddenly it sounds like a new health food! My friend really knows better; she just got "sold."

Bear in mind that when food fads come, they also go, which is another reason not to commit yourself to oat bran, rice bran, or any of the other fad foods waiting in the wings to replace it, such as psyllium, a bulking agent used for years as a laxative (in Metamucil, for example). My advice is: Stick with real food, make it low fat, and make it tasty.

Other Benefits of High-Fiber Diets

High-fiber diets can lower insulin requirements for diabetics by slowing down the absorption of glucose into the system. One study showed that a high-fiber, high-carbohydrate diet brought insulin requirements down by 25 to 50 percent. A whopping 90 percent of non-insulin-dependent diabetic patients were able to discontinue drug therapy by being on this same diet.

There are many health benefits to be derived from increasing your fiber intake. Even if you have no particular medical problems, increasing fiber is great health insurance and helps keep your weight down. And the food sources of fiber are the complex carbohydrates we should be eating anyway. Look at the high-fiber foods on the chart on the next page, then look through the recipes containing them in the recipe section. I know you'll find many appealing ways to work these healthful foods into your diet.

One caveat: Don't go overboard and eat *too* many fiber-rich foods. High-fiber diets—adding bran, for example—can reduce absorbed calcium to dangerous levels. A high concentration of fiber can also bloat you, give you gas, and cause diarrhea.

FOOD SOURCES OF FIBER

This table shows some of the best sources of dietary fiber. Total fiber is given because soluble and insoluble have not been measured separately in most foods. However, foods that *have* been analyzed and contain a significant amount of soluble fiber (at least 1 gram per serving) are marked by an *.

Gram

Wheat bran (½ cup) 13
Nabisco 100% bran (½ cup) 9
Kellogg All Bran (⅓ cup) 10
Quaker Oat Bran hot cereal (⅔ cup cooked) 4*

Pinto beans (¾ cup cooked) 8*
Kidney beans (¾ cup cooked) 14
Navy beans (¾ cup cooked) 9
Lentils (¾ cup cooked) 6*
Black-eyed peas (¾ cup cooked) 12*
Chickpeas (garbanzos) (¾ cup cooked)................................. 7*
Split peas (¾ cup cooked) 4*

Bulgur (cracked wheat), prepared (1 cup).............................. 8
Whole-wheat spaghetti, prepared (1 cup).............................. 6
Aunt Jemima Buckwheat Pancake Mix (3 pancakes) 5
Brown rice, prepared (1 cup).............................. 3

Baked potato w/skin, medium (1).. 4*
Sweet potato w/out skin, medium (1)..................................... 3*
Brussels sprouts, cooked (½ cup) 3*
Corn, cooked (½ cup) 3
Peas or winter squash, cooked (½ cup).................................. 3
Carrot, raw (1) 2
Broccoli or spinach, cooked (½ cup) 2

Figs, dried, 3 5
Apple, large 4*
Pear.. 4
Prunes, dried (5)... 4
Raisins (¼ cup) 2
Banana, medium... 2

The fiber values given in this book are based on the latest available USDA data. The USDA stresses, however, that the data are provisional because methods have not yet been developed that give exact values for Total Dietary Fiber (TDF). Legumes are particularly difficult to analyze because their age and the amount of water absorbed while cooking varies and affects the final yield. For the purposes of most consumers, however, it is sufficient to know which foods can be considered good sources of fiber and to make an effort to include a reasonable amount of them in daily meal planning.

6

BUYER BEWARE: SOME THINGS TO KNOW WHEN YOU SHOP FOR FOOD

Improving your eating habits starts when you make out your shopping list. Poultry and fish will be high on the list; meats will figure less prominently and be leaner. Stay well stocked with grains and pastas and buy the freshest, most appealing fruits and vegetables. The continuing education goes on when you shop; the supermarket is your schoolroom and the text is the nutrition labeling on the backs of packages and containers.

Recently the U.S. government has intensified its focus on the need for more complete and honest food labeling. In February 1990, Dr. Louis Sullivan, Secretary of Health and Human Services, proposed sweeping changes to update food labeling rules to reflect modern scientific thinking about diet and health. When the new proposals take effect, virtually all packaged foods will have to carry nutritional labels specifying saturated fat, fiber, and cholesterol content plus the percentage of calories derived from fat. Terms like "low-fat" and "lite" will be formally defined. With rules like this in effect, plus educated consumers, the supermarket will be less of a nutritional minefield than it is today. Until the new labeling happens, here are some pointers for your shopping.

Lower May Not Be Low

While the nutritional breakdowns now supplied on food packages by most manufacturers are an improvement over absolutely no information at all, they can be misleading. Sugar content is one area of obvious abuse that I'll tell you about. But for the moment, let's watch out for fat.

You need to keep some quick sandwich fixings on hand for family lunches, and there in the luncheon meat case is salami, labeled "only 17 percent fat," suggesting that the other 83 percent is lean, or fat-free. Sounds good. But it's not. You see, the salami is 17 percent fat *by weight*, not by calories. And a food that is 17 percent fat by *weight* can be almost *half* fat in terms of *calories*. The percentages given for fat content are given on the basis of *weight*, not calories, which are more easily translatable into fat grams.

Even a food that claims it is as much as 95 percent fat-free may still contain plenty of fat calories. I was about to put in my cart a package of Louis Rich sliced turkey ham, made from cured turkey thigh meat, banner-labeled "95 percent fat-free—5 percent fat." Then I read the back and realized that the 5 percent fat by weight was 50 percent of the fat by calories.

Here's how I figured it out. The first item I look for in the package information is the calorie and fat content of one portion, which in this case is one slice: it says a slice contains 35 calories and 2 grams of fat. There are 9 calories in 1 gram of fat and $2 \times 9 = 18$; so 18 of the 35 calories in one slice of this turkey ham are fat, or a little over 50 percent. Now, eating those 2 grams of fat in one slice won't trash your eating plan, but that's not the point. The point is that a food that is over 50 percent fat is *not* the low-fat food you thought it was. Especially if you make a hefty sandwich. The meat is presented in a way calculated to make you buy it, thinking you are getting a magical low-fat meat that is almost 100 percent fat-free. That's why learning to read labels is so important.

For our purposes, fat content per serving, which is fat as a percentage of total calories, is a more useful reference than "percentage fat free," which begs the issue.

Take low-fat yogurt: It is labeled 1.5 percent fat by weight, but a surprising 26 percent of its calories derive from fat. Place this on a yardstick with fats and oils that derive 100 percent of their calories from fat, and you'll get the idea. This one-quarter-fat yogurt is not terribly high, but neither is its fat content as negligible as that low number—1.5—makes you think.

It is helpful to remember that fat contains more than twice as many calories gram for gram, pound for pound, than any other ingredient of food. Another way to say this is that fat contains more calories for its weight than any other food. A gram of carbohydrate has 4 calories, while a gram of fat has 9. More than double. An ounce of fat has 255 calories, while an ounce of protein or carbohydrate has only 113—less than half.

The Meat Department

The picture becomes even more confusing and detrimental to the consumer where ground beef is concerned. Beef labeled "75 percent lean" is 25 percent fat, one quarter fat, which is a lot of fat. A patty made of such meat would derive more than 70 percent of its calories from fat, since fat has more than twice the calories, etc. So the words "lean" or "extra lean" on ground beef are potentially misleading. To be so labeled, a steak or other cut of beef must have no more than 10 percent fat; "extra lean" may have no more than 5 percent. *Yet these standards do not apply when meat is ground.*

The Dairy Area

Almost half the calories of whole milk are in the form of fat, even though only 3.3 percent of its weight is in fat. Similarly, 2 percent milk (2 percent by weight) misleads in proclaiming itself "98 percent fat-free." It is actually 35 percent fat, when it comes to calories.

The "low-fat" claim on some part-skim ricotta labels used to fool me too, until I checked out the difference. Part-skim is not the same thing as low-fat. A typical 2-ounce serving (¼ cup) of ricotta still contains 5 to 6 grams fat, compared to 8 grams for a serving of whole-milk ricotta. Not that much difference. Lite ricotta (Polly-O and Sorrento), with 4 grams of fat, is better. And because the fat is cut by adding whey, a nourishing byproduct of cheese making, you get an extra boost of calcium.

Hidden Fats in Packaged Foods

Something else to keep an eye out for when you shop is fat "hidden" in packaged foods, which in their non-packaged versions would be regarded as quite low-fat—like microwave-ready rice and potato dishes, packaged rice or potato mixes, microwave popcorn and the like. The label may even have that overworked line "no cholesterol" or "100 percent natural." Reading the nutritional information, however, may tell you the food is processed with tropical oils (palm, palm kernel, coconut) or hydrogenated or partially hydrogenated vegetable oils. These fats are *hidden* in the sense that the burden is on you and me, the consumers, to know that although they *sound* okay, they are saturated and therefore can raise cholesterol. Knowing this fact allows you to make the same considered choices about buying foods even when they are not obvious sources of fat.

In the other aisles, watch out for:

Peanut butter: It contains no cholesterol, but 75 percent of the 190 calories in 2 tablespoonsful derive from fat, and while mostly monosaturated, those 16.2 grams of fat make this old standby a very high-fat food to have only as a once-in-a-while treat.

Potato chips: Munching your way through 8 ounces of potato chips (about a half-pound bag) is like adding 12 to 20 teaspoons of vegetable oil (usually hydrogenated) and a teaspoon of salt to an 8-ounce potato —as much fat and sodium as most people should eat in an entire day. Try instead a box of chunky unsalted pretzels.

Nuts: Who doesn't love their crunch? A tablespoon of peanuts, however, contains 7 grams of fat. And most people I know eat them by the handful. Dry-roasted or not, they have to be strictly limited.

Crackers: Many contain saturated fat in the form of tropical oils and partially hydrogenated vegetable oils. Those addictive bagel crisps are crisped in oil and just loaded with fat.

Frankfurters or hotdogs: The "all-beef" ones have around 13 grams of fat each, way too high for 4 or 5 mouthfuls of food. Even chicken franks have around 8 grams. I never buy any kind.

Non-dairy creamers and flavored instant coffee mixes: These have tropical oils as their principal ingredients.

Ice creams: It's hard to pass these by. But the good news is that there are some delicious sherbets or sorbets on the market, made with real fruit purées, not just sugar, water, and flavoring. And the new frozen yogurts are splendid. We always keep Élan vanilla and coffee frozen yogurt on hand, and we make outrageously good treats using them and the low-fat Buttermilk Chocolate Sauce on page 260.

Breakfast cereals: Although many cold cereals are made with partly hydrogenated oil or coconut or palm oil, fat isn't the problem here; sugar is. Reading labels will tell you a lot. Don't be fooled, even if sugar isn't high up in the ingredients list. A cereal can contain sugar in 5 or 6 different forms of varying amounts, so check out the entire label. All the following are sugar too: corn syrup, high fructose corn syrup, fructose, dextrose, honey, brown sugar syrup, and molasses. *All* may actually be present in varying amounts in the same cereal! The muesli-type cereal Swiss Familia is good, especially if you grate half an apple (with the skin) into it and/or add some berries. Commercial granolas tend to be rather high in fat and sugar, and Granola Breakfast Bars are just candy bars in disguise. My Homemade Granola (page 67), however, is peerless.

So make it a habit to scan label information, *especially* when the now familiar hype words are prominently featured. Here's where being a little paranoid is an advantage. Assume the packagers are trying to put something over on you; figure it out for yourself. And if doing math in your head isn't your strong suit, I promise you it isn't mine, either; I nearly flunked math. Nevertheless, this figuring does get to be second nature, something you can do in seconds. Until there is one standard way to tell you how much fat is in the food you buy, you're going to have to be your own detective, by reading labels.

7

EATING OUT

"Stay out of restaurants" exhorted the late Nathan Pritikin; "they are the enemy camp." "Do not read the menu" advises his Diet Center. Well. I say do read the menu, assess the possibilities, and enjoy yourself.

Of course I'm not talking about fast food joints—a look at page 284 of Appendix A, The Fat, Cholesterol, and Calorie Contents of Common Foods, will tell you why. But real restaurants have chefs and most chefs know the action is in the low-salt, low-fat corner—in fact, most of those I know are eating that way themselves. So almost every menu features at least one simple broiled dish or one called "light" or "lite." Some menus even count your calories for you, and although you may not be dieting for weight loss, a low-calorie dish is usually low fat as well. But from any menu you can choose a satisfying meal that's good to your taste buds and good to the rest of you.

The old stuff—the tons-of-butter, Béarnaise/Hollandaise kind of food we used to eat before we had our fat consciousness raised—is not even on most menus anymore. But just in case, pass right over chicken Kiev, Southern fried chicken, wiener schnitzel, or any other breaded, fried foods. If you have to eat them, remove the breading. Skip anything in buttery sauces like those mentioned above. If a soup sounds good, ask if it's creamed. If it is, go on to something else.

Order broiled fish with lemon instead of butter. Look for seafoods and vegetables that are en brochette or baked in foil, or grilled, broiled, or steamed, because they require a minimal use of a fatty cooking medium. If servings are larger than you have at home, leave some on the plate.

And if there's absolutely nothing acceptable, have a baked potato and a salad.

If the gang is gung-ho for steak, and the thought makes your mouth water, have it once in a while. Order a small one, and cut yourself a 4- to 6-ounce portion, which is roughly the size of the palm of your hand. (Steak weight in ounces is often on the menu; if it isn't, ask—waiters usually know this.) Take the rest home in a doggy bag to slice thinly for a sandwich the next day. Of course you'll trim off all visible fat.

Wherever you go, ask for vegetables without butter; dress them yourself with lemon juice and herbs or see if they can be steamed in lemon juice and garlic.

Look for dishes that have been marinated, because they will have more flavor and therefore need less butter or oil. If the house salad dressing is creamy, ask if a little oil and lemon or just balsamic vinegar can be substituted.

You already know the score in the dessert department: nix those with double pie crusts, custard bases like crème brulée, custardy sauces like Sabayon or obvious heavy cream or whipped cream. Have a fresh fruit cup with Port or Cointreau. Pick a fruit sorbet instead of ice cream. If there's a mousse, you can ask if it's made with whole eggs or just whites. If the waiter doesn't know, with your nicest, most earnest smile, ask if he could find out. (You'll be doing the next patron who asks a favor.)

Italian food offers the most opportunities for eating well and staying on your low-fat plan. There is usually something to please everyone in an Italian restaurant, which is where we often end up. Pasta tops the desirable food list (many non-Italian restaurants offer it as well), but avoid pastas with creamy sauces, sausages, or cheeses such as Gorgonzola, fontina, etc. "Parmigiano" dishes, even if meatless, usually have a disproportionately high fat content in the cheese. Be modest with the grated Parmesan you add. Watch out for dishes made with cream or egg yolks like fettuccine Alfredo, spaghetti carbonara, or anything in béchamel (white sauce). Also on this list: mayonnaise and desserts like zabaglione, spumoni, or anything with a custard filling.

Generally, pasta with tomato and other vegetable-based sauces are safe choices and you can always toss on a few dried red pepper flakes for zing. Linguine with red or white clam sauce is a good bet, although it can be salty. Italian restaurants frequently also offer superb grilled vegetables.

Chinese food is very high in complex carbohydrates, but beware of fat pitfalls, too. Peking Duck, unless you can limit yourself to *just one small pancake-full*, is a no-no because of that delicious skin. (A 3½-ounce serving contains nearly 30 grams of fat!) The Chinese do wonderful things with vegetables and noodles and it's a pleasure to fill up on them. Meats and chicken are used but in relatively small amounts, and since there's no "main course" you get a good variety of foods by choosing well and sharing dishes with your dining companions.

The Oriental stir-fry technique is very healthful because it uses a minimum of oil. The food is kept moving in a very hot wok and thus has no chance to stick. The extreme heat simultaneously sears and cooks it at the same time, so that very little oil is absorbed. In addition, food cooked this way retains more vitamins.

Steamed vegetable or shrimp dumplings, garlic prawns, diced chicken dishes (usually breast meat without skin), whole poached fish with ginger and scallions, accents of fermented black bean, shredded cabbage, broccoli with oyster sauce are all good choices.

Not such a good idea are egg rolls or spring rolls, spareribs, fried rice, or any of the deep-fried foods.

Thai and Vietnamese: These cuisines offer low-fat food satisfactions similar to Chinese cooking, but do stay away from deep-fried foods or those made with coconut milk.

Japanese: With the exception of tempura and fried, breaded pork, Japanese food is extremely low fat. Sushi and sashimi, raw fish slices on rice or alone, are pleasant options. Even the fatty fishes like yellowtail, tuna belly, and eel don't add up to much because you are eating only morsels. Try the clear soup, suimono, and the many raw or slightly cooked vegetable offerings.

Mexican food has lots of good tastes, and lots of fiber, but try to avoid sour cream, which most dishes don't need anyway, cheddar or Jack cheese, and fried tortillas. Be sparing with guacamole; avocado is the one high-fat vegetable, with 17 to 19 grams of fat in one half. Go for the seafood and chicken dishes, especially those that have been marinated. If you love beef *fajitas*, eat a moderate portion and fill up on rice and beans. Or stick with chicken fajitas, made with skinless breast meat.

Indian food, with its great vegetarian tradition, can be a low-fat watcher's delight, as long as you skirt foods made with *ghee* (clarified butter) and layered breads like paratha, also full of butter. Some vegetable dishes can be very oily; if in doubt, ask. Tandoori chicken, probably the most delicious skinless chicken around, is great. The complex spicing more than compensates for the missing skin.

French food: The butter and cream that are the cornerstones of French cooking can make eating in French restaurants deliciously perilous. In fact, I find myself going to them less and less, because I now crave a different kind of food altogether, and my system is so unused to rich, buttery food that I am actually rather unwell several hours after eating it. Nor is *la nouvelle cuisine* the answer, because this food often involves reductions of cream that can be very concentrated sources of fat. French spa cooking, when well executed, is usually lighter food, which still has flavor and textural interest. One versatile French method that is low in fat involves dishes cooked *en papillote*. In this method fish or chicken are teamed with aromatic vegetables and herbs and perhaps a bit of white wine and baked in parchment or foil. The food steams in its own luscious juices, and little if any butter is required—certainly no cream.

If a dish is "à la—" ask if it's sauced, and if the sauce can be served on the side. Dishes *à la nage* are usually in their own natural broth, and therefore quite okay.

Fast food is frequently high in fat, salt, and protein; 40 to 55 percent of the calories in most fast food offerings come from fat. Most people are trying to eat less beef and more chicken and fish, yet these choices can be dietary disasters in fast food establishments. While a single hamburger may have 13 grams of fat, 6 chicken nuggets may have 20. A fish sandwich, by the time it's batter-coated, has a slice of cheese added, and is sauced, is up to 25 grams of fat. Furthermore, chicken nuggets and chicken "patty" sandwiches are often made with chicken skin, super-high in fat, and are usually cooked in an oil high in saturated fat. Thus a fast-food chicken sandwich has as much fat as a pint and a half of ice cream!

Fast-food breakfasts, by the way, like a croissant with ham and cheese or a sausage McMuffin with Egg, are out of sight from the point of view of fat (26.8 grams) and cholesterol (263 milligrams, almost your whole daily allowance)!

Take-out food: Pizza, barbecued chicken, and ribs are probably our most common take-out foods. A well-made pizza is the highest nutrient-dense, ready-to-eat food you can buy. I love it, but still only eat it occasionally, because of the fat in the cheese. I try to ask that additional oil not be poured on top; if it has been already, I make it a point to blot it up with a paper towel. To satisfy my craving, I ask for very little cheese with a topping of green peppers, onions, and fresh mushrooms, or I make a homemade version of this with commercially prepared pizza sauce. For the base I use prepared pizza crusts, which my supermarket carries, and a small amount of part-skim mozzarella.

As for barbecued chicken: Remove the skin. Ribs: Just say no. Or, try asking a restaurant whose low-fat food you know and like to make food available for take-out.

Salad bars: Selections here can add up to more calories and fat than you think. A typical small ladle at a salad bar holds about 2 tablespoons of dressing, which, if it is Italian (14 grams) or blue cheese (16 grams), can add fat to your diet you may not be considering. Two ladlesful on a large lunch salad and you're right up there with a hamburger. Since most salad dressings are primarily fat, look for one that is low-cal or "lite." And watch what you put on your plate. Concentrate on vegetables, especially dark-green leafy ones, and beans. Avoid mayonnaise-dressed salads, bacon bits, and buttered croutons. Strictly limit the amount of cheese and nuts.

8

MICROWAVE COOKING

Microwave cooking is a boon to low-fat eating, because you do not need to add fat when you cook in order to prevent foods from sticking. A hidden asset is that the microwave makes it so easy and fast to rustle up something healthful to eat that, when hunger strikes, you are less likely to indulge in high-fat, high-calorie snack food.

The speed of the microwave also encourages you to cook low-fat dishes that do well in quantity. For example, prepare Carrot Soup (page 96) or Minestrone alla Milanese (page 104) when you have time, say on the weekend, then freeze what you don't eat in single or two-portion amounts. My freezer is never without homemade chicken stock, for pilafs and risotto, tomato sauce for pasta, a hearty soup such as lentil or pea, and a "company" soup around which to build a last-minute meal. I also keep on hand Veal Loaf (page 212) made in small loaf tins. (Remove from the tin before defrosting and heating.) The quick defrosting and heating talents of the microwave make last-minute meals a cinch, with no extra pots and pans to clean.

Old-fashioned oatmeal for breakfast, baked potatoes (both sweet and white), corn on the cob, asparagus, broccoli, baked acorn squash, and baked butternut squash for puréeing are foods I regularly cook in the microwave.

I consider my microwave an additional and infinitely useful kitchen tool, but I don't try to cook everything in it. Its best application is with foods that are to be poached, steamed, or braised—in other words, for moist cooking. Fish, stews, soups, sauces, and vegetables are all good bets.

When converting a regular recipe for use in the microwave, reduce the liquid requirement by one third and add more liquid if you think you need it during cooking. There is less evaporation here than in conventional cooking.

Remember to undercook food slightly when estimating cooking times, and let it finish during standing time. Microwaved foods continue to cook or heat after they are out of the oven, and therefore must stand before being eaten. In general, small items with low density need only a few minutes of standing time; a dense food like a potato needs about 10 minutes (under an inverted bowl). Undercooking is especially necessary when cooking fish.

You can keep a variety of breakfast breads always on hand, with no worry that they will become stale and have to be thrown away. Keep sliced whole-grain loaves, rolls, and muffins, well wrapped, in the freezer and defrost one at a time in the microwave as needed. Use a paper napkin or towel as a wrapping to keep the surface of breads, rolls, and muffins dry. (This holds true for reheating, as well.) A bagel or an English muffin wrapped in a paper towel will defrost in 30 seconds on HIGH in a 650-watt oven. But don't exceed this time even by a few seconds or you'll have a rock.

9

A WEEK'S WORTH OF MENUS TO GET STARTED ON

Each of these menus has 30 percent of calories or less from fat and 10 percent or less from saturated fat. In addition, the week's total intake averages out to under 300 milligrams of cholesterol a day and fewer than 2,500 milligrams of sodium, well below the upper limit of 3,300 recommended for adults.

The caloric intake varies from day to day as it does in real life. The important thing is the weekly average.

But don't think you have to spend the rest of your life weighing and measuring to tailor your daily menus. Doing it for a few days, though, gives you a sense of portions and combinations; then gradually you'll start operating on instinct. Some days will be nutritionally more perfect than others; but you'll be ahead in your low-fat lifestyle any way you look at it. The idea is to get started.

It is frequently a problem, for example, to meet the RDA for calcium (800–1,200 milligrams daily) when you are restricting intake of dairy products, which unfortunately supply us also with a lot of unnecessary fat. If adequate calcium intake is of concern to you, especially if you are a post-menopausal woman advised to increase daily calcium to 1,500 milligrams, you may want to discuss with your physician the advisability of calcium supplements. Not all experts are convinced that increased calcium intake prevents bone loss, particularly the accelerated loss of spongy bone that occurs in women at menopause.

The daily fat supplied by these menus actually averages out to around 20 percent, with saturated fats averaging 5 percent, both the low end of the fat range, allowing you to make additions that reflect personal preferences—the teaspoon of margarine or whipped butter on toast or on your vegetables, the extra helping of a favorite food, the salad dressing you can't live without, and so on. They also help you to see how un-depriving and filling low-fat eating can be and how much room there is within sensible parameters to create your own personal low-fat lifestyle.

Day 1

BREAKFAST
½ cup orange juice
½ cup Homemade Granola,* ½ cup blueberries, 1 cup non-fat yogurt
Coffee or tea with 2 tablespoons 1% fat milk

LUNCH
1 cup minestrone soup, canned
Sardine sandwich, with squeeze lemon, 1 teaspoon reduced-fat mayon-naise, sliced purple onion and cucumber slices, lettuce, and 2 slices white or whole-wheat toast
1 sliced orange

DINNER
Grilled Lemon–Thyme Chicken Breast* (3 ounces)
Bulgur Pilaf with Currants and Pine Nuts*
Steamed or microwaved broccoli, ½ cup
Arugula/endive salad with 1 tablespoon Semi-Classic Vinaigrette*
Marinated Strawberries with Grapes*

SNACK
Oatmeal Apple Muffin*
1 cup 1% fat milk

Nutrient Analysis: 1,756 calories, as follows:

18% Protein	23% Fat	58% Carbohydrate
134 mg Cholesterol	4% Saturated Fatty Acids	2,762 mg Sodium

*Foods marked with an asterisk (*) may be found in Part II: The Recipes section.

Day 2

BREAKFAST
½ cup orange juice
½ cup Hot Oatmeal* with 1 cup 1% fat milk, 2 tablespoons raisins and
    dash cinnamon and nutmeg
1 slice whole-wheat toast with 1 teaspoon jam
Coffee or tea with 2 tablespoons 1% fat milk

LUNCH
Lean roast beef sandwich with 3 ounces meat, lettuce, tomato, mustard,
    and 2 slices rye bread or a small submarine roll
1 peach or other fruit

DINNER
Lentil Chili*
Basic Foolproof White Rice*
Cucumber Yogurt Sauce*
2 flour tortillas
OR
Pasta with tomato sauce and 2 tablespoons grated Parmesan cheese
Tossed green salad with 1 tablespoon Balsamic Vinaigrette*
½ cup each cantaloupe and honeydew balls

SNACK
½ cup fruit-flavored sorbet

Nutrient Analysis: 1,606 calories, as follows:

16% Protein	11% Fat	73% Carbohydrate
58 mg Cholesterol	5% Saturated Fatty Acids	1,754 mg Sodium

Day 3

BREAKFAST
½ grapefruit
Bagel with 1 tablespoon Breakfast Ricotta Spread*
Coffee or tea with ¼ cup 1% fat milk

LUNCH
1 cup Pasta Salad with Tuna and Snow Peas* on lettuce
1 poppy seed roll
1 cup fruit-flavored low-fat yogurt

DINNER
Tenderloin steak, 5 ounces broiled
1 medium baked sweet potato with 1 teaspoon margarine and cinnamon
    and nutmeg to taste
1 cup Zucchini Trifolati*
2 slices Italian bread
Endive/watercress salad with 1 tablespoon Balsamic Vinaigrette*
1 cup sliced fresh pineapple with 1 tablespoon Kirsch

SNACK
1 cup 1% fat milk
1 brownie (with nuts)

Nutrient Analysis: 1,551 calories, as follows:

20% Protein	20% Fat	60% Carbohydrate
148 mg Cholesterol	6% Saturated Fatty Acids	1,206 mg Sodium

Day 4

BREAKFAST
Sliced fresh orange
2 slices Low-Fat French Toast* with 2 tablespoons maple syrup
Coffee or tea with 2 tablespoons 1% fat milk

LUNCH
1 cup pea soup
Turkey breast sandwich with 3 ounces meat, lettuce, 1 tablespoon re-
    duced-calorie mayonnaise and 2 slices whole-wheat bread
1 cup 1% fat milk
1 cup grapes

DINNER
Pan-Grilled Shrimp*
Okra–Corn Stew*
Basic Foolproof White Rice*
Mixed green salad with 2 tablespoons Semi-Classic Vinaigrette*
½ cup sorbet, any fruit flavor

SNACK
1 pear

Nutrient Analysis: 1,756 calories, as follows:

21% Protein	18% Fat	61% Carbohydrate
279 mg Cholesterol	4% Saturated Fatty Acids	1,842 mg Sodium

Day 5

BREAKFAST
½ cup orange juice
Scrambled Egg Beaters with Chives on Toast,* 2 slices whole-wheat
Coffee or tea with 2 tablespoons 1% fat milk

LUNCH
Pita pocket stuffed with Chickpea Spread* and alfalfa sprouts
Carrot sticks, green pepper rings
1 cup fruit-flavored low-fat yogurt

DINNER
Veal Loaf,* 4 ounces
Low-Fat Mashed Potatoes*
Steamed carrots
Sliced tomatoes with snipped basil, black pepper, and sprinkling of bal-
   samic vinegar
Green salad with 1 tablespoon Balsamic Vinaigrette*
Oranges Marinated with Grand Marnier*

SNACK
1 cup 1% fat milk, 4 gingersnaps

Nutrient Analysis: 1,683 calories, as follows:

20% Protein	20% Fat	61% Carbohydrate
173 mg Cholesterol	8% Saturated Fatty Acids	2,011 mg Sodium

Day 6

BREAKFAST
½ cup grapefruit juice
1 Toasted English Muffin with Banana* and 1 teaspoon jam
Coffee or tea with 2 tablespoons 1% fat milk

LUNCH
Cold Veal Loaf* sandwich with 3 ounces meat, lettuce, 1 tablespoon
  reduced-calorie mayonnaise, and 2 slices rye bread
1 apple

DINNER
Teriyaki-Grilled Swordfish,* 4 ounces
Baked potato with 2 tablespoons Pico de Gallo Sauce*
Squash Purée*
Watercress and endive salad with 1 tablespoon Semi-Classic Vinaigrette*
Fresh Fruit Salad with Ginger and Citrus Syrup*

SNACK
1 cup non-fat yogurt with ½ cup blueberries

Nutrient Analysis: 1,879 calories, as follows:

21% Protein	19% Fat	60% Carbohydrate
229 mg Cholesterol	9% Saturated Fatty Acids	2,773 mg Sodium

Day 7

BREAKFAST
½ cup grapefruit juice
¾ cup raisin bran cereal with 1 cup 1% fat milk
1 small banana
Coffee or tea with 2 tablespoons 1% fat milk

LUNCH
Minestrone alla Milanese* soup, 1 cup homemade (or canned with 1
  tablespoon grated Parmesan cheese)
½ cup Reduced-Fat Tuna Salad* in sandwich, with lettuce and sliced
  tomato
2 slices whole-wheat toast spread with 1 tablespoon reduced-calorie mayonnaise
1 cup 1% fat milk

DINNER
Chicken—Mushroom Satay*
¼ cup Herbed "Instant" Couscous*
½ cup Stir-Fried Snow Peas*
½ cup sliced cherry tomatoes, 2 tablespoons chopped scallions
1 tablespoon Lemon—Mustard Vinaigrette*
1 cup grapes

SNACK
½ cup frozen non-fat vanilla yogurt with 1 tablespoon Buttermilk Chocolate Sauce*

Nutrient Analysis: 1,489 calories, as follows:

22% Protein	24% Fat	54% Carbohydrate
124 mg Cholesterol	5% Saturated Fatty Acids	3,043 mg Sodium

Menu Weekly Average

Nutrient Analysis: 1,731 calories, as follows:

20% Protein	19% Fat	61% Carbohydrate
168 mg Cholesterol	5% Saturated Fatty Acids	2,222 mg Sodium

Calcium averages 95% of the R.D.A.

Part II

THE RECIPES

About These Recipes

These recipes represent much of the food my family and I have been eating for years. This is real food for real people, not "diet" food, although I have often cut down on oil or butter requirements after I found the results were just as good. I haven't tried to make things up or reinvent food, with the exception of Mock Sour Cream. In addition, Butter Buds and Egg Beaters are substitutes readily found in supermarkets.

Food for the low-fat lifestyle has to offer a big flavor payload to compensate for the fat we used to eat. My big flavor guns are aromatic vegetables such as onions, garlic, jalapeño peppers, scallions, and leeks, seasonings such as ginger, sesame oil, soy sauce, and balsamic vinegar, and spices and herbs such as cumin and coriander. While sauces, as most people know them, are not a large part of this way of eating, condiments like Pico de Gallo (page 124) and Warm Coriander Vinaigrette (page 177) and marinades with a lemon or garlic edge add flavor excitement (without lots of calories and fat) to the simplest broiled fish or chicken.

I hope many of these recipes will become your favorites too, and that you will also use them as delicious rough blueprints to modify the foods you now eat.

About the Nutritional Analyses

A nutritional analysis, listing calories, fat (with separate figures for total, saturated, and polyunsaturated fat), and selected nutrients per serving, follows each recipe.

Figures for fat, carbohydrates, and protein are expressed in grams (g). Other nutrients are in milligrams (mg). *

The figures given are based on the following assumptions:

- Meats are trimmed of fat and poultry is skinned before cooking, unless otherwise specified in the recipe.
- When a range is given for an ingredient, as in 1 to 1½ cups, the lesser amount is calculated.
- When a marinade is used, only the amount of the marinade absorbed by the food is calculated.
- Pasta recipes do not include Parmesan cheese, which is passed separately.
- Optional ingredients, such as garnishes, are not calculated.
- When a recipe serves, say, 4 to 6, calculations are based on the average, in this case 5.

---

*Nutritional values were obtained from Hill Nutrition Associates, Inc , Fayetteville, N.Y., and Stuart, Fla.

10

BREAKFAST

HOMEMADE GRANOLA

HOT OATMEAL

BREAKFAST COUSCOUS

SCRAMBLED EGG BEATERS WITH CHIVES
ON TOAST

LOW-FAT FRENCH TOAST

ORANGE FRENCH TOAST

PANCAKES

GERMAN APPLE PANCAKE

FOUR BAGEL BREAKFASTS

TOASTED ENGLISH MUFFIN WITH BANANA

BREAKFAST RICOTTA SPREAD

OATMEAL BREAD

OATMEAL APPLE MUFFINS

Well it's true—everything your mother told you about having a good breakfast. It sets you up for the day, means you won't be starving at lunch and tempted to overeat. The catch is that some of the best and the worst foods in the American diet are served at breakfast, so high in fat that they make it easy to consume well over half anyone's desirable fat allowance for the entire day, at this one meal. Which doesn't leave you very much to play with for the next two. One good ploy is to try and plan a nutritious breakfast that has no or little fat, one that fills you but permits you to "spend" your fat grams on the rest of the day's food. (A good rule of thumb is to plan to consume no more than half your daily fat allowance on breakfast, lunch, and a mid-afternoon snack; then you'll still have plenty to spend on dinner.)

Traditional breakfast foods such as bacon, sausage, butter, and cream cheese add considerable amounts of fat, all of it saturated, to this meal, not to mention the eggs served primarily at breakfast, which provide one third of all dietary cholesterol in American eating habits. Few of us are active enough to burn up the calories and fat in, say, two fried eggs, sausage, and buttered toast (804 calories, 73 percent of them from fat). Add to this picture the doughnuts, Danish, and syrupy pancakes that add sugar and more fat and calories. The oversized muffins that have appeared on the breakfast scene in recent years may be made of whole-wheat flour and therefore perceived as "healthy," but mostly what they add is a healthy dose of calories and fat, with their eggs, sugar, nuts, and so on.

Breakfast is an easy meal to plan, since breads, cereals, and fruit are easily come by. To help stay within your fat allowance use skim milk, skim milk yogurt, and reduce the amount of butter or margarine you use as a spread. Buy the freshest, most interesting breads you can find, especially the whole-grain variety. Hot fresh bread, rolls, and bagels are delicious unbuttered or with just some apple butter or marmalade.

HOMEMADE GRANOLA

Makes 2 quarts, or 16 servings of about ½ cup each

This is one granola that deserves a wider audience; it is absolutely delicious, with less fat and sweetener than most granolas. It's good with nothing more than some skim milk, but my favorite way to eat it is mixed with blueberries, strawberries, and low-fat yogurt.

6 cups rolled oats
1 cup untoasted wheat germ
1 teaspoon cinnamon
1 teaspoon grated nutmeg
½ cup soy flour
3 tablespoons sesame seeds

3 tablespoons sunflower seeds
1 tablespoon vanilla extract
¼ cup safflower oil
¼ cup mild-flavored honey or
     malt syrup
½ cup raisins

Preheat oven to 250°F.

In a large bowl mix together the oats, wheat germ, spices, soy flour, seeds, and vanilla.

In a small bowl combine the oil and honey. Stir to blend and pour over the grain mixture. Toss thoroughly so there are no large lumps. Spread out on a large baking pan such as a rimmed cookie sheet and bake in the preheated oven for 2 hours, stirring every 20 minutes to redistribute the grains. Add the raisins during the last 20 minutes.

Cool in the pan, then transfer to a tightly sealed jar or jars and refrigerate. Will keep refrigerated for at least a month.

Calories	237	cal
Protein	9	g
Carbohydrates	34	g
Total fat	8	g
Saturated	1	g
Polyunsaturated	5	g
Cholesterol	0	mg
Sodium	3	mg

HOT OATMEAL

Serves 1

I prefer not to use instant or quick oatmeal because not only is it high in sodium, but it also does not have the flavor or texture of the old-fashioned kind. Cooking directions are on the box or package, but if you have a microwave you can make oatmeal in a jiffy.

⅓ cup rolled oats	Brown sugar
¾ cup water	Cinnamon
Salt	Skim milk

Combine oats and water in a 2-cup glass measure. (This size is important because oatmeal can boil up and over quickly.) Microwave on HIGH for 2 minutes, 30 seconds, then let stand 1 minute. Add brown sugar, cinnamon, and milk to taste.

NOTE: You can sweeten oatmeal with honey instead of brown sugar, if you prefer. Or stir in raisins, currants, prunes, or dried apricots or figs.

Calories	103	cal
Protein	4	g
Carbohydrates	18	g
Total fat	2	g
Saturated	.3	g
Polyunsaturated	.7	g
Cholesterol	0	mg
Sodium	1	mg

Banana smoothie: First peel and slice an overripe banana and freeze the slices. Blend frozen banana slices with 1 cup chilled non-fat milk until smooth. Makes a quick, filling breakfast or a cold, delicious non-fat snack.

BREAKFAST COUSCOUS

Serves 2; ¼ cup each

Pasta for breakfast? When it's this good, why not?

1 cup skim milk
1½ teaspoons Butter Buds

½ cup couscous
1 tablespoon raisins

Heat the milk in a small pot. Stir in the Butter Buds and, when blended, stir in the couscous and raisins. Cover, remove from heat, and let stand 5 minutes.

Calories	238	cal
Protein	10	g
Carbohydrates	47	g
Total fat	1	g
Saturated	.2	g
Polyunsaturated	.1	g
Cholesterol	3	mg
Sodium	196	mg

SCRAMBLED EGG BEATERS WITH CHIVES ON TOAST

Serves 1

PAM
1 teaspoon unsalted butter
½ cup Egg Beaters (equals 2
    eggs)
Salt and freshly ground black
    pepper

1 tablespoon snipped fresh
    chives
2 slices toast, cut into
    triangles
Catsup (optional)

Spray a small to medium (preferably non-stick) skillet with PAM, set over brisk heat, add the butter, and swirl it around the pan. As soon as it gets a little bubbly add the Egg Beaters and immediately lower the heat to simmer the eggs. As the eggs begin to set, push the firm part to the center with a plastic spatula and let the uncooked portion run to the edges of the pan. Don't stir. Season with salt and pepper and sprinkle with chives. At this point you can turn off the heat, since, retained in the pan, it will finish cooking the eggs in a matter of seconds. (Or, off heat, put a lid on for 20 seconds.)

Arrange the toast points on a plate and scoop the eggs on top. If you're like me, you'll add a dollop of catsup as well.

NOTE: Egg substitutes do tend to stick more than regular eggs, so stay with scrambled eggs and don't try to do an omelet.

Calories	224 cal
Protein	14 g
Carbohydrates	27 g
Total fat	6 g
Saturated	3 g
Polyunsaturated	.1 g
Cholesterol	12 mg
Sodium	447 mg

LOW-FAT FRENCH TOAST

Serves 1

2 slices French or Italian bread, cut slightly on the diagonal, about 1 inch thick
¼ cup Egg Beaters (equals 1 egg)
¼ cup skim milk

Dash vanilla extract
Pinch sugar (optional)
Pinch grated nutmeg
Optional toppings: confectioner's sugar, fruit preserves, or maple syrup

Beat together the Egg Beaters, milk, vanilla, sugar, and nutmeg in a shallow glass dish. Add the bread, let soak briefly on one side, then turn pieces over and repeat on second side. Cook on a hot, PAM-sprayed griddle or in a PAM-sprayed non-stick skillet until nicely browned, then repeat on second side. Serve hot, sprinkled with any of the toppings.

Calories	259	cal
Protein	13	g
Carbohydrates	43	g
Total fat	3	g
Saturated	1	g
Polyunsaturated	0	g
Cholesterol	3	mg
Sodium	518	mg

ORANGE FRENCH TOAST

Use ¼ cup orange juice and omit the vanilla.

Calories	286	cal
Protein	14	g
Carbohydrates	50	g
Total fat	3	g
Saturated	1	g
Polyunsaturated	.1	g
Cholesterol	3	mg
Sodium	519	mg

Make a quick, pleasing breakfast drink by blending skim milk with strawberries, orange juice, and/or low- or non-fat yogurt.

PANCAKES

Makes 12 pancakes about 4½ inches in diameter; average
serving 3 pancakes

These pancakes are thin and elegant.

1 extra-large egg	1 heaping cup unbleached
1 egg white	white or whole-wheat
1¼ cups skim milk	flour
Dash vanilla extract	1 heaping teaspoon baking
Dash salt	powder
Several gratings nutmeg	Optional toppings: maple
	syrup, confectioner's
	sugar, or fruit preserves

Beat egg and egg white lightly in blender jar or in a bowl; add milk, vanilla, salt, nutmeg, flour, and baking powder. Beat briefly. A few lumps should remain. Let batter sit a few minutes before using. Pour batter in ¼-cup portions onto a non-stick griddle lightly sprayed with PAM and cook until golden on both sides. Serve with any of the optional toppings.

Per pancake

Calories	59	cal
Protein	3	g
Carbohydrates	10	g
Total fat	1	g
Saturated	.2	g
Polyunsaturated	.1	g
Cholesterol	18	mg

Most 4-inch pancakes are calorically similar to one slice of bread, about 70 calories. The least fatty toppings are low-fat yogurt, a light sprinkling of powdered or cinnamon sugar, a tablespoon of syrup or jelly, or some sliced fruit.

GERMAN APPLE PANCAKE

Serves 2

*This is a special breakfast to make for someone you love on Sunday morning.
It is also delicious as a dessert, served with Double-Thick Yogurt (page 275)
that has been sweetened and flavored with vanilla.*

PAM
1 large egg
1 egg white
6 tablespoons unbleached
    white flour
6 tablespoons skim milk
½ large Granny Smith or
    Golden Delicious apple

2 teaspoons lemon juice
2 tablespoons dark-brown
    sugar
2 pinches cinnamon
Optional topping: maple syrup

Preheat oven to 425°F. Place a rack in the upper third of the oven.

Liberally spray two 6-inch round gratin dishes (or one 10-inch pie
plate) with PAM and set the dishes in the oven to heat.

Beat the egg and egg white slightly, then add and stir in the flour and
the milk. The batter will be lumpy.

Peel and core the apple half, slice it thinly, and toss in a small bowl
with the lemon juice, brown sugar, and cinnamon.

Divide the batter between the two dishes; divide and arrange the apple
slices in a pinwheel pattern on top of the batter. Bake for 15 to 20
minutes, until puffed and golden. Serve immediately.

Calories	236	cal
Protein	9	g
Carbohydrates	41	g
Total fat	5	g
Saturated	1	g
Polyunsaturated	.4	g
Cholesterol	139	mg

Night-before strategy for pancakes: Mix all wet ingredients in one
bowl and refrigerate; mix dry ingredients in a second one. For breakfast, simply combine contents of bowls and cook.

FOUR BAGEL BREAKFASTS

Bagels, available fresh and frozen with a variety of flavorings like onion, poppy-seed, or sesame, make good breakfast food. Their fat is negligible (½ plain bagel = ½ fat gram) and they are chewy and filling.

BAGEL BREAKFAST 1

Half a toasted poppyseed bagel spread with about 1½ teaspoons part-skim ricotta and sprinkled with cinnamon sugar. Or use the Breakfast Ricotta Spread on page 76.

BAGEL BREAKFAST 2

Tear out enough bread from the cut half of a plain bagel to make a "trench"; fill it with a mixture of finely chopped tomato, cucumber, and a little purple onion, seasoned with a little salt and pepper. You won't believe how good this is.

BAGEL BREAKFAST 3

Spread a half of your favorite bagel with 1 teaspoon whipped butter *before* toasting it in a toaster oven. The butter goes much farther this way and the bagel is absolutely delicious.

BAGEL BREAKFAST 4

If you occasionally crave protein in the morning, have 1 paper-thin slice lean ham or 1 slice lean, smoked turkey breast on an unbuttered bagel half.

Breakfast 1			Breakfast 2		
Calories	91	cal	Calories	63	cal
Protein	4	g	Protein	2	g
Carbohydrates	16	g	Carbohydrates	13	g
Total fat	1	g	Total fat	.4	g
Saturated	.4	g	Saturated	0	g
Polyunsaturated	.2	g	Polyunsaturated	0	g
Cholesterol	2	mg	Cholesterol	0	mg
Sodium	186	mg	Sodium	250	mg

Breakfast 3			**Breakfast 4**		
Calories	92	cal	Calories	94	cal
Protein	3	g	Protein	6	g
Carbohydrates	15	g	Carbohydrates	15	g
Total fat	2	g	Total fat	1	g
Saturated	1	g	Saturated	.2	g
Polyunsaturated	.1	g	Polyunsaturated	.1	g
Cholesterol	5	mg	Cholesterol	7	mg
Sodium	195	mg	Sodium	379	mg

TOASTED ENGLISH MUFFIN WITH BANANA

Serves 1

One of our favorite quick breakfasts is the invention of our friend Didi Ball. It's really better than butter!

1 English muffin
½ ripe banana, mashed

1 teaspoon blueberry or
strawberry jam

Split the muffin and toast well. Spread each half with the mashed banana and the jam.

Calories	201	cal
Protein	5	g
Carbohydrates	44	g
Total fat	1	g
Saturated	.1	g
Polyunsaturated	.1	g
Cholesterol	0	mg
Sodium	291	mg

BREAKFAST RICOTTA SPREAD

Makes 8 servings, 2 tablespoons per serving

1 cup part-skim ricotta   **2 tablespoons plain non-fat yogurt**

Combine the ricotta and yogurt in a small bowl and whisk together. Refrigerate in a tightly covered container. Use on fresh or toasted bagels, plain or with a sprinkling of cinnamon sugar.

Calories	44	cal
Protein	4	g
Carbohydrates	2	g
Total fat	2	g
Saturated	2	g
Polyunsaturated	.1	g
Cholesterol	10	mg
Sodium	41	mg

OATMEAL BREAD

Makes 3 loaves, about 16 slices per loaf

The late James Beard gave me this recipe many years ago, in response to my request for an easy, foolproof bread that a novice could make. And I've made it ever since. Oatmeal bread was almost unheard of then; it couldn't be more appropriate now. The only change I've made is to substitute whole-wheat flour for part of the flour requirement. This bread makes marvelous toast.

3 cups rolled oats
4 cups boiling water
4 cups whole-wheat flour
3½ to 4 cups unbleached all-
     purpose flour

2 packages active dry yeast
2 tablespoons salt
4 tablespoons vegetable oil
½ cup unsulphured molasses

Put the oats in a large mixing bowl and pour in the boiling water. In another large bowl combine the two flours. Add 2 cups of the flour and the yeast to the oats and stir in. Allow the dough to rise, uncovered, in a warm, draft-free spot until double in size.

Punch the dough down, add and work in the salt, oil, molasses, and enough of the remaining flour to make a stiff dough.

Turn the dough out on a floured surface and knead, adding extra flour if necessary to make a smooth, pliable, firm dough. This will take about 10 minutes of satisfying labor, but overkneading will not spoil dough. You want it to be smooth and silky and not sticky.

Butter three 9 × 5 × 3-inch loaf pans. Preheat the oven to 350°F.

Divide the dough into three parts and form into loaves in the prepared pans. Allow the dough to rise again, uncovered, until double in bulk— anywhere from 50 minutes to 2 hours, depending on variables like room temperature, humidity, etc.

Bake the loaves on the center rack of the preheated oven for 40 to 60 minutes, or until the bread sounds hollow when removed from the pans and tapped on top and bottom. Cool on racks before slicing. The bread may be frozen.

Calories	108	cal
Protein	3	g
Carbohydrates	20	g
Total fat	2	g
Saturated	.2	g
Polyunsaturated	1	g
Cholesterol	0	mg
Sodium	276	mg

In place of cream cheese: Whip 1-percent-fat cottage cheese in the food processor and use as a spread on bagels, crackers, and so forth. Add chives, favorite herbs, cinnamon sugar—whatever you want as flavor.

OATMEAL APPLE MUFFINS

Makes 12 muffins

PAM   ¾ cup raisins
1 large egg   1 cup whole-wheat flour
¾ cup skim milk   1 cup quick rolled oats
¼ cup vegetable oil   ½ teaspoon salt or to taste
⅓ cup sugar   3 teaspoons baking powder
1 medium apple, preferably   ½ teaspoon grated nutmeg
   Granny Smith or   2 teaspoons ground cinnamon
   McIntosh, peeled, cored,
   and coarsely chopped

Preheat oven to 400°F. Lightly spray 12 muffin tins with PAM. In a medium mixing bowl beat the egg lightly, then add the milk, oil, and sugar and beat lightly. Stir in the apple and raisins.

In another bowl stir together the flour, oats, salt, baking powder, nutmeg, and cinnamon; then add to the egg mixture, stirring just enough to moisten. Fill the prepared tins three-quarters full and bake 15 to 20 minutes. Let muffins cool a bit on a rack before turning them out.

Calories	169	cal
Protein	4	g
Carbohydrates	27	g
Total Fat	6	g
Saturated	1	g
Polyunsaturated	3	g
Cholesterol	23	mg

Try to keep coffee drinking to two cups a day, each with 1 teaspoon of sugar and 2 tablespoons of low-fat milk.

11

HORS D'OEUVRES AND APPETIZERS

CHICKPEA SPREAD
CURRANT MUSTARD DIP
CURRY DIP FOR CRUDITÉS
BAKED POTATO SKINS
PARMESAN CROSTINI
BAKED GARLIC
SALMON MOUSSE
BRUSCHETTA
SHRIMP AND SNOW PEA HORS D'OEUVRE
NEW POTATOES WITH CAVIAR
MUSHROOMS À LA GRECQUE

Let's face it: A cocktail or a glass of wine before dinner isn't half as festive without some food accompaniment. It is very easy, however, to eat virtually a whole day's fat allowance in peanuts consumed with a drink. The same holds true for potato chips, another bar food you can't "eat just one of." One ounce of potato chips contains 160 calories and 10 *grams* fat (plus lots of sodium)!

Almost all the food we know as "cocktail food" is disproportionately high in calories and fat. I'm thinking of all those spreads made with softened cream cheese or butter, and the deep-fried tidbits. As for cheese, our habit of serving it with crackers as an hors d'oeuvre—when people are hungriest—is not only disastrous from a fat point of view, but also not a proper pre-dinner food from any point of view. My French friends think cheese is barbaric as an hors d'oeuvre, saying that cheese "closes the stomach." What I think they mean is that cheese tends to be so rich it kills the appetite rather than stimulates it.

All this doesn't mean you have to forgo drink nibbles. Just choose differently. Baked Potato Skins (page 83) are delicious, and you can use the insides to make mashed potatoes at a meal. Crudités, or raw vegetables, provide color and crunch, and can be quite satisfying with the tasty Curry Dip for Crudités (page 82) or Chickpea Spread (page 81). Make a handsome still life by heaping a pretty basket with vegetables and using a hollowed-out purple cabbage as the dip container. Some vegetables to use are: radishes, cherry tomatoes, cauliflower florets, baby carrots, 4-inch sticks of young zucchini, cucumber, celery, red and yellow pepper strips, rounds of fresh fennel, blanched snow peas or sugar snap peas, and fresh mushroom slices. Toasted pita bread triangles also make good no-fat dipper-uppers. Cucumber rounds can be the base for smoked salmon canapés instead of buttered brown bread, and endive leaves can be used instead of crackers with the Salmon Mousse on page 86. This is one area where you can be as creative as you like, within the bounds of your own good taste!

CHICKPEA SPREAD

Makes 2 cups, approximately ¼ cup per serving

1 small onion, quartered
½ bunch Italian parsley
  leaves, rinsed
2 cups cooked garbanzos
  (1 19-ounce can
  chickpeas, drained)
¼ teaspoon ground cumin
¼ teaspoon ground coriander
  (optional)

½ teaspoon dried oregano
Salt and freshly ground black
  pepper to taste
1 small garlic clove, put
  through a press
Juice of ½ lemon (about 2
  tablespoons)
2 tablespoons olive or
  vegetable oil

In a food processor fitted with the steel blade, process the onion and parsley until finely minced. Add the rest of the ingredients and process until blended. Do not overblend.

Serve as an open-faced sandwich on toasted whole-wheat bread with cucumber and tomato slices or stuffed in a pita bread pocket. Alfalfa sprouts go nicely on top. It may also be thinned with a little chicken, vegetable, or bean stock and used as a dip with toasted pita triangles, crackers, or raw vegetables. Some toasted sesame seeds sprinkled on top add protein and flavor.

Calories	103	cal
Protein	4	g
Carbohydrates	13	g
Total fat	4	g
Saturated	1	g
Polyunsaturated	1	g
Cholesterol	0	mg
Sodium	6	mg

CURRANT MUSTARD DIP

Makes about 1 cup

This is one of those sauces people say they could eat the telephone book with. It has no fat to speak of and it's fun to make people guess what's in it. Almost everyone says "mayonnaise," and no one believes it consists of only two ingredients!

6 ounces currant jelly   **4 tablespoons Dijon mustard**

Combine the jelly and mustard together in a small bowl, and beat with a wire whisk. Small flecks of jelly will appear not to have dissolved, but in 5 minutes or so they will melt and the sauce will be smooth. Use as a dip for Shrimp and Snow Pea Hors d'Oeuvre (page 88) or crudités.

Calories	31	cal
Protein	0	g
Carbohydrates	7	g
Total fat	.2	g
Saturated	0	g
Polyunsaturated	0	g
Cholesterol	0	mg
Sodium	100	mg

CURRY DIP FOR CRUDITÉS

Makes about 1 cup
approximately 8 servings, 2 tablespoons per serving

1 cup plain non-fat yogurt
1 teaspoon curry powder,
  or to taste
½ teaspoon lemon juice,
  or to taste

½ teaspoon ground cumin
Salt and freshly ground black
  pepper to taste

Combine all the ingredients in a small bowl, mix well, and chill.

Calories	17	cal
Protein	2	g
Carbohydrates	2	g
Total fat	.1	g
Saturated	0	g
Polyunsaturated	0	g
Cholesterol	1	mg
Sodium	157	mg

BAKED POTATO SKINS

Makes 24 pieces

For a cocktail snack, allow at least 3 strips per person. Bake the potatoes ahead and season and broil the skins just before serving. Use the filling to make mashed potatoes.

6 Idaho potatoes, baked
1 packet (4 ounces) Butter
    Buds mixed with ½ cup
    hot tap water

Salt and freshly ground black
    pepper (optional)

Preheat the broiler.

Cut the potatoes in half lengthwise and scoop out the inside, leaving about one-quarter inch. (Save the potatoes to make Low-Fat Mashed Potatoes, on page 235.) With a sharp knife cut each potato shell in half, again lengthwise. Brush the flesh side with the Butter Buds, season lightly with the optional salt and pepper, place in a broiling pan, and broil 6 or 7 inches from the heat source until brown and crisp—about 5 minutes. Watch that the skins do not burn.

Calories	31	cal
Protein	1	g
Carbohydrates	7	g
Total fat	0	g
Saturated	0	g
Polyunsaturated	0	g
Cholesterol	.1	mg
Sodium	31	mg

PARMESAN CROSTINI

Serves 8
2 slices per serving

These are great with a drink and also delicious served with soup.

PAM
16 one-quarter-inch slices of
   Italian or French bread
3 tablespoons olive oil

½ cup freshly grated
   Parmesan cheese
Freshly ground black pepper

Preheat oven to 400°F. Spray a cookie sheet with PAM. Place the bread slices on the sheet and use a brush to paint each slice with olive oil. Spread each with a teaspoon of Parmesan and some freshly ground black pepper. Bake in the preheated oven for 10 to 15 minutes or until the bread crisps and the cheese is just melted. Makes 16 pieces.

Calories	101.01	cal
Protein	3	g
Carbohydrates	6	g
Total fat	7	g
Saturated	2	g
Polyunsaturated	.5	g
Cholesterol	5	mg
Sodium	172	mg

> Eating 8 ounces of potato chips is like adding 12 to 20 teaspoons of vegetable oil (usually hydrogenated) and a teaspoon of salt to an 8-ounce potato—as much fat and sodium as most people should eat in an entire day.

BAKED GARLIC

Serves 6

Garlic becomes surprisingly sweet and tender when baked, and makes a lovely appetizer for a light meal. In California I have had it served with goat cheese as a first course, followed by a big green salad.

3 whole heads plump garlic
3 teaspoons olive oil

Salt and freshly ground black
pepper

Preheat oven to 250°F.

With a sharp knife, make an incision through the outer skin of each garlic head all around the middle, about three quarters of an inch above the base. Lift off and discard the outer papery skin above this point, leaving it intact below.

Set the garlic heads on their bases in a small baking dish, just large enough to hold them. Drizzle 1 teaspoon of olive oil over each, and season with salt and pepper.

Cover the dish with heavy-duty aluminum foil and bake the garlic for 1½ hours. It should be very tender. Serve each person half a head (cut vertically), accompanied by lightly toasted sourdough or peasant bread. Each clove of garlic can be picked up and squeezed onto the bread.

NOTE: A few branches of fresh thyme, scattered among the garlic heads before baking, add a lovely note.

Calories	74	cal
Protein	2	g
Carbohydrates	12	g
Total fat	2	g
Saturated	.3	g
Polyunsaturated	.3	g
Cholesterol	0	mg

SALMON MOUSSE

Makes about 3 cups, or 9 appetizer servings
⅓ cup per serving approximately

Let your guests spread this on crackers or serve as a first course in a thick slice on shredded salad greens.

1 envelope plain gelatin
2 tablespoons lemon juice
1 small onion, sliced
½ cup boiling water
¼ teaspoon paprika
1 teaspoon chopped fresh dill
   or Italian parsley, plus
   some sprigs for garnish

2 cups cooked salmon or 1
   16-ounce can salmon,
   drained
1 cup plain low-fat or non-fat
   yogurt

Put the gelatin, lemon juice, onion, and boiling water into blender jar or food processor. Blend 40 seconds. Add the paprika, dill, and salmon and blend briefly. Add the yogurt and blend 30 seconds longer. Pour the mixture into a 3- or 4-cup mold and chill 3–4 hours or until firm.

Unmold the mousse by wrapping a hot towel around the bottom of the mold or immersing the bottom in hot water for less than a minute. Turn out onto a serving platter and garnish with sprigs of fresh dill or parsley. Serve the mousse with flatbread or other low-fat cracker.

Calories	65	cal
Protein	9	g
Carbohydrates	2	g
Total fat	2	g
Saturated	1	g
Polyunsaturated	1	g
Cholesterol	15	mg
Sodium	182	mg

Only 3 percent of the calories in popcorn come from fat, compared to 76 percent of the calories in peanuts. And popcorn is high in fiber.

BRUSCHETTA

Serves 4

This Italian snack is one of my favorite ways to quell hunger pangs.

4 teaspoons olive oil
2 slices country-style round
  Italian loaf, halved
  crosswise or 4 slices from
  a long loaf
4 garlic cloves, halved

2 large ripe tomatoes, peeled,
  lightly seeded, and finely
  chopped
¼ cup snipped fresh basil
  leaves
Coarse salt
Freshly ground black pepper

Preheat oven to 450°F.

With a pastry brush paint both sides of each bread slice with olive oil. Place the bread slices on a cookie sheet and bake for 10 minutes, or until crisp and golden.

Rub each bread slice with the cut side of a garlic half and arrange on a plate. (Discard garlic.) Mix the tomatoes and basil in a small bowl, season to taste with salt and pepper, spoon onto the bread slices, and serve.

NOTE: Some finely chopped purple onion is delicious added to the tomatoes.

Calories	179	cal
Protein	5	g
Carbohydrates	29	g
Total fat	5	g
Saturated	1	g
Polyunsaturated	.4	g
Cholesterol	.4	mg
Sodium	256	mg

SHRIMP AND SNOW PEA HORS D'OEUVRE

Makes about 36 pieces, 3 per serving

These are very easy to assemble and pretty as well as tasty. The dip makes it!

6 ounces fresh snow peas
  (about 36)
1½ pounds medium cooked
  shrimp, peeled

1 recipe Currant Mustard Dip
  (page 82)

String the snow peas. Bring a pot of salted water to a boil and blanch pods for 45 seconds from the second boil. Immediately drain and run under cold water.

Place a shrimp on a blanched snow pea pod and secure with a toothpick, or wrap the peapod around the shrimp and secure. Repeat until all are done. Serve with Currant Mustard Dip.

Per piece

Calories	22	cal
Protein	4	g
Carbohydrates	.6	g
Total fat	.2	g
Saturated	.1	g
Polyunsaturated	.1	g
Cholesterol	37	mg
Sodium	45	mg

While alcohol contains no fat, it does contain calories and can raise hypertension risk in susceptible individuals. Since there are some possible benefits to moderate alcohol consumption, the American Heart Association recommends no more than two drinks a day.

NEW P

Makes ab

Another attractive ho

**24 small, unblemish
   potatoes (abou
   pounds)**
**1 cup Double-Thi
   (page 275)**

Scrub the potatoe
preheated 350°F.
half and top each h
¼ teaspoon salmo
still warm. The re

LOW FAT AND

MUSHROOMS

90

1 pound small mushroom
   whole, or medium
   mushrooms, qu
1 cup water
1 cup chicken
½ cup dry w
½ teaspoo
2 tables
1 tabl
⅓

Calories	21	cal
Protein	1	g
Carbohydrates	4	g
Total fat	.3	g
Saturated	0	g
Polyunsaturated	0	g
Cholesterol	8	mg
Sodium	24	mg

Your favorite snack cracker may contain more fat than you think, especially if it bears no nutritional labeling. Try rubbing the cracker with a paper napkin. If it leaves a grease stain, it contains a lot of fat. Go easy.

A LA GRECQUE

Serves 8

s,	1 bay leaf, crumbled
	4 sprigs parsley
rtered	1 garlic clove, sliced in 3
	pieces
roth	2 teaspoons coriander seeds,
ite wine	crushed
salt	½ teaspoon dried thyme
oons olive oil	8 peppercorns
spoon balsamic vinegar	½ teaspoon dried hot red
up lemon juice	pepper flakes

Wipe the mushrooms clean with a towel, cut off the stems, and set the caps aside. In a stainless-steel or enameled saucepan (*not* aluminum), combine the water, broth, wine, salt, olive oil, vinegar, and lemon juice to make a court bouillon. Make a *bouquet garni* of the bay leaf, parsley, garlic, coriander, thyme, peppercorns, and hot pepper flakes by bundling them in a double-thick 3-inch square of cheesecloth and securing it tightly. Add this to the liquid and then bring to a boil. Let the court bouillon boil for 1 minute.

Add the cleaned mushrooms, a handful at a time, and simmer over low heat uncovered for 3 minutes, stirring. Remove the mushrooms with a slotted spoon to a clean glass bowl or jar.

Boil the marinade down over high heat until only 1 cup remains. Remove and discard the *bouquet garni*. Let the liquid cool, then pour it over the mushrooms and refrigerate overnight or up to 4 days.

To serve, bring the mushrooms to room temperature, scoop out onto plates, and moisten with a little bit of the marinade.

Calories	49	cal
Protein	2	g
Carbohydrates	6	g
Total fat	2	g
Saturated	0	g
Polyunsaturated	1	g
Cholesterol	0	mg
Sodium	76	mg

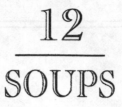

12

SOUPS

♦

SWEET RED PEPPER SOUP

CURRIED BUTTERNUT SQUASH
AND APPLE SOUP

PURÉE OF ONION SOUP

CARROT SOUP

SPLIT PEA SOUP

SHERRIED LENTIL SOUP

BLACK BEAN SOUP

SCOTCH BROTH

ESCAROLE AND RICE SOUP

CORN GAZPACHO

MINESTRONE ALLA MILANESE

FISH CHOWDER

Soups, especially homemade soups, are a wonderful way to nourish and please, and few dishes are as easy to make (once everything is in the pot, they cook themselves) or as undemanding and forgiving of their maker. You can be endlessly creative, varying your soups according to what's hanging around your kitchen—some chopped vegetables, leftover cooked rice or barley, corn, or macaroni. Peas, beans, lentils, or canned tomatoes are other pantry staples you might add; a little cut-up meat, poultry, or seafood increases not only the protein value but also the iron absorbable from the legumes. Another way to round out the protein picture of a soup containing a grain or legume would be to sprinkle some grated Parmesan cheese on top. Defatted chicken stock as part or all of the liquid requirement also boosts nutrition and flavor.

I use homemade Defatted Chicken Broth (page 273) and keep it in my freezer in quantity at all times, partly because it's easy and economical and partly because this way I control the sodium content. You may prefer to make and keep on hand Basic Vegetable Broth (page 274). I always freeze some in an ice cube tray, then knock out the cubes and keep them in a plastic bag. When sautéing onions or vegetables, I may start them in, say, a little olive oil, then add a stock cube, let it melt, cover, and continue the cooking by steaming. Through this combination method of cooking I use less fat.

I recognize that today's busy homemaker might find canned broth more convenient than homemade. Be aware that canned broth adds over 1,300 milligrams of sodium per cup that you may not want. Swanson's is lower in sodium than most, and so is Campbell's new Natural Goodness.

Tip: Keep canned broth in the refrigerator so you can spoon off the congealed fat.

As in my other recipes you will find ideas in this chapter that you can translate to create other low-fat dishes of your own, without sacrificing flavor or texture. Puréed vegetables make splendid soups, such as Purée of Onion Soup (page 95). No *roux* (flour cooked in butter) or cream is needed to give the soup texture and thickness. Try this method with purée of acorn squash, broccoli, potato and leek, carrot, cauliflower, or anything else that appeals.

SWEET RED PEPPER SOUP

Serves 6, about 1 cup each

1 tablespoon olive oil
1 medium onion,
   chopped
3 large red bell peppers,
   roasted (see page 238)
½ small jalapeño or fresh red
   chili pepper, seeded
   (optional)

4 cups defatted chicken broth,
   homemade (page 273) or
   canned
1 cup canned tomato juice
½ teaspoon salt, or to taste
Freshly ground black pepper
Garnish: chopped fresh
   coriander (optional)

In a non-stick skillet heat the oil and sauté the onion over moderately low heat, stirring, until softened. In a food processor or blender, purée the mixture with the bell peppers and the hot pepper if you are using it.

In a large saucepan combine the purée, broth, and tomato juice; bring the soup to a boil, lower the heat, and simmer, partially covered, for 15 minutes. Season with salt and pepper and serve, garnished with a sprinkling of the optional coriander.

Calories	67	cal
Protein	1	g
Carbohydrates	8	g
Total fat	4	g
Saturated	.3	g
Polyunsaturated	.3	g
Cholesterol	0	mg
Sodium	334	mg

CURRIED BUTTERNUT SQUASH
AND APPLE SOUP

Serves 4 to 6

This recipe is adapted from The Silver Palate Cookbook, *by Julee Rosso and Sheila Lukins.*

1 tablespoon unsalted butter
3 cups defatted chicken broth, homemade (page 273) or canned
2 cups finely chopped onions
1½ tablespoons curry powder
2 medium butternut squash (about 3 pounds)

2 Granny Smith apples, peeled, cored, and chopped
1 cup apple juice
Salt and freshly ground black pepper to taste

Melt the butter in a medium soup pot. Add ¼ cup of the chicken broth, the chopped onions, and the curry powder; stir together and cook, covered, over low heat until the onions are tender, about 5 minutes.

Meanwhile, peel the squash (use a potato peeler), scrape out the seeds and strings, and chop the flesh coarsely.

When the onions are tender, add the remaining chicken broth, squash, and apples and bring to a boil. Reduce heat and simmer, partially covered, until the squash and apples are very tender, about 25 minutes.

Pour the soup through a colander into a large bowl and reserve the liquid. Put the solids in the bowl of a food processor. (See NOTE.) Add 1 cup of the soup liquid and process until smooth. Return this purée to the soup pot and add the apple juice and whatever amount of cooking liquid that will give you a pleasing consistency.

Season the soup to taste with the salt and pepper, bring to a simmer, and serve immediately.

NOTE: If you like a soup with some texture, do not purée a cup or so of the solids; return these to the pot.

Calories	165	cal
Protein	3	g
Carbohydrates	35	g
Total fat	3	g
Saturated	.3	g
Polyunsaturated	.3	g
Cholesterol	0	mg
Sodium	11	mg

PURÉE OF ONION SOUP

Serves 6, about 1 cup each

It's amusing to hear your guests try to guess the main ingredient of this soup!

4 large Spanish onions, very
    fresh and hard, with
    papery brown skins
3 tablespoons light olive oil
2 10¾-ounce cans beef broth
    or consommé
Pinch sugar

Freshly ground black pepper
Salt if desired
Optional garnishes: chopped
    parsley, Mock Sour
    Cream (page 276), or
    Double-Thick Yogurt
    (page 275)

Peel the onions and slice them thinly. In a large, heavy skillet, preferably of cast iron, heat the oil and sauté the onions over moderate heat until soft and brown. Stir them frequently, watching that they do not burn. Let them cool slightly and then remove them from the pan and place in a food processor or blender. (In a blender you may have to do this in two batches.) Add ½ can of broth to the frying pan and cook, stirring over high heat, to scrape up and incorporate any brown bits. Add this to the onions, plus the balance of the can, and purée the onions until smooth.

Return the onion mixture to a large saucepan, add and blend in the other can of broth and the sugar and heat gently over low heat. Add several grindings of black pepper and a bit of salt if you think it's needed. Serve in heated soup bowls with chopped parsley or a teaspoon-size dollop of Mock Sour Cream or Double-Thick Yogurt.

Calories	126	cal
Protein	4	g
Carbohydrates	12	g
Total fat	7	g
Saturated	1	g
Polyunsaturated	1	g
Cholesterol	0	mg
Sodium	738	mg

CARROT SOUP

Serves 4 to 6

This is a low-fat version of one of my favorite soups. You won't believe how delicious such a simple concoction can be.

6 to 8 carrots
2 teaspoons salted butter
1 tablespoon olive oil
¾ cup finely chopped onion
4 cups defatted chicken broth,
    homemade (page 273) or
    canned
2 tablespoons uncooked
    long-grain rice

1 cup hot water
2 teaspoons sugar
Salt and white pepper to taste
⅓ cup skim milk
1 tablespoon Butter Buds
Optional garnishes: chopped
    parsley or chives; dill

Peel the carrots, discarding any thick, woody ends, and slice thinly. You should have about 3 cups.

Heat the butter and oil together in a heavy 3-quart pot, add the onions, and cook, stirring occasionally, until they are soft but not brown, 3 to 5 minutes. Add the carrots, broth, and rice, cover, and simmer gently about 25 minutes, or until the carrots are very soft. Put the mixture through a food mill or purée well in a food processor or blender. (You may need to do this in two batches.)

Return the purée to the pot and add the hot water, using a little more if the purée is very thick. Add the sugar and the salt, and pepper to taste. (May be prepared ahead to this point; refrigerate tightly covered.)

At serving time, put the soup over low heat, mix together the milk and butter granules, add to the soup, and bring just to a simmer. Correct seasonings. Serve plain or garnished with chopped parsley or chives or a single feather of dill.

Calories	154	cal
Protein	3	g
Carbohydrates	23	g
Total fat	6	g
Saturated	1	g
Polyunsaturated	.4	g
Cholesterol	5	mg
Sodium	115	mg

SPLIT PEA SOUP

Serves 4 to 6

I can't imagine not having this delicious soup in my freezer in winter. It's warming, filling, and comforting, and a steaming bowl for lunch on a cold day just puts me right. With the addition of garlic bread, garlic croutons, or a few slices of low-fat turkey kielbasa and a salad following, there's a light yet hearty Sunday supper. It's an easy soup to make while you're doing something else, and it makes the house smell wonderful!

1 pound dried split peas
6 cups water
4 cups defatted chicken broth,
    preferably homemade
    (page 273), or canned
1 medium carrot, peeled and
    cut into 1-inch pieces
1 medium onion, quartered
1 medium rib celery, cut into
    1-inch pieces

1 tablespoon olive oil
1 small bay leaf
1½ teaspoons ground
    cardamom
Freshly ground black pepper
    to taste
Salt to taste

Rinse the peas in a colander and pick them over. Bring the peas, water, and stock to a boil, covered, in a large, heavy soup pot. Simmer for 2 minutes, remove from heat, and let sit, covered, for 1 hour. Do not discard the liquid.

Meanwhile, process the carrot, onion, and celery to a medium chop in a food processor (about 8 pulses) or chop by hand.

Put the olive oil in a medium skillet over moderate heat. Add the chopped vegetables and cook, stirring, until they are tender, about 6 minutes. Set aside.

At the end of the hour, stir into the pot the vegetables from the skillet, the bay leaf, cardamom, and pepper. Bring the soup to a boil then lower heat, cover partially, and simmer gently, about 2 hours, stirring occasionally. Remove and discard the bay leaf.

Let the soup cool slightly; then place in the bowl of a food processor in two batches and process just until smooth, about 5 pulses. Return soup to pot. (If you like soup with texture, leave about 2 cups of unprocessed soup behind in the pot, then mix all together.)

Add salt to taste. Bring to the simmer and cook, stirring, until heated through, about 4 minutes.

| Calories | 381 cal |
| Protein | 23 g |

Carbohydrates	63 g
Total fat	5 g
Saturated	.5 g
Polyunsaturated	1 g
Cholesterol	0 mg
Sodium	30 mg

SHERRIED LENTIL SOUP

Serves 8

The sherry is optional; the soup is delicious either way!

1 large onion, chopped
2 tablespoons olive oil
2 small carrots, peeled and
   diced
1½ cups lentils (about 1
   ounce), sorted and
   washed
4 cups defatted chicken broth,
   preferably homemade
   (page 273)

2 cups water
1 large potato, peeled and
   diced
Salt and freshly ground black
   pepper to taste
1 tablespoon salted butter
1 large garlic clove, peeled and
   minced
1 teaspoon ground cumin
Medium-dry sherry (optional)

Set aside 1 tablespoon of chopped onion.

Heat the oil in a large, heavy soup pot, add the onions and carrots and cook over moderate heat until the onions are limp. Add the lentils, broth, and water, bring to a boil, cover, lower heat, and simmer for 30 minutes. Add the potato and continue to cook for another 30 minutes, or until the lentils are very soft.

Pour the soup through a colander into a deep bowl. Return the liquid to the pot. Purée the lentil mixture through a food mill into the pot. Season to taste with salt and pepper. Bring the soup to a gentle simmer while preparing the spicy addition: Melt the butter in a small skillet, add reserved tablespoon of onion and the minced garlic and sauté until just softened. Blend in the cumin and then add the mixture to the soup. Serve in warmed bowls with a splash of sherry.

NOTE: This soup freezes very well.

Calories	217	cal
Protein	11	g
Carbohydrates	30	g
Total fat	6	g
Saturated	1	g
Polyunsaturated	1	g
Cholesterol	4	mg
Sodium	28	mg

BLACK BEAN SOUP

Serves 8, about 1 cup each

This soup would be lovely either as a first course, or as a light but filling supper accompanied by garlic bread and a salad. It may also be eaten cold.

8 cups water
2 cups dried black or turtle
   beans
2 bay leaves
Several parsley stems
8 to 10 black peppercorns
1 tablespoon olive oil
2 large onions, coarsely
   chopped (about 1½ cups)
1 tablespoon minced garlic
   (about 5 fat cloves)
1 rib celery with some leaves,
   coarsely chopped

2 carrots, peeled and coarsely
   chopped
1 veal or beef knuckle
   (optional)
1 lemon, quartered
2 teaspoons salt
Freshly ground black pepper
   to taste
½ cup dry sherry
Thin lemon slices for garnish
Optional garnish: chopped
   hard-boiled egg white

Put the water in a large, heavy soup pot and bring it to a boil. Add the beans, lower heat to a simmer, skim off any froth that rises, cover, and cook for 1 hour.

Meanwhile, tie up the bay leaf, parsley, and peppercorns in a cheesecloth bag and set aside.

Heat the oil in a medium skillet, add the onions, and sauté for 2 minutes or so; then add ¼ cup of liquid from the soup pot, the garlic, celery, and carrots, turn the heat down low, and continue sautéing until the onion and celery are soft. If the vegetables do not stay moist, add a tablespoon or two more water. Set aside.

After 1 hour, add to the beans the spice bag, optional bone, vegetable mixture, lemon quarters, salt, and pepper to taste. Simmer until the beans are very soft, about 2 hours more. Remove and discard lemon quarters, cheesecloth bag, and bone if used.

Purée the beans with their liquid in batches in a food processor or blender. Return to the pot, taste for seasoning, stir in sherry, and heat. If the soup is too thick, thin with a little hot water to the consistency of heavy cream. Serve hot garnished with lemon slices and optional hard-cooked egg white.

Calories	196	cal
Protein	11	g
Carbohydrates	38	g
Total fat	1	g
Saturated	.2	g
Polyunsaturated	.3	g
Cholesterol	0	mg
Sodium	566	mg

SCOTCH BROTH

Serves 6

2 pounds lean shoulder
   and/or neck of lamb,
   with bones
3 quarts water
½ cup medium pearl barley
2 carrots, peeled and coarsely
   chopped
2 medium onions, thinly
   sliced

2 leeks, the white and 2
   inches of the green,
   rinsed and coarsely
   chopped
2 ribs celery, coarsely chopped
Salt and freshly ground black
   pepper to taste
Garnish: chopped Italian
   parsley

Combine all the ingredients but the parsley in a large, heavy soup pot. Bring to a boil and skim off the scum carefully. Cover, lower heat, and simmer 2 hours, stirring once in a while.

Remove the lamb with a slotted spoon, cut the meat from the bones into bite-sized pieces, and return to the pot. Discard the bones. Taste and adjust seasoning. Sprinkle the soup with chopped parsley before serving.

Calories	257	cal
Protein	24	g
Carbohydrates	19	g
Total fat	9	g
Saturated	5	g
Polyunsaturated	0	g
Cholesterol	79	mg
Sodium	99	mg

ESCAROLE AND RICE SOUP

Serves 6, about 1¼ cups each

In Italy minestre, *or a thick, soothing vegetable soup like this one, often constitutes the evening meal.*

1 pound escarole, or
    spinach if you can't
    get escarole
1 tablespoon olive oil
2 teaspoons finely chopped
    garlic
1 small onion, chopped
Salt

5 cups defatted chicken broth,
    homemade (page 273) or
    canned
⅓ cup Arborio rice or any
    noninstant rice
Freshly ground black pepper
Freshly grated Parmesan
    cheese to taste

Separate all the leaves of the escarole and discard any that are wilted or bruised. Soak the escarole in a basin of water and dunk up and down with your hands. Drain briefly, stack the leaves a bunch at a time, and cut crosswise into pieces about 1 inch wide. Set aside.

Heat the oil in a large, heavy soup pot and sauté the garlic and onion until the onion is pale gold—about 3 minutes. Add the escarole, sprinkle lightly with salt, and cook 3 minutes more. Add 1 cup of the broth, cover, and cook over low heat until the escarole is quite tender—10 to 15 minutes depending on how young the leaves are.

Add the balance of the broth, bring to a boil, add the rice, cover, and simmer about 15 minutes, or until rice is tender but firm to the bite. Taste and correct seasoning; add several grindings of pepper.

Off heat and just before serving, sprinkle the soup with Parmesan cheese to taste. Pass additional cheese at the table.

Calories	107 cal
Protein	2 g
Carbohydrates	16 g
Total fat	4 g
Saturated	.3 g
Polyunsaturated	.2 g
Cholesterol	0 mg
Sodium	22 mg

CORN GAZPACHO

Serves 10, about 1 cup each

Not being a great fan of green pepper, I was never fond of gazpacho until I tasted this wonderful version made with corn—the creation of a talented chef, Paolo Penati at the Fresno Restaurant in East Hampton, New York. It is not only delicious and hearty, but also ravishingly beautiful, and it makes a lovely summer lunch. Although there is a lot of initial preparation, the soup is not at all difficult.

3 cups cooked corn kernels (5 ears), freshly cut from the cob, or canned
5 ripe tomatoes (about 1¼ pounds), peeled and lightly seeded, or 1 32-ounce can Italian plum tomatoes, coarsely chopped

1 small zucchini, diced
1 medium cucumber, peeled, seeded, and diced
2 ribs celery, diced
3 to 4 scallions, the white and part of the green, finely chopped
⅓ cup finely chopped red onion

2 to 3 garlic cloves, minced
1 32-ounce can V-8 juice
Juice of 1 large lemon
Juice of 1 to 1½ limes
½ cup olive oil
1 tablespoon ground cumin,
    or more to taste

¼ teaspoon cayenne
½ teaspoon ground chili
    powder
Salt and freshly ground black
    pepper to taste
¾ cup chopped fresh
    coriander

Combine the corn, tomatoes, zucchini, cucumber, celery, scallions, red onion, and garlic in a large tureen or soup pot. Combine the V-8 juice, lemon and lime juices, and olive oil in a bowl; then stir into the vegetables.

In a small bowl, combine the cumin, cayenne, and chili powder; blend well and stir into the vegetables. Season the soup with salt and pepper to taste and add ½ cup of the fresh coriander. Refrigerate for at least 4 hours to allow flavors to mellow. Check the seasoning before serving and sprinkle the top of each serving with some of the remaining coriander.

Calories	196	cal
Protein	3	g
Carbohydrates	22	g
Total fat	11	g
Saturated	1	g
Polyunsaturated	1	g
Cholesterol	0	mg
Sodium	346	mg

MINESTRONE ALLA MILANESE

Serves 6 to 8

Long but not at all complicated—a delicious one-dish meal!

4 medium boiling potatoes,
peeled
3 tablespoons olive oil
¾ cup finely chopped onion
2 garlic cloves, minced
3 medium ripe tomatoes,
peeled and chopped, or 1
14-ounce can Italian
plum tomatoes, drained
and chopped
1 16-ounce can cannellini
beans, drained
1 medium leek, sliced, the
white and part of the
green
2 ribs celery, sliced
2 to 3 carrots, peeled and cut
into ½- × 1-inch sticks

½ cup finely chopped parsley,
preferably Italian
½ teaspoon ground sage
½ teaspoon crumbled dried
rosemary
½ teaspoon dried oregano
2 cups low-sodium beef broth
2½ quarts boiling water
1 cup finely shredded green
cabbage or Swiss chard
2 cups shelled or frozen peas
(optional)
½ cup short-grain rice,
preferably Arborio
Salt to taste
Freshly grated Parmesan
cheese

Cut 2 of the potatoes into small dice and set aside.

In a large, heavy soup pot, combine the olive oil, onion, and garlic and cook gently over low heat until the onion is soft. Add the tomatoes and cook over medium heat for several minutes.

Add the diced potatoes, the beans, leek, celery, and carrots to the pot.

Combine half the parsley with the sage, rosemary, and oregano. Divide this mixture into 2 parts and add 1 part to the vegetables. Simmer over lowest heat for 5 minutes. Add the broth and the 2 whole potatoes. Simmer covered, over low heat, for 15 minutes. Add the boiling water and simmer, covered, for 1 hour.

Mash the whole potatoes against the side of the soup pot with a fork and gently stir back into the soup. Add the remaining herb mixture, the cabbage or Swiss chard, optional peas, and rice. Add salt to taste and simmer another 20 minutes. If the soup becomes too thick, add a little more water—up to a cup—as needed.

Serve the soup steaming hot, sprinkled with the remaining parsley. Pass grated Parmesan cheese and a pepper mill and serve with good, crusty bread.

Calories	273	cal
Protein	7	g
Carbohydrates	47	g
Total fat	7	g
Saturated	1	g
Polyunsaturated	1	g
Cholesterol	0	mg
Sodium	182	mg

FISH CHOWDER

Serves 8, about 1½ cups each

Gentle, warming, soothing, delicately flavored—and low in fat!

2 pounds firm white fish such as cod, halibut, blackfish, fileted and skinned
4 to 5 medium boiling potatoes (about 1¾ pounds), peeled and cut into ½-inch cubes
½ teaspoon salt, or to taste
2 tablespoons vegetable oil

2 medium carrots peeled and cut into ¼-inch dice
1 cup coarsely chopped onion
3 tablespoons chopped parsley
⅔ cup skim milk
2 tablespoons Butter Buds
1 16-ounce can creamed corn
Freshly ground black pepper

Wash the fish and cut it into roughly 2-inch pieces. Put the fish into a large, heavy soup pot, add about 5 cups water or enough to cover the fish by 1 inch. Bring just to a boil, lower heat immediately, and simmer gently, covered, for 4 minutes. Remove the fish to a platter with a slotted spoon and set aside.

Add the potatoes to the same liquid, bring to a boil, sprinkle in the salt, cover, and cook 12 to 15 minutes, until the potatoes are at the point of breaking up. They should almost disintegrate.

While the potatoes are cooking, heat the oil in a 10-inch skillet, add the carrots and cook, covered, over moderate heat until they are slightly softened, about 4 minutes. Uncover, add the onion and parsley, and sauté, stirring, until the onion softens and takes on a slight color, about 5 minutes.

When the potatoes are ready, add the vegetable mixture to the pot; combine the milk and Butter Buds, and stir in. Add the corn. Add the fish and season to taste. Heat gently, uncovered, but do not let the soup boil, for 5 minutes.

Calories	278 cal
Protein	31 g
Carbohydrates	25 g
Total fat	5 g
Saturated	1 g
Polyunsaturated	3 g
Cholesterol	66 mg
Sodium	379 mg

13

SALAD DRESSINGS, SALADS, AND RELISHES

♦

BALSAMIC VINAIGRETTE
SHALLOT VINAIGRETTE
"ZERO" HERB DRESSING
SEMI-CLASSIC VINAIGRETTE
LEMON–MUSTARD VINAIGRETTE
GARLIC VINAIGRETTE
SESAME VINAIGRETTE

MUSHROOM AND CELERY SALAD
VINAIGRETTE OF BLACK BEANS
WITH TOMATO
VINAIGRETTE OF BLACK BEANS
WITH CORN AND TOMATO
MOROCCAN CARROT SALAD
ARAB TOMATO SALAD
OLD-FASHIONED COLE SLAW

JAPANESE SPINACH SALAD
WITH SESAME SEEDS

TUNA AND WHITE BEAN SALAD

REDUCED-FAT TUNA SALAD

WHEATBERRY SALAD

PICO DE GALLO

CUCUMBER YOGURT SAUCE (RAITA)

TOMATO–CORN RELISH

OLIVE SALSA

PEPPERHASH

Salads are a cornerstone of every eating plan, whether for losing weight or for eating healthily. And little wonder—a salad is the simplest way to get some of the vegetables we all need. Other virtues of salads are that they fill you up, so you are able to eat less of the foods you should limit; they also cleanse the palate, especially after the main course, and they are a very pleasant way to end a meal if you're not having a sweet. In fact, my husband is so enamored of his evening salad that if we are in a restaurant and no salads have been included in the dinner, he orders one to eat while others at the table are having dessert!

Salads are also easier than ever to rustle up at home. Not only are there more greens available than ever before to add interesting variety, but you can also buy fresh ingredients in a pinch at those salad bars springing up all over, thus avoiding preparation if you're rushed.

One word of warning, however: The fat calories can really add up in dressings. This part of the salad is the one item most people keeping a diet diary forget to record. Salad *sounds* so healthy and benign that it's hard to remember that one recipe of classic three-to-one vinaigrette, with its three tablespoons of olive oil, contains 42 grams of fat. This amount can easily dress a salad for three hearty salad eaters, giving them each 14 extra fat grams for that one meal alone. (If we get into blue cheese dressing, it's even higher, but of course you won't do that.)

For me, this is not the end of the world; the fat *is* unsaturated and I love a good salad so much I am willing to cut back somewhere else in order to have it dressed properly. I have played around with changing the proportions of oil and vinegar, adding chicken broth, tomato juice, thinning with water and such, all to try to find a lower-fat dressing that would please me and receive the approval of my husband the Salad Maven. Only the Semi-Classic Dressing with 2:3 proportions and the Balsamic Vinaigrette with 2:2 come close. Good balsamic vinegar has such an intense flavor that a dressing made with it can be used in very small amounts. Next best is really cutting down on the oil, using lemon juice together with vinegar to soften the bite of the latter and adding shallots for extra flavor, or extending your dressing with water. One fat-conscious person I know dresses salads by whisking Dijon mustard into an aged-five-years balsamic vinegar, with tasty results. If you can get by with lemon juice souped up with herbs, garlic, or what have you, or simply balsamic vinegar alone, go for it! You'll have all those extra fat grams to spend!

BALSAMIC VINAIGRETTE

Serves 4

2 tablespoons balsamic vinegar
1 tablespoon water
½ teaspoon salt

Freshly ground black pepper
1 teaspoon Dijon mustard
2 tablespoons olive oil

Put the vinegar and water in a small bowl, add the salt, several grindings of pepper, and the mustard and whisk in. Add the olive oil and whisk until smooth.

Calories	62	cal
Protein	0	g
Carbohydrates	.4	g
Total fat	7	g
Saturated	1	g
Polyunsaturated	1	g
Cholesterol	0	mg
Sodium	311	mg

SHALLOT VINAIGRETTE

Add 1 tablespoon finely chopped shallot to the basic recipe.

"ZERO" HERB DRESSING

Serves 8, about 2 tablespoons each

¼ cup red wine or sherry
vinegar
6 ounces (1 small can) tomato
or V-8 juice
1 pinch dried savory or
oregano
1 tablespoon chopped fresh
chives or scallion, the
white and part of the
green

1 tablespoon minced Italian
parsley
1 garlic clove, crushed
½ teaspoon salt, or to taste
Freshly ground black pepper
to taste
Dash cayenne
Pinch sugar

Combine all the dressing ingredients in a jar and shake to mix thoroughly.
Remove the garlic clove before serving.

Calories	6	cal
Protein	.2	g
Carbohydrates	1	g
Total fat	0	g
Saturated	0	g
Polyunsaturated	0	g
Cholesterol	0	mg
Sodium	220	mg

The typical small ladle for dressing at a salad bar holds about 2
tablespoons of dressing; this amount of French, Italian, or blue
cheese dressing contains from 12 to 20 grams of fat!

SEMI-CLASSIC VINAIGRETTE

Serves 6, about 1 tablespoon each

2 tablespoons red wine
    vinegar
1 tablespoon water
½ teaspoon Dijon mustard
½ teaspoon salt, or to taste

Freshly ground black pepper
    to taste
3 tablespoons extra-virgin
    olive oil

Put the vinegar and water in a small bowl. Whisk in the mustard, salt, and pepper. Add the oil and whisk until you have a smooth emulsion. Store in a covered jar in the refrigerator.

Calories	37	cal
Protein	0	g
Carbohydrates	.2	g
Total fat	4	g
Saturated	1	g
Polyunsaturated	1	g
Cholesterol	0	mg
Sodium	117	mg

LEMON–MUSTARD VINAIGRETTE

Substitute lemon juice for the vinegar in the above recipe, and increase the mustard to 1 teaspoon.

GARLIC VINAIGRETTE

Smash a garlic clove with the side of a knife and let it steep in either of the above dressings for 1 hour or so before serving. Remove before using.

SESAME VINAIGRETTE

Serves 8, about 1 tablespoon each

This is lovely over lettuces mixed with grated carrots and alfalfa sprouts. Or use any salad combination you like.

3 tablespoons reduced-sodium
   soy sauce
3 tablespoons rice vinegar

2 tablespoons mirin (a Japanese
   syrupy rice wine)
1½ teaspoons dark sesame oil

Mix the dressing ingredients together in a jar, and chill if desired. The dressing may be stored in the refrigerator for several weeks.

Calories	22	cal
Protein	.3	g
Carbohydrates	2	g
Total fat	1	g
Saturated	.1	g
Polyunsaturated	.4	g
Cholesterol	0	mg
Sodium	226	mg

MUSHROOM AND CELERY SALAD

Serves 4, about ¼ cup each

12 large unblemished
   mushrooms
1 cup sliced celery
¼ cup minced onion
¼ cup chopped sweet red
   pepper

Freshly ground black pepper
1 teaspoon vegetable oil
Juice of 1 large lemon
Salt to taste

Wipe the mushrooms with a damp paper towel, cut off the coarser part of the stem (reserve for soup), and cut mushrooms into very thin slices. Toss them in a serving bowl with the celery, onion, and red pepper.

Add a few grindings of black pepper. Stir together the oil and lemon juice, add salt to taste, pour over the salad, and toss.

Calories	46	cal
Protein	2	g
Carbohydrates	7	g
Total fat	2	g
Saturated	.2	g
Polyunsaturated	1	g
Cholesterol	0	mg
Sodium	31	mg

VINAIGRETTE OF BLACK BEANS WITH TOMATO

Serves 12, about 1 cup each

1 pound dried black beans, picked over
1 large onion, chopped
2 ribs celery, chopped
3 bay leaves
1 teaspoon dried hot red pepper flakes
1 teaspoon dried oregano
1 medium carrot, peeled and cut into chunks
2½ quarts cold water
1 teaspoon salt
1 small red onion, finely chopped
1 medium ripe tomato, peeled and cut into ¼-inch dice

3 tablespoons finely chopped fresh coriander
½ cup Lemon–Mustard Vinaigrette (page 113) with 1 tablespoon soy sauce added
1 medium cucumber, peeled, seeded, and cut into ¼-inch -dice
Freshly ground black pepper to taste
1 medium cucumber, sliced, for garnish

Put the beans in a large mixing bowl, cover with cold water, and let stand overnight.

Put the onion, celery, bay leaves, red pepper flakes, oregano, and carrot in a cheesecloth bag and tie securely. Drain the beans and transfer to a large heavy soup pot or, preferably, an 8-quart Dutch oven. Add the cheesecloth bag and the cold water.

Bring the beans to a boil, reduce heat, and simmer, partially covered, for 45 minutes. Do not stir during this time. Add the salt and continue simmering until beans are tender, about 20 minutes longer. Discard the cheesecloth bag and let the beans cool to lukewarm in the liquid, then refrigerate for at least several hours, or, if you have the time, overnight. (This improves the flavor.) Drain the beans and put them back in the pot.

In a small bowl combine the red onion, tomato, and coriander and gently toss. Add half of this mixture to the beans. Then add the vinaigrette, diced cucumber, and black pepper. Toss gently but well.

To serve the salad, make a border of unpeeled cucumber slices on a platter and mound the beans in the center. Sprinkle the top with the remaining onion mixture.

Calories	170	cal
Protein	9	g
Carbohydrates	27	g
Total fat	3	g
Saturated	1	g
Polyunsaturated	1	g
Cholesterol	0	mg
Sodium	176	mg

VINAIGRETTE OF BLACK BEANS WITH CORN AND TOMATO

Add 2 cups canned, frozen, or fresh cooked whole corn kernels. Being a grain, this enhances the protein of this dish.

Calories	192	cal
Protein	9	g
Carbohydrates	32	g
Total fat	4	g
Saturated	1	g
Polyunsaturated	1	g
Cholesterol	0	mg
Sodium	176	mg

MOROCCAN CARROT SALAD

Serves 4 to 6

Another summer standby. This salad is great with broiled chicken, on a picnic, as a first course, or just to flesh out any light meal. Note the fat content.

6 to 7 large carrots, peeled
2 shallots, finely chopped
2 to 3 tablespoons sugar
½ teaspoon salt
½ teaspoon ground cumin
Dash cayenne

Freshly ground black pepper
3 tablespoons lemon juice
½ cup minced fresh coriander
    or parsley, preferably
    Italian

Shred or julienne the carrots with the appropriate disk of a food processor. Put the carrots in a serving bowl, add the shallots, and toss. Combine in a small bowl the sugar, salt, cumin, and cayenne; then toss with the carrots. Season with liberal grindings of black pepper. Add the lemon juice and toss again. Let the carrots marinate 1 hour. Sprinkle the salad with the coriander or parsley and serve at room temperature.

Calories	80	cal
Protein	1	g
Carbohydrates	19	g
Total fat	.3	g
Saturated	0	g
Polyunsaturated	.1	g
Cholesterol	0	mg
Sodium	263	mg

ARAB TOMATO SALAD

Serves 4

1 small green pepper, halved,
  seeded and deveined
2 medium ripe tomatoes,
  peeled, seeded, and cut
  into ½-inch cubes (about
  1½ cups)
1 tablespoon finely chopped
  parsley
1 tablespoon finely chopped
  onion

¼ teaspoon minced garlic
1 teaspoon minced fresh
  coriander
Salt if desired
¼ teaspoon cayenne
⅓ teaspoon ground cumin
1 tablespoon white vinegar
2 tablespoons light olive oil

Cut the pepper into lengthwise strips about ½ inch wide; stack these and cut crosswise into thin slices. (There should be about ⅓ cup; if there is more, save for another use.)

Put the pepper strips into a bowl, add the remaining ingredients, and toss. Chill before serving.

Calories	78 cal
Protein	1 g
Carbohydrates	4 g
Total fat	7 g
Saturated	1 g
Polyunsaturated	1 g
Cholesterol	0 mg
Sodium	6 mg

OLD-FASHIONED COLE SLAW

Serves 8

There are times when nothing but this endearing favorite will do. Traditionally the dressing was made with mayonnaise (egg yolk–rich mayonnaise) and thinned with heavy cream. This dressing tastes every bit as good and has two-thirds less fat.

1 small head green cabbage, or ½ large head	3 tablespoons cider vinegar
1 small onion	1 tablespoon Dijon mustard
2 carrots, peeled	3 teaspoons sugar, or to taste
½ green pepper	2 teaspoons salt, or to taste
4 tablespoons reduced-calorie mayonnaise	Skim milk
3 tablespoons plain non-fat yogurt	2 teaspoons celery seed (optional)
	Freshly ground black pepper to taste

Cut the cabbage in quarters, trim off any coarse leaves, and remove core. Shred, using a slaw shredder or the shredding disk of a food processor. Put the cabbage in a serving bowl. Grate the onion very finely (or chop it finely in the food processor with the steel knife) and add it to the cabbage. Shred the carrots and green pepper. (The pepper you will have to do on the medium holes of a hand grater; it gets too watery in the processor.) Add these to the cabbage, and mix thoroughly with your hands or two spoons.

Combine the mayonnaise, yogurt, vinegar, mustard, sugar, and salt. Stir or whisk until smooth. Thin with milk to the desired consistency.

Add the optional celery seeds to the cabbage and toss; then pour in the dressing and toss well to coat the vegetables thoroughly. Season with pepper to taste. Refrigerate for several hours before serving.

Calories	63	cal
Protein	2	g
Carbohydrates	10	g
Total fat	2	g
Saturated	1	g
Polyunsaturated	.1	g
Cholesterol	3	mg
Sodium	689	mg

JAPANESE SPINACH SALAD WITH SESAME SEEDS

Serves 4

This makes a lovely side dish for fish.

1½ pounds fresh young
    spinach, rinsed and dried
¼ cup soy sauce
¼ cup rice vinegar

2 tablespoons mirin (syrupy
    rice wine)
1 tablespoon sesame seeds

Wash the spinach in lots of cold water to remove all traces of sand. Make several bundles of the spinach (tie stems together with kitchen twine). Have a bowl of ice water ready.

Bring a pot of lightly salted water to a rolling boil, then turn off the heat. Holding the spinach by the stems with your fingers or tongs, dip the bundles into the hot water until just wilted. Immediately plunge into the ice water to stop the cooking process. Remove the spinach from the ice water, squeeze out the excess liquid, and set aside on paper towels.

In a small bowl, mix the soy sauce, vinegar, and mirin.

In a clean dry skillet, toast the sesame seeds, shaking the pan constantly, until they begin to color slightly, or a few pop.

Combine the spinach and dressing in a serving bowl, toss gently, and garnish with the sesame seeds.

Calories	71	cal
Protein	5	g
Carbohydrates	10	g
Total fat	2	g
Saturated	.2	g
Polyunsaturated	1	g
Cholesterol	0	mg
Sodium	1,126	mg

TUNA AND WHITE BEAN SALAD

Serves 4, about 1 cup each

This is an excellent first course or easy summer lunch, to be served with fresh, crusty Italian bread. All the main ingredients can always be on hand in your larder for quick meals any time.

1 15-ounce can cannellini
   beans, undrained
1 tablespoon lemon juice
½ teaspoon salt, or
   to taste
Freshly ground black pepper
2 tablespoons good-quality
   olive oil

¼ cup finely chopped
   scallions, the white and
   part of the green
1 7-ounce can light tuna in
   water
2 tablespoons chopped Italian
   parsley
Lemon wedges

Heat the beans with their liquid slightly over low heat or for 45 seconds on HIGH in a microwave oven. Set aside.

Make the dressing by mixing the lemon juice, salt, several grindings of pepper, and the olive oil in a mixing bowl large enough to hold the rest of the ingredients.

Drain the still-warm beans and add them to the bowl. Toss gently with a wooden spoon until the beans are thoroughly coated. Stir in the scallions and set the beans aside for 1 hour, then taste for seasoning. Because the beans are absorbent, they may need additional salt, pepper, and lemon juice.

Drain the tuna and break up into large pieces. Fold these gently into the beans. Top with chopped parsley and serve garnished with lemon wedges.

Calories	23	cal
Protein	19	g
Carbohydrates	15	g
Total fat	11	g
Saturated	1	g
Polyunsaturated	1	g
Cholesterol	19	mg
Sodium	768	mg

REDUCED-FAT TUNA SALAD

Makes 4 to 5 sandwiches

1 7-ounce can light tuna in water (preferably low-sodium)
2 ribs celery, chopped
2 tablespoons sweet pickle relish, or more to taste
1 hard-cooked white of egg, chopped
1 heaping teaspoon minced onion

2 tablespoons plain non-fat yogurt
1 tablespoon reduced-calorie mayonnaise
¼ teaspoon dry mustard
Freshly ground black pepper to taste

Drain the tuna and put it in a small mixing bowl. Add the celery, relish, egg white, and onion and mix well. In another small bowl, whip together the yogurt, mayonnaise, and dry mustard. Pour over the tuna mixture and fold in gently but thoroughly. Season with the black pepper.

To make tuna sandwiches, an all-American favorite, use either sourdough bread, or whole-wheat, lightly toasted, or rye bread. Instead of slathering the bread with mayonnaise, use just a dab of the reduced-calorie kind and add thin cucumber slices and leaves of arugula or lettuce. I don't think you'll be able to tell the difference between this and a regular tuna sandwich.

The tuna salad

Calories	88	cal
Protein	14	g
Carbohydrates	4	g
Total fat	1	g
Saturated	.3	g
Polyunsaturated	.1	g
Cholesterol	19	mg
Sodium	266	mg

Three ounces of tuna packed in oil give you 7 grams of fat, even after draining; compare with 1 gram of fat in the water-packed kind.

WHEATBERRY SALAD

Serves 5, about ¼ cup each

This salad invariably becomes a refrigerator mainstay whenever I introduce it to a fat- or weight-conscious friend. (One even eats it for breakfast!) It's pretty, very filling, and makes a great low-calorie, low-fat snack.

1 cup wheatberries
3½ cups water
½ teaspoon salt

Sesame Vinaigrette
2 tablespoons soy sauce
2 tablespoons dark sesame oil
2 teaspoons rice or red wine vinegar
2 teaspoons sugar

2 scallions, chopped (the white and part of the green)
½ cup finely chopped onion
½ sweet red pepper, diced
½ sweet yellow pepper, diced (if unavailable, use 1 whole red pepper)
1 small cucumber, peeled, seeded, and diced

Soak the wheatberries overnight in the water. Drain off the soaking liquid and measure it. Add enough cold water to make 3½ cups.

Put the wheatberries in a 3-quart pot with the water and salt. Bring to a rolling boil, cover, reduce heat, and simmer for 40 minutes, or until most of the liquid is absorbed. Uncover and cook 10 minutes longer to separate the grains.

While the wheat is cooking, combine the soy sauce, sesame oil, vinegar and sugar in a small saucepan and stir over moderate heat just until the sugar dissolves. Set aside.

Drain the wheatberries, toss with a fork, and combine with the vinaigrette while still warm. Let them cool to room temperature, and then combine with the scallions, onion, peppers, and cucumber. Toss again and refrigerate for 1 hour before serving.

NOTE: Wheatberries, whole unpolished kernels of wheat, can be found principally in health food stores and are packaged under a variety of names: hard-wheat, soft-wheat, or whole-wheat kernels.

Calories	191	cal
Protein	6	g
Carbohydrates	30	g
Total fat	7	g
Saturated	1	g

Polyunsaturated	2 g
Cholesterol	0 mg
Sodium	636 mg

PICO DE GALLO

Serves 6, about ¼ cup each

This sauce could be considered the catsup of Mexico—to be used in whatever quantity and however it pleases. It is most often spooned onto tortillas to enhance whatever else they contain. It can also be used as a dip, or with fajitas, broiled fish, or just about anything else you can think of.

2 large or 4 medium ripe tomatoes, seeded and finely chopped, 1 15-ounce can Italian plum tomatoes, drained, seeded, liquid reserved
¼ cup minced scallions, the white and part of the green

2 fresh jalapeño or serrano chilis (see NOTE)
1 garlic clove, minced
¼ cup minced fresh coriander
1 teaspoon dried oregano
Juice of 1 lime
½ cup water, or the reserved liquid from tomato can
Salt to taste

Mix all the ingredients together in a bowl and season with salt to taste. Do not make the sauce more than 3 hours ahead, and refrigerate it if you're not using it immediately.

NOTE: For a very hot sauce, use the chilis unseeded. Remove the seeds if you desire a milder sauce.

Calories	43 cal
Protein	2 g
Carbohydrates	10 g
Total fat	.4 g
Saturated	.1 g
Polyunsaturated	.2 g
Cholesterol	0 mg
Sodium	15 mg

CUCUMBER YOGURT SAUCE
(RAITA)

Serves 4, about ½ cup each

This sauce is commonly served with Indian food. It allows individual diners to tone down the degree of spiciness in the rest of the meal and it also serves the important function of completing the protein picture in a vegetarian meal.

1 to 2 cucumbers, about ½ to ¾ pounds

¾ teaspoon whole cumin seeds

1 cup plain non-fat yogurt

1 teaspoon peanut or vegetable oil

½ teaspoon minced garlic

Salt to taste

Peel the cucumber and cut in half. If the seeds are large, remove them. Grate the cucumber against the largest holes of a grater and put the cucumber in a bowl.

Put the cumin seeds in a small skillet, set over low heat, and cook until the seeds take on some color and begin to "pop." Shake the skillet and remove from heat.

Add the cumin, yogurt, oil, and garlic to the cucumber. Add salt to taste, blend well, and chill before serving.

Calories	7	cal
Protein	.5	g
Carbohydrates	1	g
Total fat	.2	g
Saturated	0	g
Polyunsaturated	0	g
Cholesterol	.1	mg
Sodium	6	mg

TOMATO–CORN RELISH

Serves 8, about ½ cup each

This is good with grilled meat or fish.

2 cups fresh corn cut from
   the cob (7 to 8 ears), or
   1 16-ounce can corn
   kernels
2 pounds ripe tomatoes,
   peeled, seeded, and
   juiced, or 1 28-ounce can
   whole tomatoes, drained,
   seeded, and chopped into
   ¼-inch dice
½ cup chopped onions
½ cup diced sweet red pepper

¼ cup fresh lemon juice
1 to 2 teaspoons sugar, or to
   taste
1 fresh jalapeño pepper,
   seeded and finely chopped
2 tablespoons chopped fresh
   coriander or Italian
   parsley
½ teaspoon ground cumin, or
   to taste
Salt and freshly ground black
   pepper to taste

Combine all the ingredients in a bowl and let the relish stand in the refrigerator for at least 4 hours, stirring once or twice. Adjust the seasoning.

Calories	126 cal
Protein	4 g
Carbohydrates	28 g
Total fat	1 g
Saturated	0 g
Polyunsaturated	.3 g
Cholesterol	0 mg
Sodium	28 mg

OLIVE SALSA

Serves 6, about ½ cup each

This fresh condiment has little fat and delivers big flavor, which especially enhances grilled swordfish or tuna and is also lovely with chicken. Make it about 30 minutes before you plan to serve it. The recipe is easily halved.

6 medium ripe tomatoes
8 Sicilian or Greek olives,
   pitted
2 teaspoons chopped parsley
2 tablespoons coarsely
   chopped fresh basil

2 tablespoons finely chopped
   red onion
2 tablespoons olive oil
Salt and freshly ground black
   pepper to taste
A few dashes balsamic vinegar

Core, lightly juice, and roughly chop the tomatoes into ½-inch chunks. Combine these with the olives, parsley, basil, and red onion in a bowl and let the mixture stand for 30 minutes. Pour off any liquid that has accumulated from the salsa, add the olive oil, salt and pepper to taste, and a few dashes of balsamic vinegar.

Calories	76	cal
Protein	1	g
Carbohydrates	6	g
Total fat	6	g
Saturated	1	g
Polyunsaturated	1	g
Cholesterol	0	mg
Sodium	115	mg

PEPPERHASH

Serves 8, about ½ cup each

Growing up in Philadelphia, I didn't know that the whole world didn't eat pepperhash, which was always served in seafood houses with fried oysters. I would guess its origin is Pennsylvania Dutch, although no one has confirmed this. It has zero fat and is a lovely fresh-tasting accompaniment to fish or shellfish of any kind.

1 cup minced green pepper
½ cup minced sweet red pepper
4 cups minced green cabbage
1 cup minced celery

2 tablespoons salt, or to taste
2 tablespoons whole mustard seeds
2 tablespoons brown sugar
½ cup vinegar

Combine the green and red peppers, cabbage, celery, and salt. Let the mixture stand overnight; then drain thoroughly and put in an earthenware crock or large glass jar; set aside.

Combine the mustard seeds, brown sugar, and vinegar in an enameled or stainless-steel saucepan (non-reactive) and bring to a boil. Pour this over the drained vegetables and mix in. Let the pepperhash cool first, then refrigerate. It is best if served within three days.

Calories	43	cal
Protein	1	g
Carbohydrates	8	g
Total fat	1	g
Saturated	0	g
Polyunsaturated	.2	g
Cholesterol	0	mg
Sodium	845	mg

14

GRAINS, LEGUMES, AND BEANS

♦

BASIC FOOLPROOF WHITE RICE
RICE PILAF
BAKED PILAF
HERBED PILAF
BULGUR PILAF WITH CURRANTS
AND PINE NUTS
TABBOULEH
BARLEY–SCALLION–PINE NUT CASSEROLE
HERBED "INSTANT" COUSCOUS
BLACK BEANS AND RICE
BLACK BEAN AND RICE SALAD
BLACK BEAN AND RICE SALAD
VINAIGRETTE
FLAGEOLETS BRETONNE
SUCCOTASH
CHICKPEAS, TOMATOES, AND RICE
CURRIED LENTILS AND RICE
LENTIL CHILI
LENTILS WITH GARLIC AND TOMATOES

GRAINS

Not only are grains an abundant source of protein and many important vitamins, but also a number of them are an excellent source of dietary fiber.

If your family is unaccustomed to eating whole-grain breads, try starting them with cracked-wheat bread, served at least once a day. You'll be surprised how addictive the flavor and texture can become. Do try whole-wheat, 7-grain, pumpernickel and other whole-grain breads, but don't be fooled by light-colored brown breads that are soft and squashy; these usually contain little whole wheat and get their color mainly from caramel. If there's a good bakery or specialty food store near you, check out their whole-grain breads. The other advantage to whole-grain breads, of course, is that they are usually so good you can eat them without butter.

Apart from bread, there are many delicious grain dishes you can include in your meal planning. This section contains a good variety that are so tasty you can serve them to company without hesitation. You probably already serve white rice now and again, but think about broadening your scope to include the chewier brown rice, wheatberries (the whole unprocessed wheat kernel, which you can put into salads and meatloaf), bulgur, couscous, kasha, and barley.

Polished white rice, the rice most of us use, has been milled to remove the outer hull, germ, and bran layer. *Converted rice* is rice that has been partially cooked under pressure before the bran layer is removed, a process devised to make the rice cook up less sticky (although you pay in loss of flavor). *Brown rice* is rice that has been hulled but still has the bran and germ layer intact. It is the most nutritious rice, with a maximum of fiber, vitamin, and mineral content. Fragrant types include Texmati, and Indian rice grown in Texas, and the nutty, rust-colored Wehani, grown in northern California. Fragrant brown rices are sometimes sold in packaged blends. Luxurious, nut-flavored *wild rice* is not a rice at all, but the seed of a grass.

Rice varies widely in length and shape of grain. The longer rice, like our popular Carolina long-grain, cooks up drier and fluffier than the shorter kinds. Its length also allows it to take up flavorings, making it ideal for pilafs. I find it the best all-round rice. Medium-grain rice expands less and is stickier, and short-grain, or Oriental, rice is the stickiest of all. The latter two tend to clump a bit, making them suitable for rice puddings, molded dishes, and sauced Oriental dishes, but otherwise they are frustrating.

The plump, oval-grained Italian Arborio rice is an absolute must for making a *risotto*; it has the capacity to absorb much more liquid (hence flavoring) than ordinary rice, resulting in the fabulously flavored, creamy yet chewy rice that is the hallmark of a fine *risotto*.

Pilaf (rice cooked with stock, onions, and seasonings of one kind or another) is a wonderful dish to have in your repertoire. Full of flavor, it can stand on its own as a side dish and doesn't need a sauce. It can accompany a wide variety of foods and easily feed many people. I use it with almost any kind of chicken dish.

Barley is as simple as rice to cook—it just requires a longer cooking time. To use as a side dish, simply bring it to a boil with 3 times the quantity of water, then cover and simmer 30 to 50 minutes, or until the barley is tender and the water absorbed.

Barley is frequently hulled to remove the outer bran-like coating, in a process called "pearling"; you'll find it in the market as "medium pearl" barley, medium connoting the cooking time. Whole barley, found in health food stores, takes longer to cook but is more nutritious.

Kasha, or buckwheat, a species of grain not related to wheat, is a staple in Russia, used for both savory and sweet dishes, as a stuffing for fish, meat, and poultry, or served with mushrooms and onions with sour cream. Kasha, with its strong malt-like flavor, contains twice as much vitamin B as wheat and is the best source of protein in the plant kingdom.

Bulgur, or cracked wheat, the Middle Eastern staple, is another delicious and useful grain and is particularly high in fiber (8 grams in a 1 cup serving). The steamed and dried grains are cracked to various sizes. Since it is already partially cooked, it can be prepared just by soaking it in water until it softens.

Millet: I am not a particular fan of this light-textured, mild-flavored grain, other than in mixed-grain breads, but if you want to try it as an occasional replacement for rice, it is cooked with 2½ times its volume of liquid, for about 20 minutes.

Wheatberries are another name for whole-wheat grains. They are nutty and chewy with an unmistakable wheaty flavor. The berry of both red (hard) wheat and white (soft) wheat is available, with the former higher in protein.

Just a glance at the variety in the recipes that follow will give you some idea of the enormous versatility possible with grains.

BASIC FOOLPROOF WHITE RICE

Rice is an important component of low-fat eating, and, when perfectly cooked, a deliciously satisfying one as well. Here's what you have to know:

1. understand what rice to use for what purpose (see pages 130–31);
2. use two measures of liquid to one of rice;
3. never stir rice while it's cooking.

Time it correctly, don't have the flame too high, and you'll get perfect results every time.

I always use long-grain Carolina rice, unrinsed, and always the two-to-one liquid-to-rice proportions. The basic procedure applies to the making of any amount of rice, whether with water or broth, and with or without herbs or seasonings. Keep the same proportions, respect the technique, and you'll *never have a failure.*

1. Measure out the rice (depending on the meal, figure ⅓ to ½ cup uncooked rice per person; rice more than doubles when cooked).
2. Put *double* the amount of water on to boil.
3. Heat some olive oil or half-oil-half-butter (say 1 tablespoon total for 1 cup rice) in a heavy saucepan with a tight-fitting lid. Add the rice and stir with a wooden spoon over low heat *just until* the grains become coated and a few become opaque.
4. Now add the hot liquid all at once (it will make a fierce sizzle), add salt to taste, stir, bring to a boil, cover, turn down the heat to low, and cook for exactly 18 minutes. *Never stir the rice while it cooks.* At the end of the cooking time, fluff with 2 forks, and serve.
5. For really fluffy rice, remove the lid when the rice is finished, put a clean, folded tea towel on top of the pot, put the lid back on and let the pot sit this way anywhere from 5 to 15 minutes. The rice will not get cold and the steam it contains will be absorbed by the cloth instead of condensing inside the lid and falling back onto the rice to make it gummy. (You can also keep rice warm this way, cloth and lid in place, in a very slow oven, for as much as 2 hours.) Then fluff with a fork and serve.

Exceptions to these rules pertain to making a risotto with Italian rice and cooking Indian basmati rice. Each has its own washing, handling, and cooking requirements.

As noted in the recipe title, these instructions apply to white rice. Brown rice, which may be regular or converted, has a different yield when cooked and requires different timing, so consult the instructions on the box.

More rice cooking tips:

• Rinse the rice in a colander only if you buy it unpackaged and notice impurities or dirt.

• If rice is tender but has not absorbed all the liquid for some reason, do not continue cooking or it will become soggy. Instead, pour off the excess liquid.

• Make twice the rice you need and use the leftovers at another meal. To reheat cold rice, steam for 15 minutes in a colander set over a saucepan containing 2 inches of simmering water, covered with a lid or aluminum foil. Or sprinkle with water, cover with plastic wrap, and reheat in the microwave.

RICE PILAF

Serves 3, approximately ¾ cup each

½ tablespoon unsalted butter
1 tablespoon olive oil
1 small onion, finely chopped
1 cup long-grain white rice

2 cups hot defatted chicken
broth, preferably
homemade (page 273)
Salt to taste

In a heavy saucepan or casserole with a tight-fitting lid, melt the butter in the oil over moderate heat. Add the onion and cook until softened and faintly colored. Add the rice and cook for 2 minutes, stirring constantly, just until grains are well coated with oil but not brown. Pour in the broth all at once, add salt to taste, and bring to a boil, stirring. Cover, reduce heat to low, and simmer 18 to 20 minutes, or until rice is tender but firm to the tooth. Gently fluff with 2 forks and serve.

BAKED PILAF

This is a good way to make rice in quantity. Preheat the oven to 350°F. Prepare as above, doubling or tripling the ingredients as required, and after bringing the rice to boil, cover and place in the oven for 30 minutes.

HERBED PILAF

Omit the onion and add 1 teaspoon dried thyme or 2 tablespoons minced fresh dill (or any other herb you fancy) when you add the rice to the butter and olive oil.

Calories	251	cal
Protein	18	g
Carbohydrates	42	g
Total fat	7	g
Saturated	1	g
Polyunsaturated	.3	g
Cholesterol	4	mg
Sodium	507	mg

BULGUR PILAF WITH CURRANTS AND PINE NUTS

Serves 4, about ¼ cup each

The contrast of flavors and textures afforded by the nuts and currants makes this family favorite interesting and filling enough to be the "star" of a meatless meal. It is also marvelous as a side dish with roast chicken or lamb.

¼ cup pine nuts, toasted (*see below*)
1 tablespoon olive oil
1 small onion, finely chopped, to make ⅓ to ½ cup
1 cup medium or coarse bulgur

¼ cup currants
2 cups hot defatted chicken broth, preferably homemade (page 273)
Salt to taste

Preheat oven to 350°F. Toast the pine nuts and set aside.

In a heavy 2½- to 3-quart saucepan heat the oil over moderate heat. Add the onion and sauté, stirring, until soft but not brown, about 2 minutes. Add the bulgur and sauté, stirring constantly, until the grains are well coated with the oil. Add the toasted pine nuts, currants, broth, and salt and bring to a boil, stirring. Cover and bake in the preheated oven for 45 minutes, or until all the liquid has been absorbed and the bulgur is tender. Do not stir during this time. Fluff the pilaf by tossing it briefly with 2 forks.

To toast pine nuts:

Place pine nuts in a large, dry skillet and cook, stirring, over medium heat about 5 minutes, until lightly browned.

In a microwave: Spread nuts in a single layer in a microwave-safe dish and microwave at HIGH for 3 minutes, or until lightly golden.

Calories	240 cal
Protein	8 g
Carbohydrates	45 g
Total fat	9 g
Saturated	1 g
Polyunsaturated	2 g
Cholesterol	0 mg
Sodium	505 mg

Without pine nuts

Calories	195 cal
Protein	6 g
Carbohydrates	44 g
Total fat	4 g
Saturated	.5 g
Polyunsaturated	.3 g
Cholesterol	0 mg
Sodium	500 mg

TABBOULEH
(CRACKED WHEAT SALAD)

Serves 6 to 8, about 1 cup each

This Middle Eastern treat is traditionally eaten by scooping it up with a leaf of Romaine lettuce.

1 cup bulgur, preferably fine
1 small onion, finely chopped
1 bunch scallions, trimmed
  and finely chopped, the
  white and part of the
  green
1 cup minced parsley,
  preferably Italian
¼ cup crushed dried mint, or
  ½ cup chopped fresh
  mint

Salt and freshly ground black
  pepper to taste
¼ cup fresh lemon juice
¼ cup olive oil
Garnishes: Romaine lettuce
  leaves, black Greek-style
  olives, tomato wedges or
  cherry tomatoes, carrot
  curls

Mix the bulgur with 2 cups cold water and let stand for 30 minutes at room temperature. Drain thoroughly in a sieve, pressing any water out with your hands.

Put the bulgur in a bowl and add the onion; squeeze the two together with your hands so the onion juices penetrate the wheat. Fluff with 2 forks; then add the scallions, parsley, and mint and toss to mix. Add salt and pepper to taste. Beat the lemon juice and olive oil together, add, and toss. Taste again for seasoning. Refrigerate uncovered for at least 1 hour.

To serve, arrange the lettuce leaves on a platter to form a bed for the tabbouleh and mound it in the center. Decorate with any combination of the suggested garnishes.

Calories	150	cal
Protein	3	g
Carbohydrates	23	g
Total fat	8	g
Saturated	1	g
Polyunsaturated	1	g
Cholesterol	0	mg
Sodium	7	mg

BARLEY–SCALLION–PINE NUT CASSEROLE

Serves 6, about ½ cup each

Try this when you need a starchy side or main dish; it's a nice change from rice.

1 cup pearl barley
1 tablespoon salted butter
1 medium onion, chopped
¼ cup toasted pine nuts
    (page 135)
⅓ cup finely chopped parsley,
    preferably Italian, plus
    more for garnish

¼ cup finely chopped
    scallions, the white and
    part of the green
3 cups very hot defatted
    chicken broth, preferably
    homemade (page 273)
Salt and freshly ground black
    pepper to taste

Preheat the oven to 350°F.

Rinse the barley, drain, and set aside.

Melt the butter in a 1½-quart flameproof casserole. Add the onion and cook until softened, about 2 minutes. Add the barley and continue cooking, stirring constantly, until the barley is well coated with butter. Stir in the pine nuts, parsley, scallions, hot broth, and salt and pepper to taste. Mix well, bring to a boil, cover, and bake in the preheated oven for 1 hour and 15 minutes. Fluff with 2 forks, turn into a warm serving dish, garnish with additional chopped parsley, and serve.

Calories	206	cal
Protein	6	g
Carbohydrates	29	g
Total fat	8	g
Saturated	3	g
Polyunsaturated	1	g
Cholesterol	10	mg
Sodium	46	mg

HERBED "INSTANT" COUSCOUS

Serves 6, about ¼ cup each

Couscous, a traditional North African dish steamed over a spicy stew, is made of fine semolina wheat sprinkled with fine flour to keep each grain separate. The usual cooking method is quite time-consuming, although it produces a superior texture. This instant version is softer but just as tasty as the traditional one. Serve this couscous with any highly flavored fish or chicken dish.

2 cups defatted chicken broth,
   preferably homemade
   (page 273), seasoned
   with salt and pepper
1 tablespoon olive oil

1½ cups couscous
2 tablespoons chopped parsley
1 tablespoon minced chives
Salt and freshly ground black
   pepper

Bring the broth and olive oil to a boil, stir in the couscous, remove from the heat, cover, and set aside for 5 minutes.

Fluff the couscous with a fork, fold in the parsley and chives, and season again to taste with salt and pepper. Keep covered until ready to serve.

Calories	340	cal
Protein	9	g
Carbohydrates	56	g
Total fat	8	g
Saturated	1	g
Polyunsaturated	1	g
Cholesterol	0	mg
Sodium	11	mg

BEANS

Beans, in all their wonderful variety, play such an important role in the low-fat lifestyle that they deserve a bit of explanation. They are mankind's second most important food (the grasses—wheat, rye, rice, etc., are first), but in spite of their prominence in many foreign cuisines, most

Americans consume them infrequently. From the standpoint of flavor, versatility, cost, and healthfulness, beans—and their culinary cousins, peas—are without peer. They are full of protein, complex carbohydrates, several B vitamins, iron, magnesium, and zinc. Though fairly high in calories (higher, in fact, than some very lean meats), the trade-off is that they are low in fat, contain no cholesterol, and are very filling in small quantity. Because they combine easily with other foods, a limited amount can go a long way when added to soups, salads, and rice dishes.

If all this were not enough, beans also contain a soluble fiber that helps lower cholesterol. In fact, Dr. David A. Jenkins, professor of medicine and nutritional sciences at the University of Toronto, found that beans are as effective as oats in lowering cholesterol levels, although the decrease will vary from person to person. Jenkins found that two servings a day can lower cholesterol levels by 13 to 14 percent.

The insoluble fiber found in beans and the composition of their protein and starch make beans a "slow-release" carbohydrate food, or one that digests slowly. This factor makes them a boon to diabetics, because the correspondingly gentle rise in blood sugar requires less insulin. It is generally believed that the tendency of beans to produce flatulence can be lessened by changing the soaking water often. They should be rinsed again in a colander under running water after the soaking period.

One expert claims that simply eating beans frequently diminishes the gas problem in time. Since uncooked starch is harder to digest, cooking beans thoroughly also helps. Beans should hold their shape but be soft and mash easily; they should not be chewy.

As with other plant foods, the protein here is not as complete as that from animal sources. To obtain protein of similar quality, eat beans along with a grain food or a small amount of animal protein such as yogurt, milk, or cheese, or a bit of fish, meat, or poultry. Thus, a good bread with Split Pea Soup (page 97) or Lentil Chili (page 147) with rice will complete the protein picture. A bowl of Cuban beans and rice with a tomato pasta sauce spooned over, and a little Parmesan grated on top, is a favorite quick meal at our house. I'm sure you'll come up with your own favorite combinations.

Cooking Tips for Beans

Most dried beans (black beans, kidney beans, and so forth) double in volume and weight after being soaked. Soybeans and chickpeas usually triple. Figure that 1 cup dried beans (8 ounces) yields 2 to 2½ cups or 1 to 1¼ pounds when cooked. Count on 1 cup of dried beans to serve 4 people when combined with other foods or as a side dish.

SOAKING

Dried beans must be presoaked, using either the overnight or the "quick" method. Use at least 3 times their volume of water for soaking. Don't add baking soda to the water; it destroys nutrients. Changing the soaking water two or three times cuts down on flatulence.

Overnight method: Wash the beans and place in four parts water. Cover and let stand 4 hours or overnight.

Quick method: Bring water and beans to a boil and cook for 2 minutes. Cover, remove from heat, and let stand 1 hour.

COOKING

After presoaking by either method, discard soaking water, replace with fresh water, and boil beans gently for 1½ to 2 hours, partially covered, until soft.

Split peas and black-eyed peas can be rinsed and then cooked without soaking.

Do not add baking soda during cooking as some older cookbooks suggest. It destroys nutrients, makes beans mushy, and can cause a bitter taste. Salt, if used, should not be added until the beans are nearly cooked through and tender, since it toughens bean skins, makes them impermeable, and slows the cooking.

Pressure cooker method: If you use one, the beans can be cooked in 3 to 10 minutes after presoaking, or in 25 to 45 minutes (in three or four parts water) without presoaking. Be sure to follow your cooker's directions carefully; cooking times vary with the type of bean.

Cooked beans can be stored in the refrigerator for one week or in the freezer for several months.

Lentils: We should eat more of this pulse (another word for legume). Known as the "meat" of vegetarians, lentils are rich in vitamins and high in protein, and when served with rice, they provide more combined fiber than oats. Most varieties can be cooked in 30 to 45 minutes (no soaking necessary). The most common lentil is the brownish-green; the Egyptian, or red, lentil is smaller and it cooks faster. There are also orange and yellow lentils. They all turn brown-gray when cooked, with little noticeable flavor difference between them. Only the red and brown are available dried. One cup of dry lentils yields about 2¼ cups cooked; one pound of dried lentils will serve four.

BLACK BEANS AND RICE

Serves 4, about 1 cup each

Every Cuban cook has some slightly different take on this classic recipe known as "Moors and Christians." It goes with everything, is immensely nourishing and filling, and can even be made into a salad, by dressing it with vinaigrette. Leftover black beans may be used. The recipe is easily doubled.

2 tablespoons olive oil
1 medium onion, finely
   chopped
2 teaspoons finely chopped
   garlic
1 small green pepper, finely
   chopped
2 medium ripe tomatoes,
   coarsely chopped, or 4
   canned Italian plum
   tomatoes, drained and
   coarsely chopped

Salt and freshly ground black
   pepper
2 cups cooked black beans (or
   1 15-ounce can, drained
   and rinsed)
1 cup long-grain white rice

Heat the oil in a heavy casserole or saucepan with a tight-fitting lid. Add the onion, garlic, and green pepper and sauté over moderate heat until the onion is translucent, about 2 minutes. Add the tomatoes and cook, stirring, until the mixture is well blended and has thickened, about 3 to 4 minutes. Season to taste with salt and pepper. Stir in the beans, mixing well. Cover and let simmer very gently while preparing the rice.

In a separate saucepan bring 2 cups of salted water to a boil over high heat, add the rice, reduce heat to a simmer, cover, and cook for 18 minutes, or until all the liquid is absorbed. Serve the rice and beans in separate bowls, or make a ring of the rice around the beans on a platter.

Calories	366	cal
Protein	12	g
Carbohydrates	63	g
Total fat	8	g
Saturated	1	g
Polyunsaturated	1	g
Cholesterol	0	mg
Sodium	9	mg

BLACK BEAN AND RICE SALAD

Prepare the black beans and rice as outlined above, and mix the two together. (If you are using leftover rice and cooked black beans, stir the beans into the onion–green pepper–tomato mixture and let steep over very low heat only 5 minutes or so.) Smash a garlic clove and place in a small bowl with ½ teaspoon dried thyme and 3 tablespoons balsamic vinegar. Let this steep while the rice and beans come to room temperature. Remove and discard the garlic, splash the flavored vinegar over the rice and beans, and toss well. Serve over lettuce leaves.

Calories	368	cal
Protein	12	g
Carbohydrates	64	g
Total fat	8	g
Saturated	1	g
Polyunsaturated	1	g
Cholesterol	0	mg
Sodium	9	mg

BLACK BEAN AND RICE SALAD VINAIGRETTE

You can also omit the vinegar and use the recipe for Lemon–Mustard Vinaigrette (page 113), but don't forget to add the vinaigrette to the fat tally.

FLAGEOLETS BRETONNE
(FRENCH KIDNEY BEANS BRITTANY STYLE)

Serves 6 to 8

In France green beans are grown just for the tender, pale inner bean known as flageolet, which looks like a small lima bean and is a classic accompaniment to roast lamb. They can be bought here canned and dried and are a great treat.

2 cups dried flageolet beans,
    soaked (page 140)
1 tablespoon salted butter
1 tablespoon olive oil
½ cup chopped onion

2 garlic cloves, minced
Salt and freshly ground black
    pepper to taste
1 tablespoon finely chopped
    parsley

Drain and rinse the flageolets. Put about 4 cups water on to heat in a large pot.

Melt the butter and olive oil in a medium saucepan. Add the onion and garlic and cook until the onion is just wilted, about 2 minutes. Stir in the drained beans and cook over gentle heat for about 3 minutes, then add enough hot water from the pot to just cover the beans. Bring to a boil, cover, lower heat, and simmer for about 1 hour over gentle heat. Check from time to time to see that the liquid has not cooked away. If the beans look dry, add a cautious additional amount of hot water. Cook until the beans are tender and the liquid is absorbed. Season to taste with salt and liberal grindings of black pepper. Toss with the parsley and serve.

NOTE: You can substitute dried white navy beans or pea beans and make *Haricots blancs à la bretonne*; the result isn't as delicate but it is still delicious.

Calories	236	cal
Protein	13	g
Carbohydrates	37	g
Total fat	4	g
Saturated	1	g
Polyunsaturated	1	g
Cholesterol	4	mg
Sodium	26	mg

SUCCOTASH

Serves 4 to 5, about ½ cup each

1 tablespoon Butter Buds
⅓ cup skim milk
1 tablespoon olive oil
2 tablespoons finely chopped
　onion
10-ounce package frozen
　whole corn kernels or
　1 cup fresh corn kernels,
　from about 2 ears

½ teaspoon salt, or to taste
10-ounce package frozen lima
　beans, cooked according
　to package directions
Freshly ground black pepper

Mix the Butter Buds into the skim milk and set aside.

Heat the oil over low heat in a heavy saucepan and sauté the onion until soft, about 1 minute. Add the corn, salt, and milk mixture and simmer for 3 minutes, or until most of the liquid is absorbed. Add the lima beans, cover, and simmer gently until beans are heated through, about 3 minutes. Season with several good grindings of black pepper.

Calories	145	cal
Protein	6	g
Carbohydrates	25	g
Total fat	3	g
Saturated	.5	g
Polyunsaturated	1	g
Cholesterol	1	mg
Sodium	314	mg

CHICKPEAS, TOMATOES, AND RICE

Serves 4, about 1 cup each

Make this recipe when you have rice left over from pilaf, but not enough to go around. It couldn't be simpler, and it makes a hearty main dish if served with a green vegetable or salad. The combination of a grain and a legume gives you complete protein.

2 teaspoons olive oil
2 garlic cloves, minced
2 to 3 ripe tomatoes, peeled,
    seeded, and chopped
    (or use canned)
1 16-ounce can chickpeas,
    drained and rinsed

1 to 1½ cups cooked white
    rice, heated (page 132)
Salt and freshly ground black
    pepper to taste

Heat the olive oil over medium heat in a saucepan or skillet big enough to eventually contain the chickpeas and rice, and sauté the garlic until it takes on the slightest color. Add the tomatoes and chickpeas and cook, stirring for 7 or 8 minutes, adjusting heat as needed. Mix with the warmed rice in a warm serving bowl and toss with salt and pepper to taste.

Calories	242	cal
Protein	8	g
Carbohydrates	43	g
Total fat	4	g
Saturated	.5	g
Polyunsaturated	1	g
Cholesterol	0	mg
Sodium	345	mg

CURRIED LENTILS AND RICE

Serves 5, about ¾ cup each

This tasty, filling side dish is easily elevated to main-course status by adding bits of leftover fish, meat, or chicken.

1 cup lentils, rinsed
4 cups defatted chicken broth, homemade (page 273) or canned, or cold water
½ teaspoon salt, or to taste
1 tablespoon olive oil

2 medium yellow onions, thinly sliced
Freshly ground black pepper
½ cup long-grain white rice
2 teaspoons curry powder
1 tablespoon chopped parsley

Put lentils, broth or water, and salt in a large, heavy saucepan, cover, and bring to a boil; then lower heat and let the lentils simmer gently for 20 minutes.

Meanwhile, heat the olive oil in a non-stick skillet over low heat and sauté the onions, stirring frequently, until they are pale gold, about 5 minutes. Season liberally with black pepper and set aside.

When the lentils have cooked 20 minutes, add and stir in the onions, rice, and curry powder. Simmer, covered, for an additional 18 minutes, or until the rice is tender and liquid is absorbed. Check the saucepan from time to time to see that the mixture doesn't stick. Sprinkle with parsley and serve.

Calories	267	cal
Protein	13	g
Carbohydrates	44	g
Total fat	5	g
Saturated	.5	g
Polyunsaturated	.5	g
Cholesterol	0	mg
Sodium	229	mg

LENTIL CHILI

Serves 12, about 1 cup each

You'll never miss the meat in this super-delicious chili, and it's a great way to serve a crowd.

⅓ cup olive oil
1 medium onion, cut into
    ½-inch chunks
2 garlic cloves, minced
1 medium carrot, peeled and
    coarsely chopped
7 cups water
⅓ cup tomato paste
2 cups (about 12 ounces)
    brown lentils, rinsed
1 green pepper, cut into
    ½-inch chunks
1 sweet red pepper, cut into
    ½-inch chunks

1 19-ounce can red kidney
    beans, rinsed and drained
1 cup canned, cooked
    garbanzo beans, rinsed
    and drained
2 cups canned whole tomatoes
    in purée
⅓ cup chili powder
4 teaspoons ground cumin
¼ teaspoon dried red pepper
    flakes, or more if desired
Salt and freshly ground black
    pepper to taste

Heat the olive oil in a large, heavy pot and sauté the onion, garlic, and carrot over medium heat until the carrot is tender, about 5 minutes.

Add the water, tomato paste, lentils, green and red pepper, and the kidney and garbanzo beans. Add the tomatoes, breaking them up against the side of the pot as you do. Stir in the chili powder, cumin, and red pepper flakes. Bring to a boil and reduce heat to moderate. Cover and cook 45 minutes, or until lentils are tender but not mushy. Add more water if necessary. Adjust seasoning with salt and pepper to taste. Serve alone or over plain basic white rice (page 132).

Calories	239	cal
Protein	11	g
Carbohydrates	34	g
Total fat	7	g
Saturated	1	g
Polyunsaturated	1	g
Cholesterol	0	mg
Sodium	684	mg

LENTILS WITH GARLIC AND TOMATOES

Serves 4, about ½ cup each

This dish of Indian origin makes a pleasant change of pace as an accompaniment to fish, chicken, or veal, when the usual starches and vegetables pale.

2 tablespoons olive oil
5 garlic cloves, minced
½ pound ripe tomatoes, peeled
   and finely chopped, or 1
   14-ounce can Italian
   plum tomatoes, drained
   and chopped

1 cup lentils, rinsed
2½ cups water
¾ teaspoon salt, or to taste
1 tablespoon lemon juice

Heat the oil over moderate heat in a heavy 2½-quart pot. When hot, add the garlic and cook until it takes on some color, a minute or so. Add the tomatoes and cook, stirring frequently, for about 5 minutes, or until the tomatoes are almost reduced to a paste. Add the lentils and water, stir, and bring to a boil. Cover, lower heat, and simmer gently for 30 minutes. Add salt to taste and the lemon juice and stir to mix.

Calories	238	cal
Protein	14	g
Carbohydrates	31	g
Total fat	7	g
Saturated	1	g
Polyunsaturated	1	g
Cholesterol	0	mg
Sodium	284	mg

15
PASTA

PENNE WITH EGGPLANT

SPAGHETTI PUTTANESCA

**PASTA WITH SWEET PEPPERS
AND TOMATO SAUCE**

**ORECCHIETTE WITH BROCCOLI AND FRESH
AND SUN-DRIED TOMATOES**

LINGUINE WITH WHITE CLAM SAUCE

PASTA WITH SMOKED SALMON AND BASIL

GAEL GREENE'S SCALLOP PASTA

QUICK MEAT SAUCE FOR PASTA

PORK LO MEIN

**PASTA SALAD WITH TUNA
AND SNOW PEAS**

One of the most important foods in your low-fat plan is pasta. It's easy, fast, and filling and when not smothered in rich sauces or tons of cheese the noodle is at the top of the "recommend" list. A cup of cooked macaroni or spaghetti (about 2 ounces dry) has barely a trace of fat or cholesterol. Just about all the cup's 210 calories derive from complex carbohydrates. Combine pasta with vegetables or protein like meat, fish, or a bit of cheese and you have a well-balanced one-dish meal.

With a good variety of pastas on your shelf (stored in a cool, dry place, pasta keeps indefinitely), the ingredients for your favorite sauces on hand in the pantry or the freezer, you're never more than 15 minutes away from dinner. My most reliable favorite is the Puttanesca Sauce on page 152; the tomatoes, anchovies, and capers are easily kept on hand, and the sauce is fabulous not only on spaghetti or linguine but also on orecchiette, which "holds" the sauce nicely.

Add any lean ingredients you like to your pasta—sliced skinless chicken breast, turkey, or fish. Keep away from recipes that call for a creamy base, and be generous with zesty flavorings like dried red pepper flakes, garlic, basil, oregano, and parsley—the Italian kind. Be sparing with the olive oil—you can usually do with less than most other recipes call for. Ditto with the cheese. Use grated Parmesan sprinkled on top, rather than in the dish, and don't forget to add it to your fat count. One tablespoon has 1.8 grams of fat; ½ cup packed, about 22 grams.

There isn't too much you need to know about pasta itself; both the dried and fresh kind are made with the same ingredients—flour and water or flour and eggs. Durum wheat, the hardest, or semolina, the coarsest grind of durum, makes the best pasta—flavorful and resilient.

If you have a source for fresh pasta (it's available in the refrigerator section in many supermarkets), you may prefer its tender, lighter texture, and the way it absorbs sauces.

Cooking Pasta

To improve the taste and texture of your pasta, cook just until *al dente* ("to the bite"—firm but edible), which means frequent testing while the pasta boils. Avoid the problem of sticking by cooking pasta in a large volume of rapidly boiling, salted water (at least 4 quarts per pound of dry pasta). Leave the pot uncovered. Adding oil to the water is up to you—it's not really necessary. Fresh pasta cooks much faster than dried, so start tasting immediately after the water returns to the boil. Turn into a capacious colander (there's a special wire mesh one for pasta) and shake several times to get the water out. Don't rinse (unless you need to cool the pasta off quickly). Turn the pasta into a warmed bowl and toss with the sauce immediately.

PENNE WITH EGGPLANT

Serves 4

The eggplant makes this filling and satisfying—a good bet as a main-course pasta, followed with a mixed green salad.

1 pound penne (quill-shaped pasta)	¼ teaspoon dried hot red pepper flakes
4 tablespoons olive oil	½ teaspoon salt, or to taste
1 medium-large eggplant, about 1½ pounds, peeled and cut into 1-inch cubes	Freshly ground black pepper to taste
4 garlic cloves, finely chopped	1½ tablespoons chopped parsley, preferably Italian
35-ounce can Italian plum tomatoes, drained and coarsely chopped	Grated Parmesan cheese

Bring a large pot of salted water to the boil. Add the penne and cook until tender but slightly firm to the bite, about 12 to 15 minutes.

When you start the water, begin the sauce. In a large, preferably non-stick skillet, heat 2 tablespoons of the olive oil over medium-high heat until hot but not smoking. Add *half* the eggplant and cook, tossing frequently, until almost tender. Transfer to a heated plate. Add another tablespoon of oil and repeat with the remaining eggplant. Add it to the plate.

Add the remaining tablespoon of oil to the skillet and sauté the garlic until pale gold, about 1 minute.

Add the tomatoes, red pepper flakes, salt, and pepper to taste. Add the eggplant and cook until the sauce is thickened and the eggplant is tender, about 10 to 15 minutes. Keep the sauce hot if the pasta is not done yet.

Drain the pasta in a colander, place in a warm serving bowl, and add the sauce. Toss well, add the parsley, and toss again. Serve immediately with a bowl of grated Parmesan cheese passed separately.

Calories	629 cal
Protein	18 g
Carbohydrates	106 g
Total fat	16 g
Saturated	2 g
Polyunsaturated	1 g
Cholesterol	0 mg
Sodium	687 mg

SPAGHETTI PUTTANESCA

Serves 4

We eat pasta a lot, and this quick, tasty "harlot's" sauce is one of our favorites!

2 tablespoons olive oil
2 to 3 garlic cloves, crushed
8 anchovy filets, cut into 4
   pieces each
1 35-ounce can Italian plum
   tomatoes, drained and put
   through a food mill or a
   coarse sieve
8 black olives, preferably the
   Niçoise type, pitted and
   sliced

1 teaspoon capers
1 tablespoon chopped fresh
   basil or parsley
2 dried red chilis or ¼
   teaspoon dried hot red
   pepper flakes
1 pound spaghetti or linguine

Heat the oil in a large skillet; sauté the garlic until it is soft but not brown; add the anchovies. After several minutes, when the anchovies have broken apart and appear almost melted, add the tomatoes, stir, and simmer for 10 minutes. Stir in the olives, capers, basil or parsley, and chilis or red pepper flakes. Simmer sauce uncovered for 20 minutes or until thickened. Remove whole peppers, if used, before pouring the sauce over hot pasta.

Calories	455	cal
Protein	1615	g
Carbohydrates	77	g
Total fat	10	g
Saturated	1	g
Polyunsaturated	1	g
Cholesterol	4	mg
Sodium	781	mg

PASTA WITH SWEET PEPPERS AND TOMATO SAUCE

Serves 6

4 to 6 large sweet peppers, red and/or yellow (depending on size)
3 tablespoons olive oil
2 garlic cloves, finely chopped
2 pounds ripe tomatoes, peeled, seeded, and chopped, or 1 2-pound, 3-ounce can whole tomatoes, drained and chopped

½ teaspoon salt, or to taste
Freshly ground black pepper
Dash cayenne
2 tablespoons chopped fresh basil
1 pound rigatoni or farfalle
¼ cup finely chopped parsley, preferably Italian
Freshly grated Parmesan cheese

Roast and peel the peppers as directed on page 238. Remove the seeds and membranes and cut the peppers into 1-inch-wide strips. (This part can be done ahead.)

Put 2 tablespoons of the olive oil in a heavy skillet large enough to hold the tomatoes and peppers, swirl it around to coat bottom and add the pepper strips. Cook, stirring constantly, for 3 to 4 minutes, or until the peppers are glossy. Transfer to a heated plate and keep warm.

Put on the pasta water to boil and add a little salt.

Pour the remaining 1 tablespoon oil into the skillet and sauté the garlic until it is pale gold, about 1 minute. Add the tomatoes, salt, pepper, cayenne, and basil, and scrape up and stir in any brown bits. Simmer covered for 15 to 20 minutes. Add the peppers plus any accumulated juices and cook 5 minutes longer. Check the seasoning.

While the sauce simmers, cook the pasta in rapidly boiling water. Drain and place in a heated serving dish. Pour the pepper–tomato sauce over the pasta, sprinkle with parsley, and serve immediately in hot bowls. Pass the grated Parmesan cheese separately.

Including pasta

Calories	389	cal
Protein	4	g
Carbohydrates	68	g
Total fat	8	g
Saturated	1	g
Polyunsaturated	1	g
Cholesterol	0	mg
Sodium	199	mg

Use dry-curd or low-fat cottage cheese instead of ricotta when making lasagna or manicotti. Both are much lower in fat than even part-skim ricotta.

ORECCHIETTE WITH BROCCOLI AND FRESH AND SUN-DRIED TOMATOES

Serves 6

After trying in vain to obtain this recipe from the restaurant where I'd eaten and adored it, I came up with my own version, which is another good main-course pasta.

1 small bunch broccoli
1½ pounds fresh, ripe
   tomatoes, peeled, seeded
   and chopped, or
1 28-ounce can whole
   tomatoes, drained and
   chopped
½ cup thinly sliced scallions,
   the white and part of the
   green
¼ cup sun-dried tomatoes, oil
   rinsed off, thinly sliced

¼ cup chopped fresh basil
¼ cup chopped parsley,
   preferably Italian
2 garlic cloves, minced
½ teaspoon salt, or to taste
Freshly ground black pepper
Dash cayenne
2 tablespoons olive oil
12 ounces orecchiette or other
   small pasta, cooked
Freshly grated Parmesan
   cheese

Cut off the thick stems of the broccoli and reserve for another use. Break the remainder into very small florets—you should have about 3 cups—and boil gently in well-salted water for 3 minutes. Broccoli should be undercooked—still slightly firm. Drain well, plunge into cold water, and drain again. Set aside.

In a medium saucepan combine the tomatoes, scallions, sun-dried tomatoes, basil, parsley, garlic, salt, pepper, and cayenne. Stir in the oil. Gently mix in the reserved broccoli and heat gently. Toss the sauce with the hot pasta and serve at once. Pass the grated Parmesan separately.

NOTE: For a richer flavor, sprinkle the hot pasta with dry Butter Buds when tossing with the sauce.

Calories	319	cal
Protein	10	g
Carbohydrates	51	g
Total fat	9	g
Saturated	1	g
Polyunsaturated	1	g
Cholesterol	0	mg
Sodium	427	mg

LINGUINE WITH WHITE CLAM SAUCE

Serves 4

This classic pasta dish is filling, tasty, and low in fat!

2 6½-ounce cans minced
  clams
2 tablespoons olive oil
5 garlic cloves, minced
½ cup dry white wine
¼ cup chopped parsley,
  preferably Italian

½ teaspoon dried oregano
Freshly ground black pepper
12 ounces linguine
Optional garnish: 12 fresh
  littleneck clams, steamed
  open

Bring a large pot of salted water to the boil. Have a large heated bowl
ready, as well as individual soup bowls.

Drain the minced clams, reserving the juice, and set aside. You should
have between one-half and three-quarters cups clam juice.

While the water is heating, warm the oil in a heavy skillet over
moderate heat and sauté the garlic just until it sizzles but has not taken
on color, about 1 minute. Add the clam juice and wine, parsley, oregano,
and liberal grindings of black pepper and bring to a boil. Lower heat and
simmer partially covered for 10 minutes. Stir in the minced clams and
cook gently, just until clams have heated through.

Cook the linguine *al dente*, drain, and put in the heated serving bowl.
Add the clam sauce, toss well, and dish out into heated soup bowls. Top
each portion with 3 optional fresh clams and serve at once. No cheese
with this, please.

Calories	450	cal
Protein	23	g
Carbohydrates	68	g
Total fat	9	g
Saturated	1	g
Polyunsaturated	1	g
Cholesterol	30	mg
Sodium	116	mg

PASTA WITH SMOKED SALMON AND BASIL

Serves 2

This is a quick and elegant little pasta to feed two. There is virtually no cooking other than the pasta. You can use dried pasta in a pinch, but fresh pasta is infinitely better with all these fresh flavors. Happily, fresh pasta can now be found in most supermarkets.

1 tablespoon olive oil
2 small garlic cloves, minced
1 tablespoon finely chopped
  parsley
1 tablespoon finely chopped
  fresh basil
1 tablespoon finely chopped
  scallion

2 ounces smoked salmon,
  minced (about 3
  tablespoons)
½ pound fresh egg noodles,
  linguine or fettuccine
Salt and freshly ground black
  pepper to taste

Put a large pot of salted water on to boil for the noodles. Put the oil, garlic, parsley, basil, scallion, and salmon in a warmed bowl large enough to hold the pasta. Toss the mixture well.

When the water boils, add the noodles and cook *al dente*; this should take about 3 minutes, since fresh noodles cook very quickly. Drain the noodles, add to the bowl, and toss with the flavorings. Add salt if desired and freshly ground pepper to taste. Divide the pasta between two warm plates and serve at once.

NOTE: Don't worry about eating raw garlic; it is minced, and the heat of the pasta will wilt it considerably as it's tossed.

Calories	429	cal
Protein	20	g
Carbohydrates	64	g
Total fat	11	g
Saturated	1	g
Polyunsaturated	1	g
Cholesterol	140	mg
Sodium	255	mg

GAEL GREENE'S SCALLOP PASTA

Serves 4

As a respite from the rich food she must eat in the line of duty, food critic Gael Greene cooks simple, elegant low-fat pasta like this at home.

¼ cup flour
1 pound sea scallops,
   cut in half
1 tablespoon olive oil
2 garlic cloves, minced
¾ pound fresh linguine

8 ounces (1 bottle) clam juice
Freshly ground black pepper
¼ cup pine nuts, toasted
   (page 135)
Chopped Italian parsley

Put a large pot of salted water on to boil for the pasta.

Put the flour in a plastic bag. Add the scallops, shake well, then turn into a strainer and shake to remove excess flour.

Heat the olive oil in a large non-stick skillet, add the garlic and cook just until softened but not brown, about 1 minute. Add the scallops and over high heat sauté briefly, stirring, until the edges become pale gold, about 1 to 2 minutes. Set aside and keep warm.

Cook the linguine and drain only briefly. Immediately return it to the pot and add the clam juice. Heat briefly and season liberally with the pepper. Serve the pasta in warm bowls topped with the scallops and a sprinkling each of pine nuts and parsley.

Calories	606 cal
Protein	44 g
Carbohydrates	76 g
Total fat	15 g
Saturated	2 g
Polyunsaturated	3 g
Cholesterol	183 mg
Sodium	448 mg

QUICK MEAT SAUCE FOR PASTA

Serves 6, about ½ cup each

Everyone loves this sauce! It freezes very well, and can be used with any kind of pasta. It's especially good on shells.

¾ **pound very lean ground**
   sirloin
1 26-ounce jar marinara sauce
1 teaspoon dried oregano

2 to 3 garlic cloves
Dash cayenne
Freshly ground black pepper
½ teaspoon salt, or to taste

Heat a heavy, non-stick skillet over medium-high heat. Add the ground beef and sauté, stirring frequently, for 4 to 5 minutes, or until meat loses its pinkness. Turn the contents of the skillet into a strainer or colander lined with paper towels and allow the fat to drain off.

Put the meat into a heavy 3-quart saucepan. Add the marinara sauce and stir well. Rub the oregano between the palms of your hands to powder it slightly, and add. Put the garlic through a garlic press and add, along with the cayenne, a liberal amount of black pepper, and salt to taste. Stir well, cover, and cook over gentle heat for 20 minutes, stirring occasionally. Correct the seasoning.

Calories	195	cal
Protein	13	g
Carbohydrates	13	g
Total fat	11	g
Saturated	3	g
Polyunsaturated	1	g
Cholesterol	34	mg
Sodium	1167	mg

One tablespoon of freshly grated Parmesan cheese has 1.8 grams of fat.

PORK LO MEIN
(CHINESE NOODLES WITH PORK)

Serves 6 to 8

4 to 5 dried black Chinese
    mushrooms (optional)
½ pound lean pork loin or
    roast pork
1 head Napa cabbage
2 to 3 whole scallions
2 tablespoons peanut or
    Canola oil

½ teaspoon salt
1 pound spaghetti or Chinese
    noodles, parboiled,
    drained, and rinsed to
    stop cooking
2 tablespoons soy sauce,
    preferably Chinese or
    Tamari

Soak the mushrooms in warm water 30 to 60 minutes. Drain, rinse, and squeeze dry. Remove the stems and reserve for soup.

Slice the pork thinly and shred into matchstick-sized strips. Cut the cabbage crosswise into 1-inch pieces. Cut the scallions into 1-inch sections. Slice the mushrooms thinly.

Heat the oil until very hot in a wok or large heavy skillet; add the salt, then the scallions, and stir-fry about 45 seconds. Add the pork strips and stir-fry until they lose their pinkness, 2 to 3 minutes. (If using roast pork, stir-fry for 45 seconds.) Add the cabbage and mushrooms and continue to stir-fry with a scoop-and-toss motion about 2 minutes more. Add the parboiled noodles and soy sauce and toss gently with the stir-fried mixture. Cover the wok or skillet and cook 5 minutes over medium heat, or until noodles are warmed through.

Calories	340	cal
Protein	16	g
Carbohydrates	51	g
Total fat	7	g
Saturated	2	g
Polyunsaturated	2	g
Cholesterol	19	mg
Sodium	482	mg

PASTA SALAD WITH TUNA AND SNOW PEAS

Serves 6

½ pound fresh snow peas
4 to 5 whole scallions, trimmed
1 6½-ounce can white tuna in water, drained
10 ounces fusilli, cooked, drained

2 tablespoons reduced-calorie mayonnaise
2 tablespoons plain non-fat yogurt
¼ teaspoon dried mustard
Freshly ground black pepper to taste

Remove the tops and strings of the snow peas and blanch the vegetable for 45 seconds in boiling, salted water. Immediately drain and refresh under cold running water. With a cleaver or sharp knife cut the snow peas on the diagonal into half-inch pieces and set aside.

Chop the scallions finely. You should have a heaping ½ cup.

Put the tuna in a large bowl and flake it with a fork. Add the snow peas, scallions, and pasta and toss. Mix the mayonnaise, yogurt, and dry mustard together in a small bowl, add to the pasta mixture, and toss well—the mayonnaise mixture will be barely visible. Add black pepper to taste and refrigerate the salad for an hour or so before serving.

Calories	232	cal
Protein	14	g
Carbohydrates	37	g
Total fat	3	g
Saturated	1	g
Polyunsaturated	.3	g
Cholesterol	14	mg
Sodium	154	mg

16

FISH AND SHELLFISH

♦

STEAMED FISH WITH GINGER, SCALLIONS,
AND CORIANDER

TILEFISH IN RED SAUCE

MUSTARD-BAKED FLOUNDER

SEABASS WITH TOMATOES

HOT GINGER FISH WITH SWEET PEPPERS

SEAFOOD RAGOÛT WITH RICE AND PEAS

BOMBAY SOLE

TERIYAKI-GRILLED SWORDFISH

GRILLED TUNA WITH WARM CORIANDER
VINAIGRETTE

SALMON IN FOIL WITH VEGETABLES

BAKED RED SNAPPER WITH JULIENNE OF
VEGETABLES

MIGNONETTE SAUCE FOR OYSTERS

OYSTER PAN ROAST

MUSSELS MARINARA

POACHED SCALLOPS WITH GINGER

PAN-GRILLED SHRIMP

STEAMED SHRIMP WITH GARLIC AND
SCALLIONS

Seafood figures importantly in the low-fat eating scheme. Not only do most fish give you high protein with almost no fat, but even the "fatty" fishes are desirable because of a cholesterol-lowering factor found in fish oils. Most shellfish—shrimp, mussels, lobster, crab—are very low in fat, and although some contain more cholesterol ounce for ounce than poultry or other fish, you can eat them occasionally and still stay within the recommended guidelines of less than 300 milligrams per day. The healthfulness of fish, along with its generally brief cooking time, makes it the ideal fast food. Yet it seems the average shopper still feels insecure not only in buying fish but in cooking it.

Whether you stick to safe filets of sole, or venture forth into cooking a whole fish, you want it to be fresh. So learn what to look for and try to buy fish the day you plan to eat it. Fresh fish proclaims itself to the eye, the nose, and the touch. Skin and flesh should glisten. If the fish is whole, the gills should be bright red and clean, not sticky. The flesh should be firm and elastic. If the fish is already steaked or fileted, the flesh should not retain the imprint of fingers. Both fish and shellfish should be mild and sea-like, not fishy. Shrimp should not be mushy or have an iodine smell.

Most people I know who eat fish do it dutifully, without being exactly thrilled by what they eat. Fish *is* bland, for the most part, but in the days when lowering my husband's cholesterol and weight was a goal, I learned some dishes that have remained our favorites over the years and are every bit as satisfying as a meat or chicken dish. Tilefish (or any firm white fish) in Red Sauce (page 167), Steamed Fish with Ginger, Scallions, and Coriander (page 166), Mustard-Baked Flounder (page 168) and Steamed Shrimp with Garlic and Scallions (page 184) are our favorites.

For general cooking, the less you do to a first-class fresh fish the better. Steaming, especially with some aromatic herbs or spices, is a splendid example of a minimalist approach yielding the maximum of flavor. Try baking a whole fish in foil. It's neat, doesn't smell, doesn't dirty a single cooking vessel, and you can be as creative as you like with the flavoring combinations. Use a big piece of heavy-duty foil, spray with PAM, and choose enclosures ranging from garlic, scallions, onion slices, tomato slices, paper-thin slices of zucchini, mushrooms, chopped shallots, any seasonings you like, and a tablespoon of white wine. Close foil over fish and twist ends securely, then bake in a preheated 425°F. oven on a baking sheet, timing it 10 minutes to the inch, plus or minus any fraction thereof.

Broiling particularly suits large, thick filets and fish steaks (cross-cut slices of large, firm-fleshed fish) such as halibut, salmon, tuna, and swordfish; as swordfish tends to be dry, try marinating it in Teriyaki sauce (page 175) and baste frequently during cooking.

Just remember that regardless of the method or recipe, overcooking is the easiest way to ruin fish and make it dry. Fish should be cooked only until the translucent flesh is opaque. Actually if you remove it from the heat while there is still a hairline of translucency in the middle (check by inserting the tip of a sharp knife), it will continue to cook to perfection in its own heat. No matter what recipes say, don't cook "until fish flakes with a fork." If your fish flakes, for sure it is overcooked, and then it is too late.

For a general rule of thumb that can be applied to all cooking methods, calculate cooking time at 10 minutes per inch, plus or minus any fraction thereof. Add 5 minutes per inch if a sauce is involved or you are baking in foil.

STEAMED FISH WITH GINGER, SCALLIONS, AND CORIANDER

Serves 4

This Chinese steaming method produces an exquisitely flavored and ravishingly pretty fish with a lovely natural sauce that is delicious over rice.

1 whole seabass, weakfish, red snapper, carp, or other non-oily white fish, about 3½ to 4 pounds including head

2 quarter-size slices fresh ginger

5 to 8 whole scallions, trimmed

2 tablespoons corn or peanut oil

1 tablespoon light soy sauce

1 teaspoon dark sesame oil

Dash dry sherry

Handful finely chopped fresh coriander

Rinse the fish carefully and make sure all traces of blood and membrane are removed. Pat it dry. With a sharp knife score the fish on both sides from head to tail with 4 or 5 diagonal slashes. These should be about an inch apart and go almost through to the bone. Put the ginger slices in the cuts nearest the head. Set aside.

Cut the green tops from the scallions and set aside; cut the white parts into fine julienne strips and set aside.

Select an ovenproof platter that will hold the fish either flat or slightly curled (see NOTES). On it make a bed of the reserved green scallion tops and lay the fish on top.

Pour 2 to 3 inches of water into a deep roasting pan with a cover or a large Dutch oven and put a rack in the pan that will hold the fish above the water (see NOTE). Bring to a boil over medium heat. Using mitts to protect your hands, place the platter with the fish on the rack and cover. Turn heat up to high. Steam the fish until the flesh is translucent at the bone, about 15 minutes.

While the fish is steaming, prepare the sauce: Combine the oil, soy sauce, sesame oil, and sherry in a small, heavy saucepan and heat gently for 2 or 3 minutes over low heat, stirring constantly. Set aside.

Remove the platter from the steamer and pour the sauce over the fish. Sprinkle with the scallion juliennes and chopped coriander and serve at once.

NOTES: 1. If you do not have a platter that holds the fish and fits your steaming pan, make one of suitable size out of a double thickness of heavy-duty foil; roll up the edges for an inch all around to catch the delicious juices that will emerge from the fish as it cooks. Serve right from the foil "dish" placed on another platter. 2. If you do not have a rack that fits your pan, improvise by placing the fish platter on 3 tuna fish cans, tops and bottoms removed or 3 or 4 demitasse cups turned upside down.

Calories	210	cal
Protein	25	g
Carbohydrates	2	g
Total fat	11	g
Saturated	2	g
Polyunsaturated	6	g
Cholesterol	54	mg
Sodium	243	mg

TILEFISH IN RED SAUCE

Serves 6

This pretty, tasty dish, which I often serve to company, is of North African origin, where it is made with grouper. Our tilefish is an excellent substitute, but you could also use any firm-fleshed white fish.

3 tablespoons olive oil
1 pound ripe tomatoes, peeled, seeded, and sliced, or 1 28-ounce can whole tomatoes, drained and sliced
6 garlic cloves, crushed
1 small fresh hot red pepper, diced, or 1 dried red pepper, crumbled
Salt and freshly ground black pepper

6 1¼-inch tilefish steaks, about 2 pounds total or steaks of any other non-oily, white fish such as seabass, grouper, or cod
2 tablespoons chopped coriander (or parsley)
1 tablespoon imported Hungarian paprika

Preheat oven to 400°F.

Select a shallow, flameproof baking dish large enough to hold the fish steaks in one layer. Put 2 tablespoons of the olive oil in the bottom and swirl around to coat evenly. Make a layer of half the tomato slices, the garlic, and the hot pepper. Season lightly with salt and pepper. Put the fish steaks on this bed, top with the remaining tomato slices, season again with salt and pepper, and sprinkle with the coriander.

In a small cup mix the paprika with the remaining tablespoon of olive oil and spoon over the fish, smoothing with the back of the spoon. Set over fairly high heat on top of the stove and cook for 5 minutes; then cover with heavy-duty aluminum foil and bake for 15 minutes. Serve with rice.

Calories	210	cal
Protein	25	g
Carbohydrates	5	g
Total fat	10	g
Saturated	2	g
Polyunsaturated	2	g
Cholesterol	0	mg
Sodium	78	mg

MUSTARD-BAKED FLOUNDER

Serves 4

This dish is simplicity itself; it can be prepared hours ahead and refrigerated until needed. Boiled or steamed new potatoes and blanched snow peas make a delicious accompaniment.

1 tablespoon light olive or
    Canola oil
Salt and freshly ground black
    pepper
3 tablespoons finely chopped
    shallots
4 flounder filets, about 1¼
    pounds (or grey or lemon
    sole, or fluke)

¼ cup dry white wine
2 teaspoons Dijon mustard
¼ cup breadcrumbs
1 tablespoon unsalted butter
¼ cup finely chopped parsley,
    preferably Italian
Lemon wedges

Arrange the oven rack in the highest position. Preheat oven to 400°F.

Spread the olive oil in a baking dish large enough to hold the fish in one layer. Sprinkle the dish with some salt and pepper and the shallots.

Arrange the filets over the shallots and sprinkle them with 3 tablespoons of the wine. Blend the remaining wine with the mustard and brush the filets with the mixture. Sprinkle the breadcrumbs evenly over the filets and dot with the butter. (May be prepared ahead to this point. If refrigerated, bring to room temperature before cooking.)

Bake in the preheated oven for 5 minutes. Turn the broiler to "high," and run the filets under it just until they are lightly browned, about 40 seconds to 1 minute. Serve immediately with the lemon wedges.

Calories	300	cal
Protein	39	g
Carbohydrates	7	g
Total fat	12	g
Saturated	3	g
Polyunsaturated	1	g
Cholesterol	103	mg
Sodium	285	mg

SEABASS WITH TOMATOES

Serves 4

This simple recipe deliciously incorporates fish and vegetables in one easy-to-make dish; try it on someone who is ho-hum about fish!

2 seabass, about 3 pounds
    total, cleaned, heads and
    tails intact
Salt and freshly ground black
    pepper
1 teaspoon dried thyme or
    several branches fresh
    thyme

4 medium potatoes, peeled and
    cut into ⅛-inch slices
2 tablespoons olive oil
Juice of 1 lemon
2 medium onions, sliced
4 medium ripe tomatoes,
    thinly sliced
1 lemon, thinly sliced

Preheat oven to 425°F.

Wash fish and pat dry. With a sharp knife make 3 shallow diagonal slashes on each side of each fish. Season with salt and pepper and tuck several branches of thyme inside each fish or sprinkle insides with dried thyme.

Cook potatoes in boiling salted water for 10 minutes. Drain and turn onto a clean dish towel. Pat dry.

Put the oil and lemon juice in a shallow baking dish that will comfortably hold the potatoes and the fish. Add the onion and potato slices; turn gently with two wooden spoons to coat them and season them with salt and pepper. Lay the 2 fish on top, alternate tomato and lemon slices around them, and season lightly again. Bake in the preheated oven 15 minutes.

Calories	258	cal
Protein	23	g
Carbohydrates	26	g
Total fat	8	g
Saturated	1	g
Polyunsaturated	1	g
Cholesterol	44	mg
Sodium	87	mg

HOT GINGER FISH WITH SWEET PEPPERS

Serves 4

This is pretty enough for company!

PAM
1 3½- to 4-pound seabass, head and tail on, cleaned and backbone removed
Salt and freshly ground black pepper (optional)
½ lemon
2 tablespoons grated or finely chopped fresh ginger
½ cup chopped onion
2 to 3 long hot red peppers, seeded and chopped (about ¼ to ⅓ cup)

2 medium ripe tomatoes, seeded, juiced, and diced
Garnishes:
Cabbage or romaine lettuce leaves
1 scallion, julienned, the white and part of the green
½ green pepper, cut into ½-inch strips
½ yellow pepper, cut into ½-inch strips

Preheat oven to 450°F. Spray one side of an 18- × 18-inch piece of heavy-duty aluminum foil with PAM and set aside.

Open fish out like a book; season flesh side lightly with optional salt and pepper and squeeze the lemon over.

Mix the chopped ginger, onions, and hot peppers in a small bowl and season lightly wtih black pepper. Add the tomatoes and mix in.

Spoon this stuffing onto the fish, then close the fish and place on the oiled foil. Bring foil edges up, fold over, and down; tuck the ends under to make a neat package. Place on a baking sheet and bake in the upper third of the preheated oven for 30 minutes.

To serve, wilt cabbage or lettuce leaves under hot water and arrange attractively on a serving platter. Carefully unfold foil and slide fish onto the platter, along with any accumulated juices. Arrange the scallion julienne and pepper strips in a crisscross pattern on top of the fish and serve at once.

Calories	156 cal
Protein	26 g
Carbohydrates	7 g
Total fat	3 g
Saturated	1 g
Polyunsaturated	1 g
Cholesterol	54 mg
Sodium	97 mg

Squid, while low in fat, is the seafood highest in cholesterol; it has 220 milligrams in 3 ounces cooked.

SEAFOOD RAGOÛT WITH RICE AND PEAS

Serves 6

The major part of the preparation for this dish may be done ahead of time, up to the point of adding the fish and shrimp, which must be done at the last minute. The rice and peas may also be made ahead of time and kept warm in a slow oven.

2 pounds firm white fish filets, from such fish as seabass, rockfish, pollock, haddock, redfish, blackfish, tilefish
1 pound medium shrimp
2 tablespoons olive oil
1 large onion, coarsely chopped (about 1½ cups)
2 to 3 garlic cloves, minced
1 medium green pepper, coarsely chopped
1 medium carrot, peeled and sliced
4 medium ripe tomatoes, peeled, seeded, and coarsely chopped, or 1 35-ounce can whole tomatoes, drained, seeded, and coarsely chopped

1½ cups defatted chicken broth, homemade (page 273) or canned
1 cup dry white wine
1 jalapeño pepper, seeded or minced, or several dashes cayenne
Salt and freshly ground black pepper to taste
Rice and Peas (recipe below)
Chopped parsley

Cut the fish into pieces about 1½ inches square. Shell the shrimp. Set both aside.

Heat the oil in a large, heavy soup pot, add the onion and garlic, and cook briefly, stirring until the onion is softened and transparent. Add the green pepper, carrot, and tomatoes and stir. Add the broth, wine, hot pepper, and salt and pepper to taste. Bring to a boil, lower the flame, cover, and simmer gently for 15 minutes. (Recipe may be prepared ahead to this point.)

While the sauce cooks, prepare the rice and peas.

Just before serving, bring the sauce to a simmer and add the shrimp. Cover and cook over gentle heat just until the shrimp turn pink, about 4 minutes. Stir once or twice during this time. Season the fish and add, pushing the pieces down into the sauce. Cover and cook for 4 minutes longer, just until the fish is opaque.

Spoon out a helping of rice and peas into heated soup bowls; then spoon the stew over the rice and garnish with chopped parsley.

RICE AND PEAS

3½ cups defatted chicken
  broth, homemade (page
  273) or canned, or water
1½ cups long-grain white rice

2 cups fresh peas or 1 10-
  ounce package frozen
  peas, partly thawed
2 teaspoons unsalted butter

Bring the broth or water to a boil, add the rice, bring to a second boil, lower heat, cover, and cook for 15 minutes.

Add the peas and the butter on top of the rice, cover, and cook 8 minutes more. Toss with 2 forks and season lightly if desired.

NOTE: If using frozen peas, cook only 4 minutes after adding them.

Calories	320	cal
Protein	43	g
Carbohydrates	9	g
Total fat	12	g
Saturated	3	g
Polyunsaturated	4	g
Cholesterol	201	mg
Sodium	482	mg

Rice and Peas

Calories	241	cal
Protein	7	g
Carbohydrates	46	g
Total fat	3	g
Saturated	1	g
Polyunsaturated	.1	g
Cholesterol	3	mg
Sodium	604	mg

BOMBAY SOLE

Serves 2

1 pound filet of sole, flounder,
  or any other flatfish
1 cup plain non-fat yogurt
1 teaspoon paprika

1 teaspoon ground cumin
1 teaspoon ground coriander
Salt and freshly ground black
  pepper

Put the fish in a rectangular ovenproof glass or earthenware dish. Combine the yogurt, paprika, cumin, and coriander and mix well. Pour the marinade over the fish, smoothing it out with the back of a spoon, cover with plastic wrap, and let the fish marinate for a couple of hours in the refrigerator. Remove the plastic.

Preheat the broiler, with the grill set about 4 inches from the flame. Broil the fish for 4 minutes, turn and broil second side 4 minutes more. Season lightly with salt and pepper, and serve immediately with Rice Pilaf (page 133).

Calories	286	cal
Protein	49	g
Carbohydrates	9	g
Total fat	5	g
Saturated	2	g
Polyunsaturated	1	g
Cholesterol	116	mg
Sodium	266	mg

TERIYAKI-GRILLED SWORDFISH

Serves 6

This recipe is also wonderful with tuna or salmon steaks.

⅔ cup soy sauce
½ cup medium-dry sherry
1 tablespoon sugar
1 garlic clove, crushed
2 teaspoons finely grated fresh
    ginger

2 pounds swordfish steaks in
    2 or 4 pieces, at least
    ¾-inch thick

In a small saucepan combine the soy sauce, sherry, sugar, garlic, and ginger. Bring to a boil over moderate heat, then strain into a shallow glass or enamel pan. Marinate the fish steaks in this mixture for about 30 minutes, turning them several times. Cook them on a well-oiled grill, 10 minutes per inch of thickness, and brush them frequently with the marinade. Turn the steaks once halfway through the cooking period.

If desired, the remaining marinade may be used as a dipping sauce.

Calories	182	cal
Protein	29	g
Carbohydrates	2	g
Total fat	6	g
Saturated	2	g
Polyunsaturated	1	g
Cholesterol	56	mg
Sodium	596	mg

GRILLED TUNA
WITH WARM CORIANDER VINAIGRETTE

Serves 4

4 tuna filets, about ¾-inch thick and 5 ounces each
PAM
Salt and freshly ground black pepper

Warm Coriander Vinaigrette (recipe follows)

Heat a ridged iron griddle or large cast-iron frying pan. Spray lightly with PAM and, when quite hot, lay the tuna steaks on carefully. Cook for 4 minutes, then carefully turn each over using a broad spatula or pancake turner and cook for 4 minutes on the second side. Season with salt and pepper and serve immediately topped with Warm Coriander Vinaigrette.

NOTE: The tuna may also be cooked in a broiler preheated at least 10 minutes; adjust the rack so the fish is 2 to 4 inches from the flame. Spray the broiler rack and the top of the filets with PAM. Broil the fish for 8 minutes and do not turn.

The tuna only

Calories	208	cal
Protein	33	g
Carbohydrates	0	g
Total fat	7	g
Saturated	2	g
Polyunsaturated	2	g
Cholesterol	54	mg
Sodium	55	mg

WARM CORIANDER VINAIGRETTE

Serves 12, about 1 tablespoon each

This is excellent on grilled tuna or any fish that has been simply broiled. It's best made ahead.

½ teaspoon imported
   Hungarian paprika
¼ teaspoon cayenne
1 teaspoon ground cumin
3 teaspoons minced garlic
¼ cup fresh lemon juice or a
   mixture of lemon and
   wine vinegar

¼ cup chopped parsley,
   preferably Italian
¼ cup chopped fresh
   coriander
3 tablespoons olive oil
¼ cup tomato juice

Combine the paprika, cayenne, cumin, and garlic in a small bowl; add the lemon juice and stir. Then add the parsley, coriander, and enough olive oil to reach a spreadable consistency. Blend in the tomato juice. Refrigerate the sauce for at least 1 hour before using. (In a tightly covered jar it can be refrigerated for up to a week.) Warm the vinaigrette gently before serving. Spoon over broiled fish.

Calories	35	cal
Protein	.1	g
Carbohydrates	1	g
Total fat	3	g
Saturated	.5	g
Polyunsaturated	.3	g
Cholesterol	0	mg
Sodium	19	mg

SALMON IN FOIL WITH VEGETABLES

Serves 6

This is an easy company dish that can prepared entirely ahead and baked just before serving. The vegetables can be varied according to whim, taste, and availability.

6 salmon filets, about 5
    ounces each
Coarse salt
Freshly ground black pepper
½-inch chunk fresh ginger,
    finely chopped
Grated zest and juice of 1
    lemon
1 bulb fresh fennel, finely
    sliced

1 zucchini, cut in ½-inch
    rounds
1 large ripe tomato, peeled,
    seeded, and chopped
12 large basil leaves, finely
    chopped, or ⅓ cup
    chopped Italian parsley,
    plus additional basil or
    parsley sprigs for garnish
PAM

Put 2 rimmed cookie sheets in the oven and preheat to 400°F.

Place the salmon filets in a glass baking dish and season with the salt, coarsely ground pepper, chopped ginger, lemon zest, and lemon juice.

In a large bowl, mix the fennel, zucchini, tomato, and chopped basil or parsley and season with salt and pepper.

Cut 6 sheets of heavy-duty aluminum foil approximately 10 × 16 inches. Spray each with PAM. Distribute the vegetable mixture among them, using only half the sheet. Top with the seasoned salmon filets and any remaining lemon juice, zest, and ginger. Fold the foil into rectangular envelopes, crimping all the edges. (The recipe may be prepared to this point and refrigerated. Return to room temperature before cooking.)

Place foil packets on the cookie sheets and bake for 20 minutes in the preheated oven. To serve, place a pouch on each of 6 dinner plates, slash an X in each, garnish with basil or parsley sprigs, and serve at once with rice or couscous.

Calories	226	cal
Protein	29	g
Carbohydrates	4	g
Total fat	10	g
Saturated	1	g
Polyunsaturated	4	g
Cholesterol	78	mg
Sodium	101	mg

BAKED RED SNAPPER
WITH JULIENNE OF VEGETABLES

Serves 4

PAM
1 4-pound red snapper, head
   on, tail removed, and
   boned (about 1¾ pounds
   usable fish)
Salt and freshly ground black
   pepper
1 tablespoon olive oil
3 to 4 carrots, peeled and
   julienned

4 ribs celery, julienned
1 large onion, thinly sliced
1 teaspoon Butter Buds
1 bay leaf
¼ teaspoon dried thyme
1 cup white wine
Juice of 1 lemon
2 tablespoons finely chopped
   parsley

Preheat oven to 425°F. Spray an 8- × 12-inch oval baking dish with
PAM and set aside.

Rinse the fish inside and out and lightly season the cavity with salt
and pepper. Cut 4 or 5 diagonal slashes along one side of the fish.

Heat the oil in a large skillet, add the carrots, celery, and onion, and
cook over moderate heat until the vegetables are just soft, about 2 minutes. Sprinkle with the Butter Buds and turn gently to distribute. Spread
the vegetables over the prepared baking dish and lay the fish on top.
Add the bay leaf, thyme, wine, and lemon juice and bring to a boil on
top of the stove. Then cover with aluminum foil and bake the red snapper
for 30 minutes. Serve immediately.

Calories	513	cal
Protein	79	g
Carbohydrates	16	g
Total fat	14	g
Saturated	4	g
Polyunsaturated	2	g
Cholesterol	147	mg
Sodium	358	mg

OYSTERS

Over a hundred years ago, Americans went "oyster crazy"—the bivalves were at least as popular as hotdogs are now. Whole meals of oysters prepared a dozen different ways weren't uncommon, a gluttony that resulted in the near extinction of many species. With careful "farming," oysters are again abundant and they make good low-fat eating (only 4 grams of fat in a half-pound shucked), with the plus that they are a good source of omega-3s. Of course, battering and frying them or preparing them in the butter and cream-rich sauces of the past is out, but they are immensely satisfying served on the half shell, as the French do, with Mignonette Sauce for dipping, or as an Oyster Pan Roast, a specialty of Grand Central Station's Oyster Bar in Manhattan. In my version, 80 percent of the poaching butter called for in the original version is replaced by the oyster liquor. In oyster season, we have this almost every Sunday for lunch!

MIGNONETTE SAUCE FOR OYSTERS

½ cup mild red wine vinegar
2 tablespoons finely minced
   shallots
Salt to taste

2 teaspoons crushed or
   coarsely ground black
   pepper

Combine all the ingredients in a small bowl. Serve in individual side dishes for oyster on the half shell.

Calories	42 cal
Protein	1 g
Carbohydrates	10 g
Total fat	.2 g
Saturated	.1 g
Polyunsaturated	.1 g
Cholesterol	0 mg
Sodium	24 mg

OYSTER PAN ROAST

Serves 4 as a first course, 2 as a light lunch

Have everyone at the table; this takes 3 minutes from start to finish!

2 tablespoons unsalted butter
½ cup liquid drained from
    oysters
1 pint (1 pound) shucked
    oysters
1 tablespoon Worcestershire
    sauce

Dash cayenne
Salt and freshly ground black
    pepper to taste
Lemon juice
4 slices toasted white bread,
    sliced in half diagonally

Melt the butter in a skillet over moderate heat, but do not let it brown. Add the oyster liquor, and let it heat through for 30 seconds. Add the oysters, Worcestershire sauce, cayenne, salt and pepper to taste, and a big squeeze of lemon juice. Simmer gently, stirring constantly, until the oysters plump and puff up, 1 to 2 minutes.

Put the toast triangles in shallow soup dishes. Spoon the oysters and broth over and serve immediately.

Calories	198	cal
Protein	10	g
Carbohydrates	17	g
Total fat	9	g
Saturated	4	g
Polyunsaturated	1	g
Cholesterol	0	mg
Sodium	349	mg

MUSSELS MARINARA

Serves 4 as a hearty first course, 2 as a main course

5½ pounds mussels
1 tablespoon unsalted butter
2 tablespoons olive oil
1 small onion, chopped
2 large garlic cloves, minced
1 28-ounce can crushed
   Italian plum tomatoes

⅓ cup chopped parsley,
   preferably Italian, plus
   some for garnish
3 to 4 dashes Tabasco
½ teaspoon salt, or to taste
1 teaspoon dried oregano
⅔ cup white wine

Scrub the mussels well to remove the "beard" and sand, and soak if needed to remove sand.

Melt the butter in the olive oil in a large saucepan or pot that has a lid and is big enough to hold the mussels, and in it sauté the onion and garlic until lightly colored. Add the tomatoes, parsley, Tabasco, salt, and oregano and cook 5 minutes, stirring frequently. Add the white wine and the mussels, cover tightly, and cook over high heat 8 to 10 minutes, or until all the mussels open. Give the kettle several vigorous shakes during the cooking to redistribute the mussels. Before serving, discard any mussels that have not opened and taste the broth for seasoning.

Serve the mussels in their shells, divided among heated deep soup bowls, and spoon the broth over. Garnish with additional chopped parsley and serve with crusty bread for dunking.

Calories	291	cal
Protein	24	g
Carbohydrates	17	g
Total fat	14	g
Saturated	4	g
Polyunsaturated	2	g
Cholesterol	59	mg
Sodium	1151	mg

POACHED SCALLOPS WITH GINGER

Serves 4

This simple dish makes its own sauce and should be served over rice.

1 tablespoon unsalted butter
1 pound bay scallops, or sea
    scallops cut in halves or
    quarters
1 teaspoon finely chopped
    fresh ginger

2 tablespoons white wine
2 teaspoons finely chopped
    parsley
2 tablespoons lemon juice
Salt and freshly ground black
    pepper to taste

Melt the butter in a medium skillet, add the scallops and ginger, and sauté quickly over brisk heat, tossing, until scallops are firm and white but have not taken on any color, about 1 minute. Add the wine, parsley, lemon juice, and salt and pepper to taste and gently poach over medium heat for 1 minute more. Serve over rice.

Calories	126 cal
Protein	19 g
Carbohydrates	3 g
Total fat	4 g
Saturated	2 g
Polyunsaturated	.4 g
Cholesterol	45 mg
Sodium	213 mg

PAN-GRILLED SHRIMP

Serves 4

32 medium to large shrimp in
    their shells (about 1½
    pounds)
Juice of 2 lemons
Freshly ground black pepper

Coarse salt
2 lemons, quartered
1 bunch watercress, rinsed
    and dried

Rinse the shrimp and pat dry.

Put the lemon juice and a generous amount of pepper (but no salt) in a glass dish or pie plate and in it marinate the shrimp for 15 to 20 minutes.

Sprinkle 2 large pinches of coarse salt evenly over the bottom of a large, heavy iron skillet and put it over high heat for 3 or 4 minutes. When the skillet is very hot, add the shrimp to the pan in a single layer without crowding. (You may have to pan-fry the shrimp in 2 or 3 batches.) Fry 4 minutes, turning each shrimp over once. The shells will char slightly, adding a special flavor. Serve the shrimps in the shells, garnished with lemon quarters and sprigs of watercress.

Calories	149	cal
Protein	28	g
Carbohydrates	2	g
Total fat	2	g
Saturated	.5	gm
Polyunsaturated	1	g
Cholesterol	210	mg
Sodium	295	mg

STEAMED SHRIMP WITH GARLIC AND SCALLIONS

Serves 3, 8 shrimp each

This is one of my very favorite dishes. I serve it with Stir-fried Snow Peas (page 226) and plain rice to soak up the delicious natural sauce that results.

1 pound large shrimp
 (about 24)
3 scallions
1½ tablespoons reduced-
 sodium soy sauce
1 tablespoon rice or white-
 wine vinegar
1 tablespoon minced garlic

2 teaspoons finely grated fresh
 ginger
2 teaspoons sesame oil
1 teaspoon sugar
½ teaspoon hot red pepper
 flakes
¼ teaspoon salt

Shell the shrimp, leaving tail and first joint of shell intact. Rinse, pat dry, and set aside.

Mince the white part of the scallions, reserving the green tops. In a large bowl stir together the minced scallions, soy sauce, vinegar, garlic, ginger, sesame oil, sugar, pepper flakes, and salt. Add the shrimp, toss to coat them with the marinade, and let them marinate at room temperature, stirring several times, for 15 minutes.

Put a vegetable steamer rack in a wide, deep pot. Add enough water to come just below the rack; bring to a boil, covered.

Spread the shrimp, with marinade, over a wide, heatproof plate, such as a glass pie plate, large enough to fit inside the pot with at least 1 inch clearance around the sides. Using oven mitts, put the dish on the steamer rack over the boiling water. Steam the shrimp, covered, for 4 to 8 minutes, or until just firm to the touch. Again wearing mitts, remove the plate. Thinly slice the reserved scallion greens, and sprinkle on top. Serve the shrimp over rice.

NOTE: If you have a wok, put the shrimp in a pie plate in a bamboo steamer or flat basket. It fits nicely in the wok and you can just lift it out (taking care not to spill the delicious liquid) and set the bamboo steamer right on the table.

Calories	267	cal
Protein	39	g
Carbohydrates	9	g
Total fat	8	g
Saturated	1	g
Polyunsaturated	3	g
Cholesterol	279	mg
Sodium	994	mg

CHOLESTEROL WATCHERS: Note that this is almost your whole daily allowance, but it's worth it, because the dish is so delicious!

17

POULTRY

GRILLED LEMON–THYME CHICKEN BREASTS

CHINESE LEMON CHICKEN

PAILLARD OF CHICKEN

GRILLED ROSEMARY–LEMON CHICKEN BREASTS

MUSTARD-BAKED CHICKEN BREASTS

YOGURT-MARINATED CHICKEN BREASTS WITH CORIANDER

ORIENTAL GLAZED CHICKEN

CHICKEN–MUSHROOM SATAY

PAPRIKASH CHICKEN

POACHED CHICKEN

ADOBO CHICKEN

HERBED CHICKEN SALAD

ORIENTAL CHICKEN SALAD

TURKEY MEATLOAF

TURKEY SCALOPPINE MARSALA

Chicken and, increasingly, turkey are usually the first main-course foods people turn to when they start cutting back on meat. It is the most versatile food I know, and an important component of a satisfying, low-fat diet. But know what you are eating. To make a meaningful difference in lowering fat intake, you must be careful about portion size and the skin, which *doubles* the fat content.

As in all meats, some shrinkage takes place during cooking; how much depends on the cooking method. A recipe calling for a boneless and skinless 4-ounce portion means weight *before* cooking. You will actually end up with something closer to 3 ounces *after* cooking. The fat grams in Appendix A are given per ounce of cooked weight. I wouldn't get fanatic about this; just remember that if you eat twice as much, or use breasts that are on the large size (4 ounces = small, 6 ounces = large) you should adjust your fat gram expenditure accordingly.

When following your own recipes, always remove the skin before serving or, preferably, before cooking (except when roasting or broiling). Skinned chicken works best when marinated or used in a stew.

Chicken is easier to skin when whole. With the legs nearest you, use a paper towel with one hand to hold on to a leg, and with another grab the skin near the neck end. Pull back and off as you would a glove. (Wearing rubber gloves facilitates the job.) Also remove all the little yellow lumps of visible fat below the skin. Then cut into serving pieces if desired.

GRILLED LEMON–THYME
CHICKEN BREASTS

Serves 4

These are so easy to make and so good that we usually have them once a week! They're delicious cold too—great for a picnic.

4 small boneless chicken
    breast halves, skinned
    and slightly flattened
1 large or 2 medium garlic
    cloves, crushed with the
    side of a knife

½ cup lemon juice (about 1½
    lemons)
2 tablespoons olive oil
Pinch dried thyme
Salt and freshly ground black
    pepper to taste

Put the breasts in a glass baking dish that will hold them in one layer. Beat the remaining ingredients in a small bowl with a fork and pour over the chicken. Cover with plastic wrap and refrigerate for 2 hours. Turn the breasts once during that time.

Preheat the broiler. Remove the breasts from the marinade and broil 4 minutes on each side. Or if you have a ridged griddle, heat it over high heat until quite hot and cook the breasts 4 minutes each side, or until nicely marked.

Calories	171	cal
Protein	26	g
Carbohydrates	1	g
Total fat	6	g
Saturated	1	g
Polyunsaturated	1	g
Cholesterol	70	mg
Sodium	62	mg

About half the fat in chicken is in the skin. You can remove the skin after cooking and before eating, but do try to cut away any visible fat globules while rinsing the bird, before you cook.

CHINESE LEMON CHICKEN
Serves 6

2 quarter-size slices fresh
   ginger, minced
¼ cup reduced-sodium soy
   sauce
6 small boneless chicken
   breast halves, skinned
2 large or 3 medium lemons
3 tablespoons cornstarch
1½ teaspoons salt, or to taste
1 egg white
3 tablespoons vegetable or
   peanut oil
3 medium carrots, peeled and
   julienned

1 cup defatted chicken broth,
   homemade (page 273) or
   canned
1 small green pepper,
   julienned
1 sweet red pepper, julienned
6 scallions, the white and 2
   inches of the green,
   julienned
3 tablespoons sugar
½ cup rice or white wine
   vinegar
½ head iceberg or romaine
   lettuce, shredded

Combine the ginger and soy sauce in a large, shallow glass bowl or a plastic bag and in it marinate the breasts for 1 or 2 hours, turning them occasionally. Drain off and discard the liquid.

While the chicken marinates, peel one of the lemons carefully, removing the yellow zest only. Cut the zest into very fine julienne strips and reserve. Grate the zest of the second lemon (and third if needed) to produce around 2 teaspoons grated zest; reserve. Squeeze enough lemons to produce ¼ cup juice; reserve.

Combine 1 tablespoon of the cornstarch with the salt and egg white and toss with the breasts to coat them.

Heat the oil in a large skillet over high heat, add the breasts, and sauté them for 4 minutes per side. Remove and keep warm.

In the same pan stir-fry the carrots for 1 minute. Slowly add the chicken broth and bring to a boil. Add the reserved lemon zest julienne, cover, and cook 3 minutes. Uncover, add the green and red pepper strips, and cook, stirring, 1 minute; add the scallions and cook 1 minute more.

In a small stainless-steel or enameled saucepan (not aluminum) combine the sugar and remaining 2 tablespoons cornstarch and stir in the vinegar, lemon juice, and grated lemon zest. Heat to a boil, stirring, until thick. Add to the vegetables and cook 30 seconds.

Make a bed of the shredded lettuce on a warm serving platter. Cut the chicken breasts crosswise in strips about 1 inch thick and arrange them symmetrically over the lettuce. Pour the sauce over them and serve immediately, with boiled rice passed separately.

Calories	280	cal
Protein	30	g
Carbohydrates	20	g
Total fat	9	g
Saturated	1	g
Polyunsaturated	4	g
Cholesterol	68	mg
Sodium	1,010	mg

PAILLARD OF CHICKEN

Serves 2

2 boneless chicken breast   Salt and freshly ground black
   halves, skinned   pepper to taste
Juice of ½ lemon

Place each chicken breast half between two sheets of wax paper and flatten with a meat pounder or the bottom of a heavy skillet; the two cutlets should be of a relatively uniform thickness, somewhere between ¼ and ⅜ inch.

Heat a ridged griddle on top of the stove. Place the 2 cutlets on the grill. Over high heat, sear for 60 to 90 seconds. Loosen each breast with tongs, give a quarter turn, and replace on the grill. (Each breast is now at a 90° angle to its original position.) Cook an additional 60 to 90 seconds, depending on thickness. Watch carefully that the chicken does not overcook, or it will be dry. Season the top with salt, pepper, and a few drops of lemon juice; then turn over and repeat the above process on the second side, cooking 4 to 6 minutes in all. Season the second side and serve immediately.

Calories	140	cal
Protein	26	g
Carbohydrates	1	g
Total fat	3	g
Saturated	1	g
Polyunsaturated	1	g
Cholesterol	71	mg
Sodium	62	mg

GRILLED ROSEMARY–LEMON CHICKEN BREASTS

Serves 8

This makes pleasant summer eating served with Tabbouleh (page 136) and/or any of the vegetable salads in Salad Dressings, Salads, and Relishes.

¼ cup fresh rosemary leaves
　or 2 teaspoons dried
1 teaspoon coarsely ground
　black pepper
Grated zest from 1 lemon

2 tablespoons lemon juice
3 tablespoons olive oil
8 chicken breast halves, bone
　in, skin on

In a large glass baking dish, combine the rosemary, black pepper, lemon zest, lemon juice, and olive oil. Add chicken and toss each piece to coat well. Marinate at least 1 hour or up to 4 hours refrigerated, turning occasionally.

Light a charcoal grill and when the coals are medium-hot, pat each chicken piece dry and place it on the grill, skin side down. Grill covered for 25 to 30 minutes, or until the skin is golden and the meat firm. Turn pieces over halfway through the cooking.

Place each breast on a cutting board, remove and discard the skin and remove the meat in 1 piece from the bone. Slice into serving pieces if desired. Refrigerate if not using immediately. Serve the chicken at room temperature.

Calories	157	cal
Protein	27	g
Carbohydrates	.1	g
Total fat	4	g
Saturated	1	g
Polyunsaturated	1	g
Cholesterol	73	mg
Sodium	64	mg

MUSTARD-BAKED CHICKEN BREASTS

Serves 6

The use of non-fat dry milk with a small amount of water gives a thick, creamy coating that will stick without need of eggs.

⅓ cup Dijon mustard
¼ cup non-fat dry milk
2 tablespoons water
¾ cup fine fresh breadcrumbs, from firm-textured white bread (2 slices) or French bread

½ teaspoon chopped fresh tarragon
6 small boneless chicken breast halves, skinned
Imported Hungarian paprika
¼ cup finely chopped parsley, preferably Italian

Preheat the oven to 350°F. Arrange the oven rack in its highest position.

In a small bowl, combine the mustard, dry milk, and water and mix well. Stir in the breadcrumbs and tarragon. With a rubber spatula, spread the mixture over the top of the chicken breasts, which you've arranged in a non-stick baking pan. Sprinkle lightly with paprika, then the parsley. Bake uncovered in the upper third of the preheated oven for 20 to 25 minutes.

If you wish the tops a little browner, run the chicken breasts under the broiler for about 40 seconds, watching constantly, until some brown flecks appear.

Calories	220	cal
Protein	35	g
Carbohydrates	9	g
Total fat	3	g
Saturated	1	g
Polyunsaturated	.4	g
Cholesterol	83	mg
Sodium	753	mg

YOGURT-MARINATED
CHICKEN BREASTS WITH CORIANDER

Serves 4

3 tablespoons plain non-fat
   yogurt
Juice of ½ lemon
1½ tablespoons chopped fresh
   coriander
1 garlic clove,
   minced

4 boneless chicken breast
   halves, skinned and
   lightly flattened
Salt and freshly ground black
   pepper
PAM
1 teaspoon dark sesame oil

In a shallow glass or china baking dish combine the yogurt, lemon juice, coriander, and garlic. Season the breasts lightly with salt and pepper, place them in the marinade, and turn to coat them thoroughly. Cover and refrigerate at least 4 hours.

Spray a non-stick skillet with PAM and add the sesame oil, swirling it around. Sauté the chicken breasts lightly on each side over moderate heat until golden, but still juicy, about 8 minutes total.

Serve with Rice Pilaf (page 133) and steamed vegetables.

Calories	207	cal
Protein	40	g
Carbohydrates	1	g
Total fat	3	g
Saturated	1	g
Polyunsaturated	1	g
Cholesterol	99	mg
Sodium	119	mg

Skinless dark chicken and turkey meat contain more than twice as much fat as skinless light meat. They also have about 20 percent more calories and 10 percent less protein than light meat.

ORIENTAL GLAZED CHICKEN

Serves 4

4 boneless chicken breast
   halves, skinned
4 tablespoons finely chopped
   onion
1 tablespoon coarsely grated
   fresh ginger
1 tablespoon reduced-sodium
   soy sauce

2 tablespoons dry sherry
1½ tablespoons honey
1 teaspoon minced garlic
2 tablespoons chopped fresh
   coriander

Preheat the broiler. Line a small broiler pan or shallow baking dish with aluminum foil.

Rinse and dry the chicken breasts and put them in the broiler pan.

Combine the onion, ginger, soy sauce, sherry, honey, and garlic. Spoon about half the mixture over the chicken and broil 2 to 3 inches from the flame until the chicken begins to brown, about 5 minutes. Turn and spoon the remaining glaze mixture over the chicken and broil another 3 to 5 minutes.

Serve the chicken with the pan juices poured over plain rice and sprinkle chopped coriander on top.

Calories	227	cal
Protein	40	g
Carbohydrates	10	g
Total fat	2	g
Saturated	1	g
Polyunsaturated	1	g
Cholesterol	99	mg
Sodium	262	mg

When the label of a food such as chicken franks lists a poultry part as "chicken breast" or "chicken leg," it means the food contains the meat *and* the fatty skin! Breast *meat* or leg *meat* means only the flesh.

CHICKEN–MUSHROOM SATAY

Serves 6

6 boneless chicken breast
  halves, skinned
1 sweet red pepper, seeded
18 small mushrooms
3 tablespoons olive oil

2 tablespoons fresh lime juice
Several grindings black pepper
Dash cayenne
½ teaspoon ground cumin
1 teaspoon minced garlic

Rinse the chicken breasts and pat dry. Cut each into 4 squarish pieces. Cut the red pepper into 2-inch squares. You should have about 18 pieces.

Wilt the mushrooms slightly by placing in a steamer basket over boiling water for 2 minutes. Remove.

Divide and alternate the chicken pieces, peppers, and mushrooms equally on 6 skewers. (Push the skewer through the top of the mushroom cap rather than the underside, so it doesn't break.) Place in a shallow glass, stainless-steel, or enameled baking dish—not aluminum.

Combine in a small bowl the olive oil, lime juice, pepper, cayenne, cumin, and garlic and pour this over the skewers, turning them so everything is nicely coated with the mixture. Refrigerate, covered, for at least 30 minutes.

Preheat the broiler. Place the skewers on the broiler rack and broil about 6 inches from the heat for about 10 minutes, turning them once and basting several times. Serve with Herbed Pilaf (page 134).

Calories	186 cal
Protein	28 g
Carbohydrates	3 g
Total fat	7 g
Saturated	1 g
Polyunsaturated	1 g
Cholesterol	73 mg
Sodium	66 mg

PAPRIKASH CHICKEN

Serves 6

This family favorite was threatened with extinction until I discovered how to make a low-fat substitute for sour cream that could be used in cooking. Boiled noodles or rice, sweet-and-sour purple cabbage, and cucumber salad are essential accompaniments.

2 large onions, chopped
1 garlic clove, minced
3 tablespoons olive or vegetable oil, or a combination
½ green pepper, shredded
2 tablespoons imported Hungarian paprika (or more to taste)
2 3½-pound broiler-fryer chickens, cut up, backbones removed

Salt to taste
1 small ripe tomato, peeled, seeded, and chopped (may be canned)
1¼ cups defatted chicken broth, homemade (page 273) or canned
1 cup Mock Sour Cream (page 276) or Double-Thick Yogurt (page 275)

Sauté the onions and garlic in the oil until softened in a large heavy pot or in a Dutch oven. Add the green pepper and the paprika and mix well.

Sprinkle the chicken pieces with salt, add to the pot, then add the tomato and 1 cup of chicken broth. Stir, bring to a boil, then cover, lower heat, and simmer slowly, until the chicken is tender, about 25 minutes. Turn the chicken pieces from time to time so they cook evenly. Taste and adjust seasoning.

Transfer the chicken pieces to a warm platter. Add the remaining ¼ cup of broth to the pot and bring to a boil, scraping up bits from the bottom and sides. Add the "sour cream" or yogurt, more paprika if desired, and stir until smooth. Pour the sauce over the chicken and serve at once with noodles or rice.

Calories	367	cal
Protein	52	g
Carbohydrates	7	g
Total fat	14	g
Saturated	3	g
Polyunsaturated	2	g
Cholesterol	154	mg
Sodium	484	mg

POACHED CHICKEN
(POULE AU PÔT)

Serves 4 to 6

This homestyle French classic makes a perfect low-fat staple.

1 whole chicken, about
5 pounds
6 cups defatted chicken broth,
homemade (page 273) or
canned
1 carrot, peeled and cut into 3
or 4 pieces
1 rib celery
Several parsley stems
(no leaves)
1 yellow onion,
peeled and stuck with
2 cloves

Garnishes:
3 parsnips, peeled, cut in 2
or 3 pieces
2 white turnips, cut into
eighths
2 carrots, peeled, cut in half
lengthwise, then each
length cut into 3 pieces
6 new potatoes in their
jackets
½ pound small green beans
1 3-ounce jar prepared
horseradish

Rinse the chicken thoroughly, place in a large heavy pot, cover with cold water, and bring to the boil. Boil uncovered for 5 minutes, then discard the water. Cover the chicken with the broth and add the carrot, celery, parsley stems, and studded onion. Simmer, partially covered, until the leg moves easily and the chicken is tender, about 45 minutes to 1½ hours, depending on size. Let the chicken cool in the broth. Then remove it, discarding the cooking vegetables. Strain the broth and remove the fat.

While the chicken is cooling, cook separately each garnish vegetable and set aside. (A microwave is handy for this, and I like to cook each in some of the chicken broth, which imparts a lovely flavor.)

When the chicken is cool, remove the skin, cut meat off bone, slice, and arrange on a platter with the vegetables arranged around. Heat the broth again, season, and serve it as a first course. Follow with the chicken and vegetables, passing the horseradish separately.

Calories	546	cal
Protein	53	g
Carbohydrates	61	g
Total fat	9	g

Saturated	2 g
Polyunsaturated	2 g
Cholesterol	153 mg
Sodium	251 mg

ADOBO CHICKEN

Serves 4 to 5

Adobo is a style of cooking that can be applied not only to chicken, but also to foods such as pork, fish, shellfish, and vegetables. Used in the Philippines, the adobo preparation, which signifies food stewed in vinegar, soy sauce, and garlic, is not only simple and tasty but also eminently suited to cooking chicken without the skin, since the flesh is kept moist and it absorbs flavor while cooking.

Those on sodium-restricted diets should check the sodium content because of the soy sauce.

½ cup reduced-sodium soy
    sauce
¼ cup white vinegar
8 to 10 garlic cloves, lightly
    smashed

1 to 2 bay leaves (optional)
1 3-pound chicken, skinned
    and cut into serving
    pieces, breasts cut in half

In a large, heavy non-reactive pot or Dutch oven, combine the soy sauce, vinegar, garlic, and optional bay leaves. Bring to a boil, add the chicken pieces, and simmer, covered, over low heat for 45 minutes to 1 hour. Turn pieces over in the sauce frequently so they take on some color from the sauce. Serve hot, with the sauce spooned over boiled white rice. Accompany with a green salad.

Calories	180	cal
Protein	30	g
Carbohydrates	5	g
Total fat	4	g
Saturated	1	g
Polyunsaturated	1	g
Cholesterol	92	mg
Sodium	1,748	mg

HERBED CHICKEN SALAD

Serves 6

My husband says this is the best chicken salad he's ever eaten—largely attributable, I believe, to the way the chicken breasts are poached. You can do them in water, but they are incomparably better done in chicken broth, which intensifies the flavor. The method is extremely simple, but you do need to plan on cooking them well in advance of serving the salad.

6 chicken breast halves, bone
    in, skin on
3 to 4 scallions, the white and
    part of the green
3 heaping tablespoons
    reduced-fat mayonnaise
3 heaping tablespoons plain
    low-fat or non-fat yogurt

½ teaspoon dry mustard
Salt and freshly ground black
    pepper to taste
Snipped fresh tarragon or
    chopped parsley,
    preferably Italian

Preheat the oven to 350°F. Place the breasts in a baking pan that will hold them comfortably in one layer. Pour in enough chicken broth, water, or a combination of the two so they are almost submerged. Place the pan in the center of the preheated oven and adjust heat so the liquid just shivers but does not boil, for a good 45 minutes. Remove the pan from the oven and let the chicken cool in the broth.

Skin the breasts and tear, rather than cut, the meat into bite-sized pieces. Place them in a mixing bowl and spoon some of the broth over each layer of chicken pieces. Refrigerate for several hours.

Strain the remaining broth and refrigerate or freeze for another use.

Toss the chilled chicken pieces with two wooden spoons. Chop the scallions finely and add. Put the mayonnaise in a small bowl, add the yogurt and dry mustard, and beat briefly. Add the dressing to the chicken and toss to coat. Season to taste and add a sprinkling of fresh tarragon or a handful of chopped parsley. Only fresh herbs will do in this salad.

Calories	171	cal
Protein	28	g
Carbohydrates	2	g
Total fat	5	g
Saturated	1	g
Polyunsaturated	1	g
Cholesterol	76	mg
Sodium	122	mg

ORIENTAL CHICKEN SALAD

Serves 6 to 8

A different kind of chicken salad that does not rely on mayonnaise.

1 medium yellow onion,
    halved and stuck with 4
    cloves
2 carrots, peeled and cut into
    3 pieces
1 bay leaf
Several parsley stems
12 whole black peppercorns
Salt to taste 6 chicken breast
    halves, bone in, skin on
⅓ cup virgin olive oil
⅓ cup red wine vinegar

¼ cup soy sauce
½ medium red onion, finely
    chopped
2 scallions, the white and part
    of the green, chopped
2 cornichon pickles, sliced
    thinly on the diagonal
½ cup fresh coriander leaves,
    chopped, or watercress
Freshly ground black pepper
    to taste

Measure 4 quarts of water into a large, heavy pot. Add the onion, carrots, bay leaf, parsley stems, peppercorns, and salt to taste. Bring to a boil, reduce heat, and simmer uncovered for 15 minutes.

Add the chicken breasts, bring again to the boil, reduce heat, and simmer partially covered for 20 minutes. Remove from the heat and let the chicken cool in the broth.

Remove the breasts (strain and reserve broth for another use), discard the skin, and pull the meat from the bones. Tear the chicken into large pieces and turn them in a bowl with the olive oil. Let the chicken stand at room temperature for 1 hour.

Add the vinegar, soy sauce, red onion, scallions, cornichon pickles, and coriander, toss, and season with freshly ground black pepper. Serve the chicken salad immediately.

Calories	277	cal
Protein	28	g
Carbohydrates	6	g
Total fat	15	g
Saturated	2	g
Polyunsaturated	2	g
Cholesterol	73	mg
Sodium	798	mg

TURKEY MEATLOAF

Serves 4

This recipe is easily doubled. You could cook a second loaf, then wrap and freeze it for another meal.

1¼ pounds lean ground
    turkey
⅓ cup breadcrumbs
⅓ cup skim milk
1 egg white, lightly beaten
1 small onion, finely chopped
    or grated
1 fat garlic clove, put through
    a garlic press
½ small green pepper, finely
    chopped

3 tablespoons catsup or low-
    sodium tomato sauce
½ teaspoon dried oregano
½ teaspoon ground cumin
Salt and freshly ground black
    pepper to taste

Glaze:
3 tablespoons brown sugar
¼ cup catsup
1 teaspoon dried mustard

Preheat the oven to 350°F. Place the turkey in a bowl and break it up with your hands or a fork. Combine the breadcrumbs and milk in a small bowl; then mix into the turkey. Add the egg white and incorporate. Thoroughly mix in the onion, garlic, green pepper, catsup, oregano, cumin, and salt and pepper to taste. Pour into a 9 × 5 × 3-inch loaf pan, rap once on the counter to settle the meat, and smooth the top lightly with the back of a fork.

Bake the meatloaf in the preheated oven for 40 minutes. (The loaf will have shrunk a bit and a savory liquid collected in the dish; carefully pour this out to spoon over as gravy later on.) Combine the glaze ingredients and spread over the top of the meatloaf. Bake 20 minutes more; Then let the loaf stand 5 minutes or so before slicing. Serve with Low-Fat Mashed Potatoes (page 235).

Calories	236	cal
Protein	23	g
Carbohydrates	10	g
Total fat	12	g
Saturated	5	g
Polyunsaturated	0	g
Cholesterol	77	mg
Sodium	281	mg

(Glaze, not included in nutritional analysis)

TURKEY SCALOPPINE MARSALA

Serves 4

½ pound mushrooms
⅓ cup flour
Salt and freshly ground black
  pepper
1 pound turkey cutlets
PAM

1 tablespoon margarine or
  vegetable oil
¼ cup Marsala or semi-sweet
  sherry
Garnish: chopped parsley

Wipe the mushrooms with a damp paper towel, slice them thinly, and set aside.

Shake the flour with some salt and pepper in a plastic bag, then turn out onto a piece of wax paper.

Dip each turkey cutlet into the flour until well coated. Then fry them in a heated non-stick skillet coated with PAM until lightly colored on both sides, about 2 minutes per side, turning once. (Cutlets will not be very brown, but will take on color subsequently from the sauce.) Remove to a warm plate.

Melt the margarine or oil in the same skillet. Sauté the mushrooms over high heat until they wilt slightly, about 3 minutes, keeping them moving with a wooden spoon. Cover the skillet, lower heat, and cook until tender, about 6 minutes.

Over high heat add the Marsala to the skillet, scrape up any brown bits, and stir until slightly thickened; then return the cutlets and mushrooms to the skillet, lower flame and heat through. Arrange on a platter and garnish with chopped parsley. Serve with mashed potatoes.

Calories	216	cal
Protein	29	g
Carbohydrates	12	g
Total fat	5	g
Saturated	1	g
Polyunsaturated	1	g
Cholesterol	70	mg
Sodium	113	mg

Skinless turkey contains about one third less fat than skinless chicken.

18
MEAT

LONDON BROIL
BEEF FAJITAS
STIR-FRIED BEEF WITH PEPPERS
AND SNOW PEAS
BEEF SQUASH POT
FIREHOUSE CHILI
VEAL LOAF
BRAISED VEAL CHOPS
WITH PEPPERS AND POTATOES
ROAST LEG OF LAMB
TURKISH LAMB
LAMB KEBABS
ROAST MARINATED LOIN OF PORK
PHILIPPINE GRILLED PORK TENDERLOIN
HAM AND POTATO PIE

There's no question that the American diet relies much too heavily on meat, and that many of our national ills stem in part from our overindulgence in this high-protein and high-fat food. Many people have in fact given meat up, believing it is bad for them. But the good news is that meat can be a part of our lives; it simply has to play a minor role. Here, as elsewhere, moderation and variety are the key words. Look for recipes that use meat as a flavoring but fill you up with carbohydrates —Firehouse Chili (page 211) is a good example, as are Beef Squash Pot (page 210)and Turkish Lamb (page 215). Even Beef Fajitas (page 208) let you fill up with beans, salsa, tortillas, and so forth while enjoying the satisfying taste of beef. And when cooking and ordering meat, consider these "lean" methods: broil, grill, braise, stew with liquid (for non-tender cuts), roast or bake on a rack, stir-fry or sauté in a non-stick skillet.

Another good ploy to have beef in your low-fat lifestyle is to look for that labeled USDA "Select" grade when you shop. It's the lowest in fat and calories. Next in line are "Choice" (the grade of most supermarket meat) and "Prime," the top grade, the tenderest, and also the fattiest and highest in calories. Use the "loin/round" rule of thumb for lower fat beef and "loin/leg" for pork, lamb, and veal. These cuts are the lean choices.

LONDON BROIL

Serves 10

Flank steak is one exception to the rule that meat to be cooked should be brought to room temperature before cooking. And do pay close attention to the carving instructions! I serve this with ratatouille or sliced tomatoes, purple onions and cucumbers, and, in summer, corn—but almost any vegetable could accompany it.

½ cup reduced-sodium soy
    sauce
¾ cup dry red wine
Freshly ground black pepper
Fresh ginger, about the size of
    your first thumb joint,
    grated or finely chopped

3 cloves garlic, finely chopped
2½ pounds flank steak,
    "Choice" grade, trimmed
    of all fat, or first-cut top
    round, very well-trimmed
    of fat

Make the marinade: in a glass baking dish, combine the soy sauce, wine, pepper, grated ginger, and garlic. Marinate the flank steak in this mixture for several hours, turning occasionally. Keep refrigerated until cooking time.

To cook, preheat broiler, remove meat from marinade, and broil quickly, about 5 to 6 minutes per side. Remove to a cutting board. Holding a well-sharpened carving knife at an angle and almost flat along the top of the meat, slice thinly *on the diagonal* through to the bottom. Meat should be rare in the center.

Calories	175	cal
Protein	23	g
Carbohydrates	.5	g
Total fat	8	g
Saturated	6	g
Polyunsaturated	55	g
Cholesterol	56	mg
Sodium	189	mg

BEEF FAJITAS

Serves 6

Fajitas is Spanish for "ribbons," referring to the narrow strips of meat in this simple but delicious Mexican dish. Serve with Black Beans and Rice (page 141) and Pico de Gallo (page 124), and follow with a crisp, green salad.

1½ pounds flank steak, skirt steak, or round steak, ½-inch thick, in 1 piece
½ cup lime juice (about 3 to 4 limes)
2 to 4 garlic cloves, thinly sliced

Freshly ground black pepper
6 flour tortillas (available in frozen food section of many supermarkets)
Pico de Gallo (page 124)

Trim the steak of any visible fat and pound to ¼-inch thickness. Place in a plastic bag. Sprinkle the lime juice, garlic, and pepper over the steak, tie the bag up securely, and marinate in the refrigerator for 6 to 8 hours or overnight, turning the bag over occasionally.

Preheat the broiler. Drain the steak, discarding the marinade, and broil fairly close to the flame about 3 minutes per side. Carve slightly on the diagonal into 12 thin slices. Arrange on a hot platter.

Heat the tortillas by placing them in a moist towel, wrapping it in aluminum foil, and placing this in a slow oven (200°F.) for 20 minutes, or until the tortillas are soft.

To eat, place two slices of the meat in a warm tortilla and spoon in some of the Pico de Gallo. Fold up the tortilla and eat it.

For the traditional presentation of the meat, heat a stainless-steel platter or a cast-iron skillet over an open flame for 2 minutes. Add the meat and squeeze the juice of a lemon or lime over so it sizzles as it is brought to the table.

Calories	289	cal
Protein	26	g
Carbohydrates	25	g
Total fat	9	g
Saturated	4	g
Polyunsaturated	.4	g
Cholesterol	56	mg
Sodium	278	mg

STIR-FRIED BEEF WITH PEPPERS AND SNOW PEAS

Serves 2

½ pound flank steak, trimmed
    of all visible fat
3 teaspoons soy sauce
1 tablespoon peanut oil
1 scallion, the white and part
    of the green, minced
1 to 2 tablespoons finely
    slivered fresh ginger

1 garlic clove, minced
½ sweet red pepper, cut into
    ½-inch strips
15 snow peas (about 2
    ounces), tops and strings
    removed
1 tablespoon oyster sauce
    (found in Oriental stores)

Holding a sharp knife at a 45° angle, slice the steak into thin strips. Toss with 1 teaspoon of the soy sauce in a bowl and let stand for 20 minutes.

Heat a large, heavy skillet or wok over high heat for 30 seconds. Add the oil and swirl to coat the surface of the pan evenly. Continue heating until the oil just starts to smoke. Add the scallions, ginger, and garlic and stir-fry until fragrant, about 20 seconds. Add the beef and stir-fry until lightly browned, about 1 minute. Add the pepper strips and snow peas and stir-fry until the peppers wilt, about 20 seconds. Stir in the remaining 2 teaspoons soy sauce and the oyster sauce. Cook and stir just until the meat is cooked through, about 1 minute. Serve immediately with rice.

Calories	273	cal
Protein	25	g
Carbohydrates	7	g
Total fat	15	g
Saturated	5	g
Polyunsaturated	2	g
Cholesterol	57	mg
Sodium	958	mg

BEEF SQUASH POT

Serves 6

This is a good one-dish summer meal, when fresh vegetables are available.

1 pound very lean ground
  sirloin
2 medium onions, coarsely
  chopped
3 garlic cloves, minced
¼ cup chicken broth or water
½ teaspoon dried oregano
½ teaspoon ground cumin,
  or more to taste
2 cups fresh corn kernels (3
  to 4 ears) or 1 16-ounce
  can whole corn kernels

2 green peppers, cut into
  1-inch strips
3 young yellow squash, cut
  into ½-inch slices
3 small zucchini, cut into
  ½-inch slices
3 ripe tomatoes, lightly
  seeded, coarsely chopped
1 8-ounce can tomato sauce
2 tablespoons chili powder
Salt and freshly ground black
  pepper to taste

Preheat the oven to 375°F.

Heat a large, heavy, non-stick skillet over medium heat. Crumble the ground beef into the skillet and cook, stirring occasionally, until no longer pink, about 3 to 5 minutes. Pour the meat into a colander or strainer lined with paper towels and allow the fat to drain out.

Add onions, garlic, and broth to the skillet and sauté over medium heat, stirring, until the onions are limp, about 2 minutes. Add the oregano and cumin and cook for 30 seconds more, stirring.

Put the meat and onion mixture in an ovenproof casserole with a lid. Add the corn, green peppers, squash, zucchini, tomatoes, tomato sauce, chili powder, and salt and pepper to taste. Mix together gently but thoroughly, cover, and bake for 30 minutes. Serve with plain rice.

Calories	273	cal
Protein	20	g
Carbohydrates	28	g
Total fat	11	g
Saturated	4	g
Polyunsaturated	1	g
Cholesterol	46	mg
Sodium	313	mg

FIREHOUSE CHILI

Serves 10

Hearty chili is great for informal entertaining and can always be extended by the "extras" you serve with it: red kidney or pinto beans, plenty of fluffy white rice and a bowl of raw chopped onions. This recipe freezes well.

3 pounds lean beef, such as top round or flank "select" grade in one piece, trimmed of all visible fat

2 tablespoons olive oil

5 cups water

1 35-ounce can whole tomatoes, drained and chopped

8 to 10 chili pequins (small dried red peppers, found in specialty food stores), or 2 teaspoons dried hot red pepper flakes

1 tablespoon salt, or to taste

14 garlic cloves, finely chopped

1 teaspoon ground cumin, or more to taste

1 teaspoon dried oregano

1 teaspoon cayenne

1 tablespoon sugar

3 tablespoons imported Hungarian paprika

2 tablespoons flour

5 tablespoons yellow cornmeal

Partially freeze the beef to facilitate cutting, then slice into thin strips about 1½ to 2 inches long.

Heat the olive oil in a large, heavy pot. Add all the meat and sear over high heat, stirring constantly, until the meat loses its pinkness but is not brown.

Add 4 cups of the water, cover, and cook at a bubbling simmer until the meat is quite tender, about 1½ to 2 hours. Then add the tomatoes, chili pequins, salt, garlic, cumin, oregano, cayenne, sugar, and paprika and cook 30 minutes longer, uncovered, at a bubbling simmer.

Mix the flour and cornmeal with the remaining 1 cup water and add to the chili. Stir to prevent lumps and cook until thickened. Taste, and play with the spices and seasonings if you like.

Calories	274	cal
Protein	29	g
Carbohydrates	8	g
Total fat	13	g
Saturated	5	g
Polyunsaturated	1	g
Cholesterol	68	mg
Sodium	921	mg

VEAL LOAF

Serves 6 to 8

2 pounds lean veal, ground
   twice
1 cup fresh breadcrumbs,
   soaked in 1 cup skim
   milk
2 eggs
1 medium onion, grated

1 heaping tablespoon flour
Salt and freshly ground black
   pepper
1 cup tomato sauce, or
   marinara sauce thinned to
   tomato sauce consistency
   with tomato juice

Preheat over to 350°F.

Mix the veal, soaked breadcrumbs, eggs, onion, and flour with your hands. Then beat with a wooden spoon until the mixture appears light and frothy. Add salt and pepper and beat again.

Form the mixture into a loaf in a 9 × 12-inch baking dish, cover with the tomato sauce, and bake for about 1½ hours. Baste several times during the baking with the sauce. Serve warm, or slice thinly and serve at room temperature.

Calories	287	cal
Protein	29	g
Carbohydrates	9	g
Total fat	14	g
Saturated	7	g
Polyunsaturated	.1	g
Cholesterol	132	mg
Sodium	366	mg

If you broil fatty hamburger meat on a grill that allows the fat to drip off, or if you drain the fat after frying, you'll end up with as little fat as you'd get from lean ground beef—at a nice price savings, too.

BRAISED VEAL CHOPS
WITH PEPPERS AND POTATOES

Serves 4

A delicious one-dish meal, and such a tasty way to treat family or friends with this expensive cut. The slow cooking blends the flavors beautifully. Serve with a good Italian red wine and a salad.

PAM
4 half-inch thick loin veal
    chops, about 8 ounces
    each
½ cup chicken broth or white
    wine
2 tablespoons olive oil
1 medium onion, sliced

3 large green peppers, cut into
    ½-inch strips
2 garlic cloves, chopped
4 to 5 medium potatoes,
    peeled and thinly sliced
Salt and freshly ground black
    pepper
Chopped Italian parsley

Select a skillet large enough to hold the chops and the vegetables. Spray with PAM and heat well. Add the chops and brown them quickly on both sides. Remove and keep warm.

Add the broth or wine to the pan and, over high heat, scrape up the brown bits and cook stirring until reduced to a syrupy glaze. Lower heat to medium, add and stir in the olive oil and add the onion, peppers, garlic, and potatoes. Stir frequently and gently with a wooden spoon. When the peppers and potatoes are browned and softened, about 7 minutes, season with salt and pepper and add the veal chops and any juices that have accumulated in the plate. Season the chops. Cover and cook slowly over low heat for about 20 minutes, or until the veal and potatoes are tender. Serve right from the skillet, sprinkled with chopped parsley, even for guests.

NOTE: An 8-ounce veal chop, well trimmed, will net about 4 ounces of meat, allowing for the bone

Calories	432	cal
Protein	35	g
Carbohydrates	38	g
Total fat	15	g
Saturated	4	g
Polyunsaturated	1	g
Cholesterol	120	mg
Sodium	126	mg

ROAST LEG OF LAMB

Serves 12

This is our meat splurge dinner. There are few easier ways to feed a number of diners and, for my money, no meat is tastier than lamb. Accompany with Flageolets Bretonne (p. 143) and broiled tomatoes. Trimmed leg meat is fairly low in fat, but remember to watch portion size. You can get at least three meals from a leg, depending, of course, on how many people you have to feed. See NOTE below.

1 leg of spring lamb, 6 to 8 pounds, bone in, sirloin cut off (see NOTE), trimmed of visible fat, but with the fell, or outer membrane, intact

4 garlic cloves, sliced
1 tablespoon coarse salt
1 teaspoon dried thyme
Freshly ground black pepper
2 teaspoons olive oil

Preheat the oven to 450°F. Have the lamb at room temperature.

Wipe the lamb with damp paper towels and dry. Make several small, angled incisions with a sharp-pointed knife and insert the garlic. Mix the coarse salt, thyme, and several grindings of black pepper together in a small bowl. Brush the lamb with the oil and rub the seasoning mixture all over. Place the meat on a rack in a roasting pan with the fell, or filament side, up. Insert a meat thermometer, if you are using one, in the fleshiest part of the meat, not touching the bone.

Cook for 30 minutes in the preheated oven, then turn heat down to 350°F. and continue cooking for 30 to 50 minutes longer (145°–150° on a meat thermometer) for medium rare. For well-done meat, cook 1½ hours more (160°). It is not necessary to baste. Let the meat rest on a cutting board for 10 to 20 minutes before carving. Slice thinly, moisten meat with natural juices, and serve on hot plates.

NOTE: The sirloin piece can be frozen whole and used as a small roast for another meal. Alternatively, the meat may be removed in chunks from the sirloin bone and frozen for kebabs. Treated in this manner, you will end up with a leg yielding about 3½ pounds of usable meat before cooking. This does not apply to New Zealand legs of lamb, which are smaller and usually purchased frozen.

Leftover cooked leg of lamb can be used to make Turkish Lamb (page 215) at another meal.

Calories	210	cal
Protein	33	g
Carbohydrates	0	g
Total fat	8	g
Saturated	3	g
Polyunsaturated	0	g
Cholesterol	102	mg
Sodium	540	mg

TURKISH LAMB

Serves 3 to 4

This quick-to-prepare dish utilizes a small amount of leftover lamb. It is a perfect example of how to eat meat satisfyingly in small quantity, backed up by carbohydrates (the rice).

2 cups leftover lean, rare roast lamb, all visible fat removed, cut into ½-inch cubes (about ¾ pound meat)
1 teaspoon minced garlic
Salt and freshly ground black pepper to taste
1 tablespoon olive oil
1 14-ounce can Italian plum tomatoes, drained and cut into ½-inch wide strips, or 4 very ripe tomatoes, peeled, lightly juiced, and seeded

1 teaspoon grated lemon zest
½ cup chopped scallions, the white and part of the green
½ cup chopped parsley, preferably Italian
Basic Foolproof White Rice (page 132) or Rice Pilaf (page 133)

In a bowl combine the lamb and garlic with salt and pepper to taste.

Brush the olive oil evenly over the bottom of a 10-inch heavy skillet (preferably non-stick) and heat until almost smoking. Add the lamb mixture and brown quickly, stirring constantly, over high heat. Add the tomatoes, lower heat slightly, and cook 2 minutes more. The tomatoes should be barely cooked and retain their original texture.

Push the lamb and tomatoes to the center, sprinkle with the lemon zest and scatter the scallions and parsley around the edges. Cover tightly and remove from heat. Let sit a few minutes until some juices collect, then stir gently and serve over rice. Accompany the dish with a good crusty bread.

Calories	229	cal
Protein	24	g
Carbohydrates	6	g
Total fat	12	g
Saturated	4	g
Polyunsaturated	1	g
Cholesterol	74	mg
Sodium	221	mg

LAMB KEBABS

Serves 4

This lamb dish goes beautifully with Rice Pilaf (page 133) and Cucumber Yogurt Sauce (page 125).

20 1½-inch cubes lean lamb
  (about 1½ pounds
  purchased weight),
  preferably meat from the
  leg, completely trimmed
  of visible fat
1 teaspoon finely chopped
  garlic
2 teaspoons finely chopped
  fresh ginger
2 tablespoons lemon juice
3 tablespoons peanut or
  vegetable oil

½ teaspoon ground turmeric
½ teaspoon ground coriander
½ teaspoon ground cumin
Dash cayenne
Salt and freshly ground black
  pepper to taste
1 tablespoon grated onion
16 ripe cherry tomatoes or 2
  ripe tomatoes cut into
  eighths

Either cube the lamb yourself or have the butcher do it. Put the cubes in a bowl. Add all the remaining ingredients except the cherry tomatoes, mix well, and let the lamb marinate for about 1 hour.

Preheat the broiler. Arrange the meat cubes and tomatoes alternately on four skewers. Brush or spoon some of the marinade over the tomatoes.

Place the skewers about 4 or 5 inches from the flame. Cook, turning as needed to cook meat evenly, for about 10 minutes.

Calories	321 cal
Protein	36 g
Carbohydrates	3 g
Total fat	18 g
Saturated	4 g
Polyunsaturated	4 g
Cholesterol	109 mg
Sodium	111 mg

ROAST MARINATED LOIN OF PORK

Serves 8, about 4 ounces each

Pork is not a meat you think of as being low in fat, but the boneless center cut of the loin is as lean as you can get. Its compact form gives you a great quantity of thin slices and the marinade and the glaze produce a delicious flavor, so that a moderate portion is very satisfying. Horseradish Applesauce (page 278) is a delicious accompaniment.

3-pound boneless pork loin
    roast, center cut, all
    visible fat removed
Dry mustard
Dried thyme
½ cup medium sherry
½ cup low-sodium soy sauce
    plus 1 tablespoon

3 garlic cloves, finely chopped
2 tablespoons grated fresh
    ginger
6 ounces currant jelly
Garnishes: sliced tomatoes,
    cucumbers, purple onion

Rub the meat with dry mustard and thyme. In a small bowl combine the sherry, ½ cup of the soy sauce, garlic, and ginger. Place the meat in a large plastic bag, pour in the marinade, tie securely, and refrigerate. Let the pork marinate for 2 to 3 hours, turning the bag several times.

To cook, preheat the oven to 325°F., remove the pork from the marinade, insert a meat thermometer if you wish, and cook on a rack in a roasting pan—allowing 25 minutes per pound or until an internal temperature of 145° is reached. Baste occasionally with the marinade.

Remove the meat to a board and let it cool a bit while making the glaze. Melt the jelly in a small, heavy saucepan over medium heat and, when bubbly, add 1 tablespoon soy sauce. Let this glaze cook until smooth, stirring constantly. Spoon it over the pork and continue to let cool. Do not refrigerate.

Serve the pork at room temperature, thinly sliced, garnished with the sliced tomatoes, cucumbers, and purple onion.

Calories	298 cal
Protein	32 g
Carbohydrates	19 g
Total fat	10 g
Saturated	3 g
Polyunsaturated	1 g
Cholesterol	87 mg
Sodium	771 mg

Don't be misled by the fat gram listing on packaged deli meats. The figure may look acceptably low, but remember that a single slice is considered "a serving" . . .

PHILIPPINE GRILLED PORK TENDERLOIN

Serves 6

Extremely easy and utterly delicious! The medallions go well with either rice or mashed potatoes.

2 pounds lean pork
    tenderloin, all visible fat
    removed
¾ cup white vinegar
½ cup soy sauce

2 tablespoons minced garlic
Freshly ground black pepper
    to taste
1 teaspoon dried hot red
    pepper flakes

Cut the pork into ½-inch thick medallions. You should have about 12 slices.

In an oblong glass baking dish mix together the vinegar, soy sauce, garlic, and pepper. Add the pork slices and let them marinate 4 to 5 hours, in the refrigerator, turning occasionally.

Preheat the broiler. Broil the medallions 7 minutes on each side about 4 inches from flame. (These are also delicious on a charcoal grill; cook over a medium fire 5 minutes on each side, then 10 minutes covered.)

While the pork is cooking, bring the marinade to a boil in a small saucepan, add the hot pepper flakes, and reduce by one quarter. Strain and serve as a dipping sauce with the meat.

Calories	185	cal
Protein	33	g
Carbohydrates	4	g
Total Fat	4	g
Saturated	1	g
Polyunsaturated	.4	g
Cholesterol	98	mg
Sodium	761	mg

HAM AND POTATO PIE

Serves 5, about 1¼ cups each

Like a shepherd's pie made with ham, this is a savory, low-fat way to use up leftover holiday ham. Of the traditional holiday meats, ham is one of the lowest in fat, calories, and cholesterol.

PAM
¾ cup finely chopped onion
½ cup finely chopped green
   pepper
½ cup defatted chicken broth,
   homemade (page 273) or
   canned
Salt and freshly ground black
   pepper to taste
1 tablespoon Worcestershire
   sauce

1½ cups finely chopped lean
   ham, all visible fat
   removed
2 cups creamed corn
   (1 17-ounce can)
2 cups seasoned Low-Fat
   Mashed Potatoes
   (page 235)

Preheat the oven to 425°F.

Spray a large non-stick skillet with PAM and sauté the onion over medium heat until softened, about 2 minutes. Add the green pepper, chicken broth, salt, pepper, and Worcestershire sauce and simmer uncovered for 10 minutes.

In a bowl, stir the ham, corn, and onion mixture; then spoon this into an ungreased baking dish. Cover with the mashed potatoes, roughen the surface with a fork, and bake uncovered for 30 minutes, or until the top is flecked with brown. If necessary, run the dish under the broiler to brown.

Calories	276 cal
Protein	16 g
Carbohydrates	49 g
Total Fat	3 g
Saturated	1 g
Polyunsaturated	1 g
Cholesterol	23 mg
Sodium	853 mg

19
VEGETABLES

◆

BROCCOLI ITALIAN STYLE
STIR-FRIED BROCCOLI
FRENCH PEAS
STIR-FRIED SNOW PEAS
STIR-FRIED SNOW PEAS WITH GINGER
STIR-FRIED SUGAR SNAPS
GREEN BEANS AND CABBAGE PAPRIKASH
BRAISED ENDIVE
CORN PUDDING
EGGLESS CORN PUDDING
CORN PANCAKES
OKRA–CORN STEW
BROILED TOMATOES
BAKED POTATOES
STUFFED BAKED POTATO
LOW-FAT MASHED POTATOES
ROASTED NEW POTATOES WITH ROSEMARY
OVEN "FRIED" POTATOES

ROASTED MARINATED PEPPERS
WITH CAPERS
SQUASH PURÉE
SQUASH AND SHRIMP
SQUASH AND SHRIMP WITH GREEN BEANS
ZUCCHINI WITH TOMATOES
ZUCCHINI TRIFOLATI

Vegetables were always the "poor cousins" on our dinner plate, frequently overcooked and flavorless. It was assumed you ate them for some obscure health reasons that had nothing to do with pleasure.

Now that vegetables (and grains) have become part of a new and healthy lifestyle, we are learning that they can be flavored and prepared in, if anything, a greater variety of taste combinations and presentations than meat. And they give us the fiber and complex carbohydrates we need, not to mention all manner of vitamins and minerals. Official dietary guidelines urge the daily consumption of deep yellow and dark green leafy vegetables such as winter squashes, carrots, spinach, and broccoli, plus members of the cabbage family like cauliflower, kale, and Brussels sprouts, which are thought to contain certain cancer-inhibiting substances.

You don't have to like them all; but do explore and expect some pleasant surprises. If you like corn on the cob, try Corn Pudding (page 229) or Okra–Corn Stew (page 231); don't just steam or boil broccoli, stir-fry it or have it the Italian way with garlic. (You can use both these recipes for cauliflower as well.) There are dozens of ways to eat zucchini: try two of my favorites, with tomatoes (page 241) and Trifolati (page 242), in a blizzard of garlic, scallions, and parsley, a wonderful dish you can eat hot or at room temperature.

The point is—don't let vegetables be an afterthought. Start a collection of a few you really love. (I hope some of them come from this section!)

BROCCOLI ITALIAN STYLE

Serves 3 to 4

1 large bunch broccoli
Salt, if desired
2 tablespoons olive oil
2 to 3 garlic cloves, finely
    chopped

Freshly ground black pepper
Handful chopped parsley,
    preferably Italian

Cut off the thick stems and reserve for another use. Break the broccoli into small flowerets and boil gently in salted water for 5 to 6 minutes. Broccoli should be undercooked, still slightly firm. Drain well, run cold water over, and drain again.

Heat the olive oil in a skillet. Add the garlic and, when it sizzles but is not brown, add the broccoli and cook over moderate heat, stirring and shaking the pan frequently, for 4 or 5 minutes. Add pepper and salt to taste, sprinkle with chopped parsley, and serve at once.

Calories	84	cal
Protein	2	g
Carbohydrates	5	g
Total fat	7	g
Saturated	1	g
Polyunsaturated	1	g
Cholesterol	0	mg
Sodium	21	mg

STIR-FRIED BROCCOLI

Serves 4 to 5

1 large or 2 small bunches
    broccoli
2 tablespoons peanut or corn
    oil
½ teaspoon salt
1 teaspoon sugar

½ cup water
1 teaspoon cornstarch
    combined with 2
    tablespoons cold water
    (optional)

Break the broccoli into small flowerets with small stems. Peel and then cut the large stalks on the diagonal into thin slices about 1½ inches long. You should have about 6 cups in all. Rinse and drain.

Heat a wok or large, heavy skillet until hot, add the oil, and when it is hot add and stir-fry the broccoli for about 2 minutes until bright green. Sprinkle with the salt and sugar, toss, then add the water down the side of the pan or wok and cover. Cook over high heat for 2 minutes, stirring once. Serve immediately.

Calories	102 cal
Protein	5 g
Carbohydrates	10 g
Total fat	6 g
Saturated	1 g
Polyunsaturated	2 g
Cholesterol	0 mg
Sodium	268 mg

FRENCH PEAS

Serves 4

During that brief moment when bright green fresh peas appear in your market, put this Lucullan way of eating them on the menu. The sweet moisture that comes from the lettuce leaves and onions does lovely things to the peas. French Peas go with everything, but they are particularly elegant with salmon.

1 small head Boston lettuce
¼ cup water
4 to 6 small white onions
    peeled, or ½ yellow
    onion, cut into eighths
2 pounds unshelled peas

1 sprig parsley with stem
Pinch dried thyme
1 teaspoon sugar
4 teaspoons butter, each cut
    in half
Salt

Rinse the lettuce well, and use the leaves to line a medium heavy-bottomed saucepan. Add the water.

Cut a cross in the stem end of each white onion to ensure even cooking. Place the onions in a small saucepan with cold water, bring to a boil, and blanch 5 to 6 minutes. Drain and put the onions in the pan with the lettuce leaves.

Shell the peas and add them to the saucepan. Add the parsley, thyme, sugar, and the pieces of butter. Cover, bring to a boil, lower heat slightly and cook briskly for 4 to 5 minutes. Add salt and cook 4 to 5 minutes more. Serve immediately.

Calories	120	cal
Protein	5	g
Carbohydrates	16	g
Total fat	4	g
Saturated	2	g
Polyunsaturated	.3	g
Cholesterol	10	mg
Sodium	48	mg

STIR-FRIED SNOW PEAS

Serves 3 to 4

Everybody loves snow peas, and they go with just about everything. Best of all, they couldn't be simpler to make. The recipe is easily doubled.

½ **pound fresh snow peas**   1 **teaspoon dark sesame oil**
2 **teaspoons vegetable or**
   Canola oil

String the pea pods, drop them into a large quantity of salted water, boil for 30 seconds (from the time the second boil is reached), then drain them immediately and run them under cold water. This will stop the cooking and set the pretty green color. Pat dry and set aside. (This may be done hours ahead.)

Just before serving, heat the oils in a heavy, non-stick skillet, add the peas, and stir-fry about 45 seconds to heat the peas through and coat them with the oil. Adjust heat if necessary to prevent scorching. Serve immediately.

STIR-FRIED SNOW PEAS WITH GINGER

Add 2 teaspoons minced fresh ginger and a dash of salt to the oil and quickly stir-fry for several seconds before adding the snow peas.

STIR-FRIED SUGAR SNAPS

Follow the master recipe using sugar snap peas. Remember to string them.

Calories	54	cal
Protein	2	g
Carbohydrates	4	g
Total fat	4	g
Saturated	.5	g
Polyunsaturated	2	g
Cholesterol	0	mg
Sodium	2	mg

GREEN BEANS AND CABBAGE PAPRIKASH

Serves 4

1 tablespoon unsalted butter
1 small onion, minced
2 cups fresh green beans,
    trimmed and cut into
    1-inch pieces
1 garlic clove, minced
1 cup defatted, unsalted
    chicken broth, reduced to
    ½ cup

1½ teaspoons imported
    Hungarian paprika
½ cup tomato sauce
3 cups coarsely chopped green
    cabbage
Lemon juice to taste
Freshly ground black pepper
    to taste

Melt the butter in a large skillet or wok over medium-high heat, add the onion and stir-fry until lightly browned, about 2 minutes. Add beans and garlic and stir-fry 1 minute. Stir in the reduced broth, the paprika, and tomato sauce. Cover and bring to a boil. Reduce heat and cook until the beans are crisp-tender, about 6 minutes. Add the cabbage, cover, and cook 2 minutes more. Uncover and continue cooking over high heat until the liquid is reduced to a glaze. Season to taste with lemon juice and black pepper and serve immediately.

Calories	86 cal
Protein	2 g
Carbohydrates	12 g
Total fat	4 g
Saturated	.5 g
Polyunsaturated	.5 g
Cholesterol	0 mg
Sodium	199 mg

BRAISED ENDIVE

Serves 4

Try this when you need an elegant vegetable accompaniment that will not add much fat to the meal. The sugar and lemon pleasantly counteract the slight bitterness natural to endive

4 heads Belgian endive   ½ teaspoon sugar
2 teaspoons unsalted butter   ½ cup water
Salt and freshly ground black
     pepper

Trim off any browned rim around the stem ends of the endive.

Put the endives in a saucepan that will hold them snugly in one layer. Add the butter, salt, pepper, sugar, and water and cover tightly. Bring to the boil, then lower heat and cook slowly about 30 to 45 minutes, or until the endives are tender and the liquid has evaporated. Toward the end of the cooking time, uncover, raise heat, and brown the endives lightly on two sides.

Calories	27 cal
Protein	1 g
Carbohydrates	2 g
Total fat	2 g
Saturated	1 g
Polyunsaturated	.1 g
Cholesterol	5 mg
Sodium	23 mg

CORN PUDDING

Serves 4 to 6

2 whole eggs and 2 egg whites
2 cups frozen or fresh corn
   kernels (cut from 4 to 5
   ears) or 1 16-ounce can
   creamed corn
3 tablespoons flour

1 tablespoon sugar
Salt and freshly ground black
   pepper
1 cup skim milk
1 tablespoon melted butter
PAM for casserole

Preheat the oven to 325°F.

Beat the eggs until thick; then stir in the corn. In another bowl, combine the flour, sugar, salt, and several liberal grindings of pepper. Slowly stir in the milk, then add the butter. Stir this mixture into the egg and corn mixture.

Spray a 1½-quart casserole with PAM and pour the corn pudding into it. Bake about 1 hour and 20 minutes, or until a knife inserted near the center comes out clean.

Calories	160 cal
Protein	8 g
Carbohydrates	22 g
Total fat	5 g
Saturated	2 g
Polyunsaturated	1 g
Cholesterol	92 mg
Sodium	98 mg

EGGLESS CORN PUDDING

Substitute 1 container (8 ounces) Egg Beaters for the eggs and egg whites.

Calories	133 cal
Protein	6 g
Carbohydrates	22 g
Total fat	3 g
Saturated	1 g
Polyunsaturated	3 g
Cholesterol	7 mg
Sodium	83 mg

CORN PANCAKES

Serves 4, 3 3-inch pancakes each

These are lovely as a side dish with grilled fish or chicken.

¾ cup unbleached flour
1 tablespoon baking powder
1 teaspoon salt
Several grindings black pepper
Dash cayenne
1 egg, lightly beaten

1⅓ cups fresh cream-style
corn kernels (4 ears) (see
NOTE) or 1 10½-ounce
can creamed corn
PAM

In a bowl, mix the flour, baking powder, salt, pepper, and cayenne. Blend in the egg. Add the corn and mix well. Using a tablespoon, drop the mixture into a hot PAM-sprayed skillet or onto a griddle a few at a time. Cook until golden; turn with a spatula and cook the second side. Keep the pancakes warm in a slow oven until all are cooked.

NOTE: To make fresh cream-style corn, cut down the *center* of each row of kernels with a sharp knife; then scrape into a bowl with the back of the knife.

Calories	152	cal
Protein	6	g
Carbohydrates	28	g
Total fat	2	g
Saturated	.5	g
Polyunsaturated	.5	g
Cholesterol	53	mg
Sodium	894	mg

OKRA–CORN STEW

Serves 4

*Served over rice and accompanied by a salad, this stew makes a wonderful
meatless meal. It is also excellent with grilled shrimp or roast chicken.*

2 tablespoons olive oil
1 medium onion, chopped
1 to 2 garlic cloves, minced
1 small fresh hot green
  pepper, finely chopped
1 red chili pepper, seeded and
  minced, or dash cayenne
  added during last 5
  minutes of cooking

1 14-ounce can Italian plum
  tomatoes, chopped, liquid
  reserved
½ pound small okra, cut into
  ½-inch slices
2 cups corn kernels, fresh or
  canned
Salt and freshly ground black
  pepper to taste

Heat the olive oil in a flameproof casserole over moderate heat and sauté
the onion until wilted, about 1 minute. Add the garlic, green pepper,
and chili pepper and sauté until soft, another minute or so. Add the
tomatoes, okra, and a tablespoon or so of the tomato liquid from the
can. Cover and cook over gentle heat for about 15 minutes, or until the
okra is tender. Add the corn, season to taste with salt and pepper, cover,
and cook 5 minutes longer.

NOTE: If a chili pepper is not available, use several dashes cayenne pepper, added during the last 5 minutes of cooking.

Calories	179	cal
Protein	5	g

Carbohydrates	26 g
Total fat	8 g
Saturated	1 g
Polyunsaturated	1 g
Cholesterol	0 mg
Sodium	179 mg

BROILED TOMATOES

Serves 4

When ripe tomatoes are available, a broiled tomato makes a lovely garnish to any food.

4 ripe, nicely shaped tomatoes
Salt and freshly ground black
   pepper to taste

1 to 2 teaspoons olive oil
Snipped Herbs (optional):
   basil, rosemary, thyme, or
   parsley

Preheat the broiler. Slice the tomatoes in half horizontally. Arrange the halves in a shallow PAM- or oil-sprayed baking dish; sprinkle each with salt, pepper, and oil, smearing the oil on top with the back of a spoon. Add the optional herbs at this point.

   Place the tomatoes under the broiler, about 3 inches from the flame, and broil about 5 minutes, or until the edges blacken slightly and the tomato is heated through. Do not turn.

Calories	38 cal
Protein	1 g
Carbohydrates	5 g
Total fat	2 g
Saturated	.3 g
Polyunsaturated	.3 g
Cholesterol	0 mg
Sodium	10 mg

BAKED POTATOES

It tickles me to see that baked potatoes are being offered at many quick-lunch places around Manhattan. A baked potato also makes a great mid-afternoon mini-meal. To bake potatoes, of any kind, scrub the skins well and pierce with a fork in a few places to allow steam to escape and prevent bursting. If baking them in the oven, don't wrap them in foil, since this steams them and makes them soggy.

In the oven:

At 400°F., a medium white potato, yam, or sweet potato will take about 40 to 45 minutes. The potato is done when it yields readily to the pressure of your fingers or is pierced easily with a fork.

In the microwave:

One medium potato of any kind, 7 to 8 ounces, will bake on high in 3 to 5 minutes. To cook 2 or more, arrange like the spokes of a wheel, at least an inch apart. Two medium potatoes need 8 minutes, three, 10 minutes, four, 12 to 13 minutes. Prick as above, place the fattest end toward the middle and elevate off the floor of the oven if you can, by using a microwave browning pan or several chopsticks with a paper towel on top. After 4 minutes, wrap the potato in aluminum foil, shiny side in, and let it stand 5 to 10 minutes before eating, to even out and complete the cooking. Or put the potato under an inverted bowl and let it stand 5 to 10 minutes.

Serving suggestions:

There are several interesting low-fat sauces in this book that go beautifully with baked potatoes. Try Pico de Gallo (page 124), Mock Sour Cream (page 276) with snipped chives or dill, or Cucumber Yogurt Sauce (page 125). Or try plain low-fat yogurt with snipped fresh chives, or with crushed caraway seeds. A few toasted sesame seeds are interesting, and if you crave a butter flavor, use Butter Buds.

The vegetable highest in fiber is a baked potato with the skin.

STUFFED BAKED POTATO

Serves 1

Yes, yes I know bacon has no place in low-fat living—except v-e-r-y occasionally. Here's a wonderful, filling way to indulge and get the most out of just one slice. Have it with a salad to make an easy, light meal!

1 large baking potato per
   person, skin scrubbed

For each potato:
   ¼ cup skim milk, heated
   2 tablespoons low-fat yogurt
   3 teaspoons grated Romano
     or Parmesan cheese

1 teaspoon minced scallions
1 thin slice crisply cooked
   bacon, crumbled
Salt and freshly ground
   black pepper to taste
Chopped parsley

Place an oven rack in the uppermost position. Stretch a sheet of aluminum foil on the floor of the oven (this produces a crisp skin) and preheat oven to 300°F.

Place scrubbed, dried potatoes on the oven floor and bake for at least 1¼ hours.

Cut a 1½-inch lengthwise "lid" from each potato. Scoop out the flesh into a small bowl, taking care not to break the skin. Mash the flesh, and stir in enough heated milk to make a smooth purée. Beat in the yogurt, 2 teaspoons of the cheese, the scallions and the bacon. Season to taste with salt and pepper and pile back into the shell. Sprinkle the top with the remaining teaspoon of cheese and return to the rack in the oven to heat the potato through and brown the cheese—about 10 minutes. Sprinkle the top with parsley and serve at once.

Calories	263	cal
Protein	12	g
Carbohydrates	43	g
Total fat	5	g
Saturated	2	g
Polyunsaturated	.4	g
Cholesterol	14	mg
Sodium	229	mg

LOW-FAT MASHED POTATOES

Serves 4

Amounts here are loose—the onion is not vital but it does add a pleasant flavor to the potatoes. (Figure, approximately, half an onion per pound of potatoes.) Your preference regarding the taste and texture of mashed potatoes will govern the amount of Butter Buds and milk you use.

4 large, all-purpose potatoes
Half an onion, peeled
   (optional)
½ teaspoon Butter Buds per
   potato, or more to taste

½ cup evaporated skim milk,
   or more to taste
Salt and freshly ground black
   pepper to taste
Nutmeg (optional)

Peel the potatoes, quarter them, and put them in a pot with the optional onion; cover with cold water and boil covered until just tender, about 20 minutes. (Check with the tip of a sharp knife.) Don't overcook, or the potatoes will be waterlogged.

Drain the potatoes in a colander, discard onion if used, return potatoes to pot and briefly shake dry over heat. Sprinkle with Butter Buds, cover, and let sit 5 minutes. Mash the potatoes, then switch to a whisk and beat in enough milk to give a pleasing consistency. Season to taste with salt and pepper, more Butter Buds if you wish, and several gratings of nutmeg if you like.

Calories	162	cal
Protein	6	g
Carbohydrates	35	g
Total fat	.2	g
Saturated	.1	g
Polyunsaturated	.1	g
Cholesterol	1	mg
Sodium	89	mg

ROASTED NEW POTATOES WITH ROSEMARY

Serves 6

2¼ pounds small
(about 2½ inches in
diameter) red-skinned
new potatoes
PAM

1 tablespoon minced fresh
rosemary, or 1 teaspoon
dried
Salt
Freshly ground black pepper

Preheat oven to 450°F.

Scrub the potatoes but do not peel them. Cut them into halves or quarters depending on size.

Spray a glass baking dish with 2 generous sprays of PAM and place in the oven to heat for 3 minutes or so. Add the potatoes, salt lightly if desired, sprinkle with rosemary, and toss well to distribute seasoning. Roast the potatoes about 45 to 55 minutes depending on size, or until tender but not mushy. Stir to redistribute once or twice during cooking. Season with pepper and serve hot, warm, or at room temperature.

Calories	140	cal
Protein	3	g
Carbohydrates	31	g
Total fat	1	g
Saturated	0	g
Polyunsaturated	0	g
Cholesterol	0	mg
Sodium	13	mg

OVEN "FRIED" POTATOES

Serves 6 to 8

I confess to a terrible weakness for French fries, which are, of course, high in fat. These allow me to indulge with no guilt, and they are as good as the real thing. (And they are great with catsup!)

4 large baking potatoes   **Salt and freshly ground black**
PAM   **pepper**

Preheat the oven to 375°F. Peel the potatoes and put them in cold water. Have ready two cookie sheets, preferably with rims.

Cut a small lengthwise slice from the side of one potato. Put the potato cut side down on a work surface, then cut lengthwise into quarter-inch slices. Cut each slice into quarter-inch strips; you want French-fry-size pieces. Repeat with the remaining potatoes. If necessary, dry potato strips with paper towels.

Spray the cookie sheets liberally with PAM. Arrange the potatoes on the sheets so they do not overlap—overcrowding "steams" rather than browns them. Bake the potato strips for 1 hour in the upper third of the preheated oven, turning them over with a spatula at 15-minute intervals. Season with salt and pepper and serve while hot.

Calories	79	cal
Protein	2	g
Carbohydrates	17	g
Total fat	.4	g
Saturated	0	g
Polyunsaturated	0	g
Cholesterol	0	mg
Sodium	6	mg

ROASTED MARINATED PEPPERS WITH CAPERS

Serves 6 to 8

With beautiful sweet peppers now available in red, yellow, orange, and even black, roasted peppers make a handsome first course. (Don't use green ones, though—the flavor is too intrusive.) Serve with plenty of crusty bread for mopping up the delicious juices.

6 to 8 well-shaped sweet peppers (red, yellow, or a combination)
Red wine vinegar
Salt and freshly ground black pepper to taste

2 to 3 tablespoons capers (optional)
2 to 3 tablespoons virgin olive oil

Heat the broiler, and position the rack so the peppers will be 2 or 3 inches from the flame. Lay the peppers on the hot rack and turn frequently with tongs or two wooden spoons as blisters form, until completely charred. This will take anywhere from 5 to 10 minutes.

Immediately put the peppers in a brown paper bag and twist tightly to seal. Set aside for 10 to 15 minutes. Then slip off the charred skin and pull out the stems; most of the seeds should come with it. Cut the peppers open and discard remaining ribs and seeds. Do not rinse the peppers. It is all right if some charred patches remain.

Cut or tear each pepper into manageable halves or quarters and layer them in a shallow glass dish. Add any collected juices. Sprinkle with a teaspoon or so of vinegar, a light dash of salt if desired, and several good grindings of pepper; continue layering until all are used up. (Several tablespoons of capers may be added when layering.) Add just enough olive oil to thinly cover the top layer. Cover the dish with plastic wrap and refrigerate at least 4 hours. Let the peppers come to room temperature and add generous grindings of black pepper before serving.

Calories	56	cal
Protein	.5	g
Carbohydrates	3	g
Total fat	5	g
Saturated	1	g
Polyunsaturated	1	g
Cholesterol	0	mg
Sodium	2	mg

SQUASH PURÉE

Serves 6 to 8, about ¼ cup each

3 pounds butternut or
  Hubbard squash
2 teaspoons Butter Buds, or
  more to taste
6 teaspoons brown sugar, or
  to taste

1 teaspoon salt, or to taste
¼ teaspoon powdered ginger
½ cup evaporated skim milk,
  heated

Preheat oven to 375°F.

Rinse and dry the squash, cut in half, and remove seeds and strings. Place cut side down on a rimmed cookie sheet and add ¼ cup water so the squash does not stick. Bake until the squash is tender when pierced with a toothpick. Allow 1 hour, but start checking after 40 minutes.

Remove the squash from the oven, peel, and purée the flesh in a food processor or blender. You should have about 6 cups of purée. (If more or less, adjust seasonings accordingly.)

Return the purée to the processor. Add the Butter Buds and let sit a few minutes with the top on. Then add the brown sugar, salt, ginger, and evaporated milk and blend with 3 or 4 pulses, until fluffy. Do not overprocess.

Calories	104	cal
Protein	3	g
Carbohydrates	25	g
Total fat	.2	g
Saturated	.1	g
Polyunsaturated	.1	g
Cholesterol	1	mg
Sodium	367	mg

SQUASH AND SHRIMP

Serves 4

I serve this as part of a meatless dinner with Rice Pilaf (page 133) and a green vegetable.

1 medium butternut squash
2 tablespoons vegetable oil
2 teaspoons minced garlic
⅓ cup chopped onion
½ pound medium shrimp,
    shelled and deveined, cut
    in half

1 cup water
Salt and freshly ground black
    pepper to taste

Snap off the stem of the squash and split the squash by working the blade of a heavy chef's knife into it and striking the back of the knife near the handle with a mallet. Scoop out and discard the seeds and fibers and peel each half. Cut the flesh into ¾-inch cubes. You should have about 3 cups squash.

In a large, heavy casserole heat the oil over moderate heat, add the garlic and onion, and sauté until the onion is transparent. Add the shrimp and squash, stir to mix, add the water, and stir again. Season with salt and pepper to taste. Cover, bring to the boil, adjust heat to low, and simmer 4 minutes, or until the squash is tender but not too soft. Uncover and cook over high heat for 1 minute to reduce liquid slightly. Serve immediately, with rice.

SQUASH AND SHRIMP WITH GREEN BEANS

This dish can also be prepared with fresh green beans in addition to the squash; the color combination is very attractive. Simply add ¼ pound fresh young green beans, cut into 1½-inch pieces, to the onion–garlic mixture and cook, partially covered, for 3 minutes, before adding the squash and shrimp and proceeding with the recipe.

Calories	151 cal
Protein	10 g
Carbohydrates	11 g
Total fat	8 g
Saturated	1 g
Polyunsaturated	4 g

Cholesterol	71 mg
Sodium	72 mg

ZUCCHINI WITH TOMATOES

Serves 4

This is an easy and attractive vegetable dish that cooks without supervision while you're getting the rest of the meal ready.

4 to 5 small to medium zucchini	Salt and freshly ground black pepper to taste
4 teaspoons olive oil	Dash cayenne
1 medium onion, thinly sliced	½ bay leaf
2 garlic cloves, minced	1 teaspoon dried oregano
2 ripe tomatoes, peeled, seeded, and chopped, or 4 canned Italian plum tomatoes, drained and chopped	

Rinse the zucchini, remove ends, and cut the rest into ½-inch slices.

Heat the olive oil in a large, preferably non-stick skillet. Sauté the onion over moderate heat until slightly brown, about 2 minutes. Stir in the garlic and tomatoes and cook 5 minutes longer. Add the zucchini, salt and pepper, cayenne, bay leaf, and oregano, cover, and cook gently for 20 minutes, or until tender. If after 15 minutes there appears to be a great deal of liquid in the pan, remove the cover for the last 5 minutes or so of cooking. Taste for seasoning, remove bay leaf, and serve.

Calories	81	cal
Protein	3	g
Carbohydrates	9	g
Total fat	5	g
Saturated	1	g
Polyunsaturated	1	g
Cholesterol	0	mg
Sodium	10	mg

ZUCCHINI TRIFOLATI

Serves 4

1 pound zucchini (3 to 4
    medium zucchini)
Salt
1 fat clove garlic, peeled
2 whole scallions, trimmed,
    white and part of the
    green

1 tablespoon virgin olive oil
¼ cup chopped parsley,
    preferably Italian
Freshly ground black pepper
    to taste

Rinse the zucchini, cut off and discard the ends, and slice into ½-inch rounds. Put the slices in a colander, sprinkle with salt, mix by hand, and let stand 30 minutes. Shake the colander occasionally.

Cut the garlic in half lengthwise, then slice as thinly as possible. (There should be about 1 heaping teaspoonful; if not, add enough to make up this amount.) Set aside.

Cut the scallions in half lengthwise, then slice crosswise as thinly as possible. There should be about ¼ cup. Set aside.

Put the oil in a large skillet and place over medium-high heat. Add the garlic, and when it just begins to sizzle but is not brown, add the zucchini. Lower heat to medium and cook, tossing, for 5 to 7 minutes, until zucchini softens a bit and takes on a bit of color. Remove from heat, add the scallions, parsley, and pepper. Toss gently to combine and turn out onto a platter. Serve hot or at room temperature.

Calories	48 cal
Protein	2 g
Carbohydrates	4 g
Total fat	4 g
Saturated	.5 g
Polyunsaturated	.3 g
Cholesterol	0 mg
Sodium	5 mg

20
DESERTS

◆

RASPBERRY COULIS

POACHED PEACHES WITH
RASPBERRY SAUCE

PEARS POACHED IN RED WINE

SUMMER FRUIT COMPOTE

FRESH FRUIT SALAD
WITH GINGER AND CITRUS SYRUP

GINGERED BANANAS

ORANGES MARINATED
WITH GRAND MARNIER

MARINATED STRAWBERRIES WITH GRAPES

QUICK STRAWBERRY SOUFFLÉ

MANGO SORBET

PINEAPPLE–ORANGE SORBET

STRAWBERRY SORBET

CHOCOLATE SORBET

BUTTERMILK CHOCOLATE SAUCE

CHOCOLATE STRAWBERRY DUNK

CHOCOLATE PINEAPPLE DUNK

CHOCOLATE BANANA DUNK
CHOCOLATE FRUIT COMBO
ANGEL FOOD CAKE
LOW-FAT LEMON CHEESECAKE
CHOCOLATE MOCHA CAKE
PEACH CRISP
BLUEBERRY COBBLER
TUILES
VANILLA WAFERS
ZUCCHINI BREAD

A delicious dessert can add immeasurably to your sense of satiety, and banish any lingering feeling that your new lifestyle is going to mean deprivation. Yet this is the one area in which you are going to have to make some sacrifices. Most of the desserts we are accustomed to eating contain 10 to 20 grams of fat per serving. For our purposes, a low-fat dessert is one that contains no more than 3 grams of fat per serving. (You could go up to 5, if the fat consumption the rest of the day has been low.)

The trick is to choose desserts that you like, but ones that do not involve dairy products (apart from low- or non-fat yogurt), nuts, chocolate, or pastry. Any sweet with a crust means lots of fat calories, whether from butter, lard, or margarine. Desserts made with eggs mean a lot of concentrated fat. And those with a custard base (including ice cream), such as tarts with custard under the fruit, cakes other than angel food, pastries, pies, cheesecake, etc., have such a disproportionately high amount of calories from fat (and saturated, at that) that in the larger scheme of things, you will find yourself examining them to see if their deliciousness is worth it. If you're out for dinner or dining at a friend's home where a really delectable dessert is presented and you feel like indulging, do—but have a moderate portion. You'll have some idea of the fat content, and you'll make it up by being extra prudent at the next meal, or, if forewarned, earlier in the very same meal. When dining out, you can of course select satisfying desserts that are relatively low in fat (you only have to learn what they are) or, if cooking at home, make them, and save the pies and cakes for occasional indulgences.

I frequently serve one or more scoops of fruit sorbet arranged on a white plate along with a small arrangement of fruits, say a cluster of raspberries and several slices of kiwi. This needs only the accompaniment of a good cookie (without a high butter content), such as the delicate, French cookies known as *tuiles*, or "tiles," because they are shaped like French roof tiles. It's hard to find good cookies without fat, so this treat has to be limited, but one or two with a fruit sorbet can be a real joy. Try to find or make thin ones (they go farther), such as the Tuiles (page 268).

The desserts in this section are all low in fat per portion (some even contain an egg or two), but they are "real" desserts, not low-calorie versions of something else. I think you'll be surprised at how pleasing the choice is. Sorbets are so easy to make in one of the new machines that you might find this a good investment. If you want to do a fancy dessert for guests, you can combine several of these desserts on a plate, which makes a voluptuous presentation. Combine small scoops of three different kinds of sorbets, or do variations on a theme, such as poached pears with pear sorbet or fresh strawberries with strawberry sorbet, decorated with a mint sprig. Serving several desserts together is very luxurious—not at all the overkill it seems, since each element is small.

I feel I must particularly address chocolate, which I adore. There's no getting around it: Chocolate is, of itself, high in fat (a 1-ounce square of bittersweet cooking chocolate has 11 fat grams), and the overwhelming number of chocolate desserts also involve butter, eggs, sweet or sour cream, or nuts, making them even less acceptable. So try not to think chocolate. If you are a chocoholic, as I am, here's what to do: (1) Save chocolate desserts for very occasional treats. (The Buttermilk Chocolate Sauce (page 260), made with cocoa and buttermilk, is quite low in fat and *fabulous* over non-fat vanilla yogurt when the urge to binge burns.) (2) Don't eat more than a taste of a chocolate dessert that is served you unless it is *really* A-Number One first-class terrific. (It's surprising how many aren't.) (3) Either after, or in place of, a low-fat dessert, treat yourself to *a piece* of chocolate—a really good one—and ENJOY it!

RASPBERRY COULIS

Serves 8, 2 tablespoons each

Spoon this elegant sauce over poached peaches, whole strawberries, or lemon sorbet.

**2 10-ounce boxes frozen
    raspberries, thawed**
⅔ cup sugar

**2 tablespoons Cointreau
    (optional)**

Drain the raspberries of syrup, which may be reserved for another use, such as a drink or a gelatin dessert. Purée the berries in a food processor or blender, push through a sieve, then return the purée to the blender or processor, add the sugar, and process until the sugar has dissolved. Add Cointreau if desired.

Calories	137 cal
Protein	.5 g
Carbohydrates	35 g
Total fat	.1 g
Saturated	0 g
Polyunsaturated	.1 g
Cholesterol	0 mg
Sodium	1 mg

POACHED PEACHES WITH RASPBERRY SAUCE

Serves 6 to 8

The peaches as well as the sauce may be prepared hours ahead, then assembled at serving time. A thin, elegant cookie, such as a tuile (page 268) goes nicely with this dessert.

6 cups water
1½ cups sugar
1 tablespoon vanilla
    extract

6 to 8 medium ripe, but firm,
    peaches
Raspberry Coulis (page 247)
Mint leaves (optional)

Combine the water, sugar, and vanilla in a stainless-steel or enamel-lined (*not* aluminum) saucepan large enough to hold the peaches comfortably. Simmer for a few minutes until the sugar is dissolved and the syrup is clear. Add the peaches and cook at a very gentle simmer for 8 to 10 minutes, depending on size and ripeness. Carefully remove the peaches with a slotted spoon and drain them on a rack. Peel while still warm, then chill.

Serve each peach in an individual bowl, masked with a tablespoon of Raspberry Coulis and garnished with a mint leaf.

NOTE: The vanilla syrup may be strained, refrigerated, and used again for poaching fruit. It will keep for at least a month. It can also be used to macerate other fresh fruit, or be puréed with berries to make a quick fruit "Fool."

Peaches only

Calories	228	cal
Protein	1	g
Carbohydrates	58	g
Total fat	.1	g
Saturated	0	g
Polyunsaturated	.1	g
Cholesterol	0	mg
Sodium	.4	mg

PEARS POACHED IN RED WINE

Serves 6

6 well-shaped ripe, but firm,
    pears with stems, such as
    Bartlett or Bosc
4 tablespoons lemon juice
4 cups red wine
1 cup water

1½ cups sugar
2 strips lemon zest
½ teaspoon cinnamon
5 black peppercorns, smacked
    with the side of a heavy
    knife

With a corer, core the pears, but leave the stems intact; do this by coring the pears through the bottom, leaving about ¾ inch of the stem at the top intact. Then peel the pears. Put them in a bowl of water with half the lemon juice and set aside.

Put the wine, water, sugar, lemon zest, cinnamon, and peppercorns in a stainless-steel or enameled (*not* aluminum) pot large enough to hold the pears comfortably. Bring to the boil and simmer for 5 minutes, or until the sugar dissolves. Add the pears and cook at just below the simmer for 10 minutes, or until tender when pierced with a toothpick. (Timing will vary according to the size and ripeness of the pears; do not overcook, or they will be mushy and disintegrate.) As the pears cook, turn them gently so they color evenly. Let them cool in the syrup for 20 minutes.

Remove the pears carefully with a slotted spoon to a plate. Strain the poaching liquid, return it to the pot, and boil briskly over high heat until it becomes slightly syrupy and is reduced to 1 cup. Stir in the remaining lemon juice.

Put the pears in individual serving dishes and coat each with some of the wine sauce. Serve at room temperature.

Calories	306	cal
Protein	1	g
Carbohydrates	78	g
Total fat	1	g
Saturated	0	g
Polyunsaturated	.1	g
Cholesterol	0	mg
Sodium	11	mg

SUMMER FRUIT COMPOTE

Serves 6 to 8

This is lovely alone or served with Double-Thick Yogurt (page 275), flavored with honey and cinnamon if you like.

1 cup sugar
1 cup water
2 11-ounce cans Mandarin
    orange slices, drained,
    juice reserved
1 pound purple or small red
    plums, halved, pits
    removed

1 pint blackberries
1 pint raspberries
1 small bunch black grapes
    (about 20)
⅓ cup Ruby Port
Garnish: fresh mint leaves

Have all the fruit at room temperature. Select a large, pretty serving bowl.

In a saucepan big enough to hold the fruit, one type at a time, combine the sugar, water, and 1 cup of the reserved Mandarin orange juice. Bring to a boil over medium heat and stir until sugar is dissolved. Simmer the syrup 3 minutes.

Add the plums and poach 30 seconds, then scoop them out with a slotted spoon into the serving bowl. Add the blackberries and raspberries to the syrup, poach for 15 seconds, and transfer to the bowl. Then poach the grapes for 45 seconds and add to the bowl. Add the Mandarin oranges to the serving bowl and gently toss the fruit to distribute attractively.

Boil the poaching syrup over brisk heat until reduced by half and allow to cool. Stir in the Port and spoon over the fruit. Chill. Garnish with mint leaves.

Calories	245	cal
Protein	1	g
Carbohydrates	59	g
Total fat	1	g
Saturated	0	g
Polyunsaturated	.2	g
Cholesterol	0	mg
Sodium	5	mg

FRESH FRUIT SALAD
WITH GINGER AND CITRUS SYRUP

Serves 12, for about 10 cups fruit

Fruit salads can be disappointingly bland, but this one is a delicious exception because of its citrus-ginger underpinnings. It's great when you have a lot of people to serve, and the dressing can be made up to ten days ahead and refrigerated.

The dressing:

1 lemon	1½ cups sugar
1 lime	¾ cup cold water
1 unblemished orange	¼ teaspoon cream of tartar
5 quarter-size slices fresh ginger, each about ¼-inch thick	

Remove the zest of the lemon, lime, and orange in thin strips, using a swivel-bladed potato peeler. Try to leave behind the white pith. Set aside the citrus fruits for some another use. Cut the zest into fine julienne slivers and place in a small saucepan.

Cut the ginger into similar julienne strips and add to the zests in the saucepan. Cover with cold water, bring to a boil, then simmer gently 5 to 7 minutes. Pour through a strainer and rinse with cold water. Set aside.

Combine the sugar, water, and cream of tartar in a saucepan. Bring to the boil and stir until the sugar dissolves and the syrup is clear. Add the zest mixture to the syrup, bring to a second boil, and simmer 5 minutes. Cool and refrigerate the syrup until ready to use.

The fruit:

fresh blueberries	strawberries (hulled, left whole if small, halved if large)
cantaloupe balls or bite-sized pieces	
honeydew balls or bite-sized pieces	bite-size pieces of any of the following:
canned Mandarin oranges, drained, or fresh orange segments	crisp, unpeeled apple
	fresh pineapple
green seedless grapes	banana
	fresh mint leaves (optional)

Make a mixture of any or all of the following, using your own judgment as to the amounts of each. Do not use watermelon, since its juices dilute the syrup too much. You will be making 10 cups of fruit.

Place the fruit in a serving bowl, add enough ginger–citrus syrup to coat well, and toss thoroughly. Refrigerate for at least 1 hour before serving. Garnish with mint leaves if desired.

Calories	171 cal
Protein	1 g
Carbohydrates	44 g
Total fat	.4 g
Saturated	0 g
Polyunsaturated	.1 g
Cholesterol	0 mg
Sodium	6 mg

GINGERED BANANAS

Serves 4

3 to 4 large, just-ripe bananas   ¼ cup sugar
   (about 1½ pounds)   ¼ cup water
¼ teaspoon powdered ginger   2 tablespoons lemon juice

Slice the bananas into ¼-inch rounds. Arrange half the rounds close together in a shallow glass serving dish, sprinkle with half the ginger, and then repeat with the second layer of bananas.

In a saucepan combine the sugar and water and simmer until the sugar dissolves, about 3 minutes. Add 2 tablespoons lemon juice, pour the syrup over the bananas, and let the fruit cool. Chill before serving.

Calories	152 cal
Protein	1 g
Carbohydrates	39 g
Total fat	1 g
Saturated	.2 g
Polyunsaturated	.1 g
Cholesterol	0 mg
Sodium	3 mg

ORANGES MARINATED
WITH GRAND MARNIER

Serves 4

Fresh fruit in winter is hard to find, but, happily, this is when the best oranges are available, making this simple dessert a perfect fat-free choice.

6 navel oranges	2 strips lemon zest (about 1
1 teaspoon honey	inch long)
1 tablespoon water	¼ cup Grand Marnier
¼ teaspoon cinnamon	Fresh mint leaves (optional)

Prepare the orange sections as follows: Using a sharp knife, cut the skin off, including the white pith; then carefully cut between the membranes separating each segment, right to the core. Work over a bowl to catch any juice that falls and drop the orange sections into it as you work.

When all the oranges are sectioned, pour off the juice and strain it into a small saucepan. Add the honey, water, cinnamon, and lemon zest, bring to a boil over medium heat, and boil for about 3 minutes, or until the liquid is reduced by half and is thick and syrupy.

Remove the liquid from the heat, discard the lemon zest, and stir in the Grand Marnier. Cool to lukewarm.

Pour the sauce over the oranges and toss to coat. Cover and chill for at least 1 hour or up to 24. Let the fruit come to room temperature before serving. Arrange attractively in goblets or on dessert plates and decorate if desired with a sprig of mint.

Calories	144	cal
Protein	2	g
Carbohydrates	31	g
Total fat	.2	g
Saturated	0	g
Polyunsaturated	0	g
Cholesterol	0	mg
Sodium	2	mg

MARINATED STRAWBERRIES
WITH GRAPES

Serves 4

It's hard to imagine an easier dessert than this one, and the firm tartness of the grapes balances the soft sweetness of the berries in a very appealing way.

2 pints unblemished
  strawberries
3 tablespoons sugar

3 tablespoons fresh lemon
  juice
1 bunch seedless green grapes

Wipe the strawberries with a damp paper towel. Remove hulls and halve or quarter berries, depending on the size. Place them in a serving bowl, sprinkle them with the sugar and lemon juice, and mix gently. Refrigerate for an hour or so. Just before serving, add two good handfuls of grapes, mix again gently, and serve.

Calories	121 cal
Protein	1 g
Carbohydrates	30 g
Total fat	1 g
Saturated	.1 g
Polyunsaturated	.4 g
Cholesterol	0 mg
Sodium	2 mg

QUICK STRAWBERRY SOUFFLÉ

Serves 6, about ¼ cup each

This recipe specifies individual soufflés, but it may also be made in a 1½-quart soufflé dish.

1 cup chopped ripe strawberries	PAM 4 egg whites at room
4½ tablespoons sugar	temperature
1½ tablespoons brandy	

Put the strawberries in a small bowl, mix with 1 tablespoon plus 1 teaspoon sugar, or to taste, add the brandy and let them macerate for 30 minutes.

Put a cookie sheet on the center rack of the oven, and preheat the oven to 350°F. Spray 6 small soufflé dishes 4 inches in diameter (about 1¼-cup capacity) with PAM. Dust each with 1 teaspoon sugar, and tap out any excess.

Beat the egg whites until soft peaks form, sprinkle on top 1 tablespoon sugar, and continue beating until the whites are firm but not dry. Pour off and discard excess liquid from the strawberries and, working fast, add the strawberries to the egg whites and quickly fold in with a rubber spatula. The fruit should be well distributed, but the mixture should still look "streaky."

Spoon the mixture into the prepared soufflé dishes, put them on the cookie sheet, and bake in the middle of the oven for 12 to 15 minutes, or until the soufflés have risen above the rims and the tops have browned. Serve immediately.

Calories	56	cal
Protein	2	g
Carbohydrates	11	g
Total fat	0	g
Saturated	0	g
Polyunsaturated	0	g
Cholesterol	0	mg
Sodium	37	mg

SORBETS

Sorbet is simply the French word for sherbet. A sherbet is a smooth mix of water, sugar, and a flavoring, usually fruit, to which sometimes milk, gelatin, or egg whites may be added for additional smoothness. In this country sorbet has come to mean a fine-textured mix of the former without the latter.

Several machines have come on the market in recent years that make it easy to create delicious sorbets at home. I have an Il Gelataio, which comes with a built-in electric refrigeration system, a breeze to use. You just turn it on, pour in your mixture, set the churn, and in 20 minutes you have snowy, evenly frozen sorbet. There are other moderately priced small manual freezers, such as the Donvier, that turn out great sorbet with a slightly coarser texture.

Sorbets are best served shortly after being made. They get hard and icy after several days in the freezer, but they *can* be restored by whipping them up in a food processer and refreezing them until firm.

MANGO SORBET

Serves 6, about 1 quart

½ cup sugar
½ cup water

4 ripe mangoes
¼ cup lemon juice

Put the sugar and water in a saucepan and simmer until the sugar is dissolved and the syrup is clear, about 3 minutes. Cool to room temperature before using.

Peel and pit the mangoes. Purée the flesh in a food processor or a blender. You should have about 3½ cups of purée. Stir in the syrup and lemon juice. Force the mixture through a fine sieve.

Pour the mixture into the bowl of an ice cream maker and freeze according to the maker's directions. Or, pour into an 8-inch-square metal baking pan and freeze for 2 hours or until mushy. Remove from the freezer, beat with an electric mixer, until light and smooth and return to the freezer for 1 hour longer or until firm. Transfer to a covered container for longer freezer storage.

Calories	117	cal
Protein	1	g
Carbohydrates	31	g
Total fat	.3	g
Saturated	.1	g
Polyunsaturated	.1	g
Cholesterol	0	mg
Sodium	2	mg

PINEAPPLE–ORANGE SORBET

Serves 6, about 1 quart

4 cups ripe pineapple chunks
   or 32 ounces canned
   chunks, drained
2 cups strained *freshly*
   squeezed orange juice

¼ cup superfine sugar
3 tablespoons orange liqueur
   (Triple Sec or Cointreau)

Purée the pineapple in two batches in a food processor or blender. Put the purée in a bowl with the orange juice, sugar, and liqueur, and stir until the sugar is dissolved. Follow the freezing instructions for Mango Sorbet on page 256.

Calories	141	cal
Protein	1	g
Carbohydrates	32	g
Total fat	1	g
Saturated	0	g
Polyunsaturated	.2	g
Cholesterol	0	mg
Sodium	2	mg

STRAWBERRY SORBET

Serves 6, about 1 quart

2 10-ounce packages frozen
   strawberries packed in
   syrup

½ cup sugar
½ cup water
3 tablespoons lemon juice

Let the strawberries defrost partially while you prepare the syrup as directed for Mango Sorbet (page 256).

Purée the strawberries with their syrup in a food processor or blender. Stir in the syrup and the lemon juice. Follow the freezing instructions given for Mango Sorbet.

Calories	118 cal
Protein	.4 g
Carbohydrates	31 g
Total fat	.1 g
Saturated	0 g
Polyunsaturated	0 g
Cholesterol	0 mg
Sodium	2 mg

CHOCOLATE SORBET

Serves 5 to 6, makes 2½ to 3 cups, ½ cup per serving

This is so decadent and satisfying that no one will believe it is low in fat! It is the creation of Michel Richard of the popular Los Angeles restaurant Citrus.

½ cup sugar, or a little more to taste
1¼ cups unsweetened cocoa

2 cups warm water
⅓ cup Port

Mix the sugar and cocoa together in a bowl. Whisk in the water, a little at a time, until smooth. Add the Port.

Process the sorbet in an ice cream maker according to the manufacturer's instructions. If not using it immediately, freeze the sorbet and then process for a few seconds in a food processor to soften before serving.

Calories	158	cal
Protein	4	g
Carbohydrates	33	g
Total fat	4	g
Saturated	2	g
Polyunsaturated	0	g
Cholesterol	0	mg
Sodium	3	mg

BUTTERMILK CHOCOLATE SAUCE

Makes ¾ cup, 12 1-tablespoon servings

When nothing but chocolate will do . . . cocoa gives you great chocolate taste without the fat content of semi-sweet, German, milk chocolate, and the like. Serve this with fresh fruit or over frozen yogurt.

⅓ cup Dutch-processed cocoa, such as Droste or Lindt (not Hershey's)
¼ cup firmly packed light-brown sugar

½ cup non-fat buttermilk
2 teaspoons Grand Marnier or other orange-flavored liqueur

Off heat, combine the cocoa and brown sugar in a small saucepan. Gradually add the buttermilk, stirring to blend smoothly with a wooden spoon. Place the pan over medium heat, switch to a whisk, and cook, stirring, until the sugar dissolves, about 2 minutes. Remove from the heat and stir in the liqueur. The sauce will thicken as it cools. It will keep in the refrigerator for several weeks in a tightly closed container.

Calories	30 cal
Protein	1 g
Carbohydrates	6 g
Total fat	1 g
Saturated	.3 g
Polyunsaturated	0 g
Cholesterol	.4 mg
Sodium	29 mg

CHOCOLATE STRAWBERRY DUNK

Serves 4

1 quart handsome ripe   Buttermilk Chocolate Sauce
    strawberries, stems on   (page 260)

Do not wash the berries, but wipe them with a damp towel. Divide the
Buttermilk Chocolate Sauce between 4 small Pyrex custard dishes or
other small dishes and place each on a dessert plate. Divide the strawberries among the plates, heaping them around the sauce dish.

CHOCOLATE PINEAPPLE DUNK

Substitute ripe pineapple spears for the strawberries.

CHOCOLATE BANANA DUNK

Substitute peeled, ripe unblemished bananas, cut in half and then in
half lengthwise.

CHOCOLATE FRUIT COMBO

Serve with all the above fruits.

Calories	137 cal
Protein	3 g
Carbohydrates	30 g
Total fat	2 g
Saturated	1 g
Polyunsaturated	.3 g
Cholesterol	1 mg
Sodium	89 mg

ANGEL FOOD CAKE

Serves 12

Angel Food Cake should be in every low-fat repertoire. It has no fat or cholesterol, very few calories, yet is festive and very versatile. Serve it with Marinated Strawberries (page 254), Raspberry Coulis (page 247), or any other fruit or fruit sauce.

1 cup sifted cake flour
1½ cups twice-sifted superfine
   sugar
1 teaspoon cream of tartar
½ teaspoon salt
1½ cups egg whites (about 12
   large eggs) at room
   temperature

1 teaspoon vanilla extract
½ teaspoon almond extract
1 teaspoon lemon juice

Preheat the oven to 325°F.

Sift the measured, already sifted flour again 5 or 6 more times with ½ cup of the already sifted sugar. Hold the sifter high to incorporate as much air as possible. Set the flour aside.

Sprinkle the cream of tartar and salt over the egg whites and beat in a very large, clean bowl, using a hand-held beater or an electric one (see NOTE 1), until stiff peaks form. Sift a little of the remaining cup of sugar over the whites and gently fold in with a whisk. Repeat gradually until all the sugar is incorporated. Then sift a little of the reserved sugar–flour mixture over and fold in. Repeat gradually until it is all incorporated.

Finally, fold in the vanilla and almond extracts and the lemon juice.

Turn the batter into an *ungreased* 10-inch tube pan. Bake about 1 hour, then test by pressing lightly in the center—if the cake springs back it is done. If not, bake up to 15 minutes more, testing at 5-minute intervals.

Remove the pan from the oven, invert it, and let the cake cool for 1½ hours. The pan must be raised from the counter top at least 1 inch or so while this takes place (see NOTE 2). When thoroughly cooled, remove the cake from the pan by loosening the sides with a metal spatula.

To serve, pierce with a fork at intervals to mark portions, and pull apart with two forks to avoid mashing the cake.

NOTES: 1. Beating by hand gives greater volume but it is not absolutely necessary. 2. Many angel food pans have "legs" or else a high center tube for this purpose. If yours doesn't, rest the pan upside down with the rim on 4 upside-down teacups or put the tube over a thin bottle neck and hang the cake upside down. 3. Angel food cake cannot be frozen successfully.

Calories	142	cal
Protein	4	g
Carbohydrates	32	g
Total fat	.1	g
Saturated	0	g
Polyunsaturated	0	g
Cholesterol	0	mg
Sodium	138	mg

LOW-FAT LEMON CHEESECAKE

Serves 12

If you thought there was no place for cheesecake in low-fat living, this will be a nice surprise!

PAM
2 tablespoons margarine
½ cup finely crushed graham
   crackers
2 cups 1-percent-fat cottage
   cheese
1 cup plain non-fat yogurt or
   Double-Thick Yogurt
   (page 275)

¾ cup sugar
3 tablespoons all-purpose flour
2 eggs, slightly beaten
¾ cup skim milk
2 tablespoons lemon juice
1 teaspoon grated lemon zest
Pinch salt

Have all the ingredients at room temperature. Preheat the oven to 350°F.

Choose a 9 × 3-inch springform pan with a removable bottom; spray only the bottom with PAM. Melt the margarine, cool, and combine in a bowl with the crumbs; blend with your fingers or a fork until well combined. Pat this over the bottom of the pan and press down slightly. Place the pan in the freezer for 15 minutes.

Put the cottage cheese in a food processor and process until smooth, scraping the sides down as needed; this will take about 2 minutes. Add the yogurt, sugar, and flour, and pulse several times at 1-second intervals to blend. Add the eggs, one at a time, and process 3 seconds each to blend. Add the milk, lemon juice, lemon zest, and salt and process several seconds to blend. Carefully ladle the mixture into the crust (do not pour, to avoid creating air bubbles). The pan will be only half full.

Bake in the center of the oven for 40 to 50 minutes, or until a wooden pick inserted near center comes out clean. The cake will not rise very much and the top will appear moist.

Turn off the oven, and with the door ajar, let the cake remain there for 1 hour. Remove to a rack and complete cooling. Refrigerate, covered, for several hours. When throughly chilled, run a sharp knife around the edge of the cake, loosen, and remove the sides of the pan.

Calories	153	cal
Protein	9	g
Carbohydrates	20	g
Total fat	4	g
Saturated	1	g
Polyunsaturated	1	g
Cholesterol	38	mg
Sodium	312	mg

CHOCOLATE MOCHA CAKE

Serves 12

Don't be put off by the long list of ingredients. This cake is easy to make and richly chocolate-y.

PAM
Flour
½ cup cocoa
1 tablespoon instant coffee
⅔ cup boiling water
8 tablespoons reduced-calorie
    margarine
1½ cups sugar
¼ cup honey
1 egg yolk
1 teaspoon vanilla extract
1 tablespoon cornstarch
1 cup non-fat yogurt

2 cups flour
1 teaspoon baking soda
1½ teaspoons baking powder
2 egg whites
Pinch cream of tartar

Glaze:
⅓ cup cocoa
¼ cup evaporated skim
    milk
1 cup confectioner's sugar
1 teaspoon vanilla extract

Preheat the oven to 350°F. Spray a 9- or 10-inch tube pan with PAM and dust with flour, tapping out any excess. Set aside.

In a large bowl, mix the cocoa and coffee with the boiling water; add the margarine and stir until melted. Stir in the sugar, honey, egg yolk, and vanilla and continue stirring until well blended.

In another bowl, combine the cornstarch with ¼ cup of the yogurt, then mix in the rest of yogurt. Add this to the cocoa mixture.

Sift together the flour, baking soda, and baking powder. Add to the cocoa mixture and stir well.

With an electric beater beat the egg whites until frothy. Add the cream of tartar and continue to beat until the mixture is stiff but not dry.

Fold the egg whites gently into the batter. Pour the batter into the prepared pan and bake for 45 to 55 minutes, or until the cake pulls away from the sides of the pan and a toothpick inserted in the cake tests clean. Cool for 30 minutes on a rack, unmold, and cool to room temperature before glazing the cake.

Glaze:

Combine all the ingredients, mix thoroughly, and let sit a few minutes.

Spread the glaze over the top of the cake with a knife or plastic spatula and let it dribble down the sides.

Calories	309	cal
Protein	5	g
Carbohydrates	63	g
Total fat	6	g
Saturated	1	g
Polyunsaturated	2	g
Cholesterol	18	mg
Sodium	244	mg

PEACH CRISP

Serves 6

If ripe peaches are not available, this can be made with nectarines. It's a wonderful, homey dessert.

PAM
7 large peaches
2 to 3 tablespoons lemon juice
1 teaspoon grated lemon zest
Several gratings nutmeg

2 tablespoons unsalted butter
⅔ cup sifted all-purpose flour
½ cup rolled oats
⅔ cup tightly packed light-
    brown sugar

Preheat the oven to 325°F. Spray a 9 × 9-inch ovenproof dish with PAM.

Fill up a small pot with water and put it on to boil. Dip each peach in the water for 30 seconds, then peel it and remove the pit. Slice the peaches thinly and put the slices in the prepared dish. Sprinkle with the lemon juice, grated zest, and nutmeg and toss gently.

Cut the butter into 5 or 6 pieces and put these in a bowl with the flour, oats, and brown sugar. Mix together, using a pastry blender or two knives. When crumbly, spoon the topping over the peaches, trying to cover them evenly. Bake for 30 minutes, or until the peaches are tender. If you would like the top to be a little browner, run the dish under the broiler for 40 seconds or so, and watch constantly. Serve at room temperature.

Calories	213	cal
Protein	3	g
Carbohydrates	45	g
Total fat	3	g
Saturated	2	g
Polyunsaturated	.3	g
Cholesterol	8	mg
Sodium	6	mg

BLUEBERRY COBBLER

Serves 6 to 8

Another simple, homey dessert that doesn't mind being in the oven when other food is cooking. Be sure to use flavorful berries. You can also make this with blackberries.

PAM
¼ cup sugar
2 tablespoons cornstarch
Grated zest of 1 large
  orange
2 pint boxes blueberries,
  picked over, washed and
  dried

Batter:
3 tablespoons stick
  margarine
½ cup sugar
Pinch salt
1 large egg
½ cup skim milk
1½ cups sifted cake flour
2 teaspoons baking powder

Preheat the oven to 425°F. Spray a 9 × 12-inch Pyrex baking dish with PAM. Mix together the sugar and cornstarch and orange zest, toss with the berries and put in baking dish.

Cream together the margarine and sugar, add a pinch of salt and blend in the egg. Add milk and mix well. Stir in flour and baking powder, beat briefly and briskly to make a thick, soft batter; spoon over the berries, leaving about a one-inch border of berries visible (batter spreads). Bake in the preheated oven for 20 to 25 minutes, or until top is dappled with gold. Serve warm with frozen non-fat vanilla yogurt if desired.

Calories	330	cal
Protein	4	g

Carbohydrates	67	g
Total fat	1	g
Saturated	1	g
Polyunsaturated	1	g
Cholesterol	31	mg
Sodium	222	mg

TUILES
(ALMOND TILE COOKIES)

Makes 48 cookies, 1 cookie per serving

3 tablespoons unsalted butter,
  softened
⅓ cup sugar
3 egg whites
1 teaspoon vanilla extract
Pinch salt

3 tablespoons unbleached
  all-purpose flour
2 tablespoons cake flour
½ cup ground blanched
  almonds

Preheat the oven to 425°F. Place the oven rack in the center position. Grease 2 baking sheets well, sprinkle lightly with water, and shake off excess. Have handy a metal spatula and an old-fashioned, fat rolling pin or an empty wine bottle from which the label has been removed.

With a hand-held or regular electric mixer (not a food processor) thoroughly cream the butter and sugar together. Add the egg whites, vanilla, and salt and continue beating until the mixture is light and fluffy. Add the flours and blend well.

Drop the batter by ½ teaspoons onto the prepared baking sheets, spacing well apart, since the cookies will spread. Using the back of a small spoon, spread the batter into 2½-inch circles thin enough to see the baking sheet through them. Sprinkle the tops of the cookies with the ground almonds. Bake, one sheet at a time, until the edges are dark brown, about 5 to 6 minutes. Remove from the oven, let stand for 30 seconds, then turn the cookies over quickly with a metal spatula. Return the sheet to the oven for 2 minutes more.

Then, working very quickly, remove each cookie from the sheet and place almond side *up* around the rolling pin or bottle so that the cookie hardens into a curve. When the tiles have cooled enough to hold their shape, remove to a rack until completely cool. Then stack together carefully and store in an airtight container.

NOTE: You can also get the required gentle curve by putting the cookies over the bottom of an upside-down ring mold.

Calories	22 cal
Protein	.4 g
Carbohydrates	2 g
Total fat	1 g
Saturated	.5 g
Polyunsaturated	.1 g
Cholesterol	2 mg
Sodium	6 mg

VANILLA WAFERS

Follow the recipe for Tuiles on the preceding page but omit the almonds and do not curve.

Calories	21 cal
Protein	0 g
Carbohydrates	3 g
Total fat	1 g
Saturated	0 g
Polyunsaturated	0 g
Cholesterol	3 mg
Sodium	8 mg

ZUCCHINI BREAD

Makes 2 loaves, 12 slices per loaf, 1 slice per serving

This low-fat take on an old favorite freezes very well and is delightful as a tea bread or a sweet snack.

PAM
1 large egg
2 egg whites
⅓ cup vegetable oil
⅔ cup skim milk
2 cups granulated sugar
2 cups grated zucchini, tightly
    packed
1 teaspoon vanilla

3 cups all-purpose flour
1 teaspoon baking soda
1 teaspoon baking powder
½ teaspoon salt
1 teaspoon ground ginger
1 teaspoon ground cinnamon
¼ teaspoon ground cloves
½ cup chopped walnuts
    (about 2 ounces)

Preheat oven to 325°F. Spray two 5 × 8-inch loaf pans with PAM.

Combine the egg, egg whites, oil, milk, and sugar in a large bowl. (This can be done in an electric mixer.) Stir in the zucchini and the vanilla.

In another bowl, sift together the flour, baking soda, baking powder, salt, ginger, cinnamon, and cloves. Stir in the nuts. Add to the zucchini mixture and stir lightly to blend.

Divide between the prepared pans and bake for 1 hour. Cool for 20 minutes on a wire rack before removing from pan. Keep refrigerated, wrapped in foil, or freeze.

Calories	172	cal
Protein	3	g
Carbohydrates	30	g
Total fat	5	g
Saturated	1	g
Polyunsaturated	3	g
Cholesterol	9	mg
Sodium	109	mg

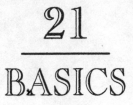

21
BASICS

♦

DEFATTED CHICKEN BROTH
VEGETABLE BROTH
GRAVY
DOUBLE-THICK YOGURT
MOCK SOUR CREAM
APPLESAUCE
HORSERADISH APPLESAUCE

DEFATTED CHICKEN BROTH

Makes about 7 cups

This is wonderful to have on hand and easy to prepare. Freeze in ice cube trays, then store the cubes in a plastic bag. When freezer space is a problem, reduce the broth by boiling and "reconstitute" it before use by adding water.

**Approximately 3 pounds
  assorted chicken bones
  and parts (carcasses,
  necks, wings, backbones,
  etc.)
About 10 cups cold water
1 teaspoon salt
1 large onion, quartered**

**2 carrots, peeled and cut into
  thirds
1 to 2 ribs celery
4 to 5 parsley sprigs, stems
  only
1 bay leaf
Large pinch dried thyme**

Rinse the chicken parts and remove any visible fat. Put them in a large, heavy soup pot and add enough water to just cover them. Bring the water to a boil over high heat, lower heat at once, and cook for a few minutes, skimming off any gray froth that rises. Add the remaining ingredients and simmer, partially covered, for 1 hour. Do not permit the liquid to boil rapidly or it will be cloudy.

Let the broth cool slightly, then remove chicken parts and solids. Strain the broth by pouring it into a bowl through a sieve lined with a double layer of dampened cheesecloth or a white paper towel. Refrigerate until the fat hardens on top. Remove the fat and discard. Alternatively, defat with the Gravy Strain (see Special Products, page 305).

Calories	40 cal
Protein	1 g
Carbohydrates	6 g
Total fat	2 g
Saturated	0 g
Polyunsaturated	0 g
Cholesterol	0 mg
Sodium	5 mg

Defat commercial chicken or beef broth by removing can lid and refrigerating until the fat hardens. Scoop off and discard.

VEGETABLE BROTH

Makes about 10 cups

You can play with this broth as you wish, adding pea pods, carrot tops, mushroom stems, etc., or fresh tomatoes for color. Use for added nourishment and flavor, in place of water, as when boiling rice or other grains, or anywhere chicken broth is called for.

About 10 cups cold water
2 medium onions, quartered
2 carrots, coarsely chopped
2 ribs celery, coarsely chopped
2 leeks, well washed, the
    white and all the green,
    or leek greens only
1 parsnip (optional)
5 garlic cloves, peeled

5 sprigs parsley, stems only
1 bay leaf
¼ teaspoon thyme
2 cloves
6 to 8 whole black
    peppercorns
2 teaspoons reduced-sodium
    soy sauce or Tamari

Combine all the ingredients in a large, heavy soup pot. Bring slowly to a boil, then adjust heat and simmer, partially covered, for 1 hour. Strain or put through a *chinois* (a cone-shaped strainer), pressing down on the vegetables to release all the juices. Discard the vegetables and spices. If the flavor seems weak, reduce the liquid by boiling. Correct seasoning.

GRAVY

Serves 4, about 3 tablespoons each

1 tablespoon cornstarch
1 cup defatted chicken or beef
    broth at room
    temperature

Freshly ground black pepper
    to taste
½ teaspoon Butter Buds
    (optional)

Combine the cornstarch and broth in a jar with a tight lid. Shake together, then use to deglaze a cooking pan: Pour the liquid into the pan in which you have sautéed food and, over high heat, scrape up any brown bits on the bottom. Then let the liquid reduce a bit. You could also simply heat the broth–cornstarch mixture in a small saucepan, season with pepper, and use as is. Enrich if you like with a sprinkling of Butter Buds.

Calories	17	cal
Protein	.1	g
Carbohydrates	3	g
Total fat	.4	g
Saturated	0	g
Polyunsaturated	0	g
Cholesterol	0	mg
Sodium	1	mg

DOUBLE-THICK YOGURT

Makes about 2 cups

Reminiscent of the wonderful, thick Middle Eastern yogurt labani, *this is simply yogurt thickened by having its whey, or liquid, drained off. Use it to extend high-fat spreads like cream cheese, to replace sour cream in recipe favorites like Beef Stroganoff, as well as to top foods where a dab of whipped cream is the usual garnish.*

1 quart plain non-fat yogurt

Line a colander with double-thick cheesecloth and set it over a large bowl. Spoon the yogurt into the prepared colander and refrigerate for 8 hours or overnight. Discard the whey. The yogurt may be kept for up to 10 days if refrigerated in a tightly closed container.

Calories	26	cal
Protein	3	g
Carbohydrates	3	g
Total fat	0	g
Saturated	0	g
Polyunsaturated	0	g
Cholesterol	1	mg
Sodium	31	mg

MOCK SOUR CREAM

Makes about 1 cup

1 cup low-fat cottage cheese   1 tablespoon lemon juice
2 tablespoons skim milk

Purée the cottage cheese in a blender, about 2 minutes, and thin to desired consistency with the skim milk and the lemon juice.

Calories	11	cal
Protein	2	g
Carbohydrates	1	g
Total fat	.1	g
Saturated	.1	g
Polyunsaturated	0	g
Cholesterol	1	mg
Sodium	59	mg

Make your own non-fat fruit-flavored yogurt by adding to the yogurt Applesauce (page 277) or any puréed fruit. Be inventive: Try adding a little vanilla, cinnamon, ground cardamom, and so forth.

APPLESAUCE

Makes 3 to 4 quarts

Homemade applesauce is a wonderful meal enhancer to have on hand. I use it on corn pancakes instead of syrup and as a side dish with turkey or chicken. My younger daughter loves to mix it into low-fat yogurt and sprinkle cinnamon sugar on top. You can do these things with commercial sauce as well, but homemade is better.

I learned this cooking method from my mother-in-law. Since no water is involved, it produces a thick, silky sauce that is rich in flavor, and freezes very well.

Wash 5 to 6 pounds Early McIntosh or Cortland apples. Do not peel them. Cut them into quarters, removing the stem and blossom ends. Put ½ cup lemon juice in a large, heavy stainless-steel or enameled pot (*not* aluminum) and add all the apples. Cover and cook over very low heat (use a flame tamer if necessary to prevent scorching), stirring occasionally, until the apples are reduced to mush. This will take about 1 hour.

Put the contents of the pot through a food mill and discard the skins, seeds, and cores that are held back. Sweeten the purée to taste with sugar, add cinnamon or a dash of nutmeg if you like, and return briefly to low heat and cook stirring just until the sugar is melted. Serve at room temperature; applesauce should never be served ice cold.

Sugar not included

Calories	88 cal
Protein	0 g
Carbohydrates	23 g
Total fat	0 g
Saturated	0 g
Polyunsaturated	0 g
Cholesterol	0 mg
Sodium	2 mg

HORSERADISH APPLESAUCE

Serves 6, about ½ cup each

Add ¾ cup prepared white horseradish to 2 cups chilled applesauce, homemade (page 277) or commercial. Serve with cold Roast Marinated Loin of Pork (page 217) or cold chicken.

Calories	35	cal
Protein	.3	g
Carbohydrates	9	g
Total fat	.2	g
Saturated	0	g
Polyunsaturated	0	g
Cholesterol	0	mg
Sodium	15	mg

Part III

APPENDIXES

APPENDIX A

The Fat, Cholesterol, and Calorie Contents of Common Foods

NOTE: TR = trace; pcs. = pieces; LN = lean

Food	Serving Size	Calories	Fat (g)	Sat. Fat (g)	Chol. (mg)
BEANS AND LEGUMES					
Black-eyed peas, cooked	(½ cup)	99	TR	TR	0
Kidney beans, red, cooked	(⅔ cup)	151	TR	TR	0
Lentils, cooked	(⅔ cup)	154	TR	TR	0
Lima beans, cooked	(½ cup)	105	TR	TR	0
Navy beans, cooked	(½ cup)	129	TR	TR	0
Black beans, cooked	(½ cup)	114	TR	TR	0
Chickpeas (garbanzos), cooked	(½ cup)	134	2	TR	0
Pinto beans, cooked	(½ cup)	117	TR	TR	0
CHEESE					
American	(1 oz)	106	9	6	27
Blue	(1 oz)	100	8	5	21
Brick	(1 oz)	105	8	5	27
Brie	(1 oz)	95	8	N/A	28
Camembert	(1 oz)	85	7	4	20
Cheddar	(1 oz)	114	9	6	30
Colby	(1 oz)	112	9	6	27
Cottage cheese (1% fat)	(½ cup)	81	1	1	5
Cottage cheese (2% fat)	(½ cup)	102	2	1	9

Food	Serving Size	Calories	Fat (g)	Sat. Fat (g)	Chol. (mg)
Cottage cheese (4% fat)	(½ cup)	108	5	3	16
Cream cheese	(1 Tb)	49	5	3	16
Cream cheese, whipped	(1 Tb)	32	3	2	10
Edam	(1 oz)	101	8	5	25
Feta	(1 oz)	75	6	4	25
Gouda	(1 oz)	101	8	5	32
Gruyère	(1 oz)	117	9	5	31
Monterey Jack	(1 oz)	106	9	N/A	25
Mozzarella	(1 oz)	80	6	4	22
Mozzarella (part skim)	(1 oz)	72	5	3	16
Muenster	(1 oz)	104	9	5	27
Neufchâtel	(1 oz)	74	7	4	22
Parmesan (grated)	(1 Tb)	23	2	TR	4
Parmesan (hard)	(1 oz)	111	7	5	19
Provolone	(1 oz)	100	8	5	20
Ricotta (whole milk)	(½ cup)	214	16	10	63
Ricotta (part skim)	(½ cup)	170	10	6	38
Romano	(1 oz)	110	8	N/A	29
Roquefort	(1 oz)	105	9	5	26
Swiss	(1 oz)	107	8	5	26
Cheese Whiz spread	(1 oz)	80	6	3	20
CHIPS AND SNACKS					
Corn chips, Fritos	(1 oz)	154	10	2	0
Potato chips	(1 oz)	148	10	3	0
Pretzels	(1 oz)	111	1	TR	0
Tortilla chips, Doritos	(1 oz)	140	7	N/A	0
COMBINATION FOODS					
Chicken à la king	(1 cup)	468	34	13	186
Chicken and noodle casserole	(1 cup)	367	18	6	96
Chili con carne, w/beans, canned	(1 cup)	339	16	7	43
Chop suey, beef and pork, w/o noodles, canned	(1 cup)	155	8	3	30
Chow mein, chicken, w/o noodles, canned	(1 cup)	95	TR	N/A	8
Macaroni and cheese, homemade	(1 cup)	430	22	9	42
Pâté, chicken liver	(2 Tb)	52	3	N/A	N/A
Pizza, cheese ½ of 10″ pie	(1 slice)	140	4	1	10
with pepperoni N/A	(1 slice)	N/A	N/A	N/A	N/A

Food	Serving Size	Calories	Fat (g)	Sat. Fat (g)	Chol. (mg)
Pot pie, chicken	(⅓ of 9" pie)	545	31	11	72
with beef	(⅓ of 9" pie)	517	30	8	44
Spaghetti with meatballs and tomato sauce, canned	(1 cup)	258	10	2	2
Stew, beef and vegetable, canned	(1 cup)	194	8	2	34
CONDIMENTS					
Mayonnaise	(1 Tb)	99	11	2	8
Mayonnaise, imitation	(1 Tb)	34	3	TR	4
Mayonnaise, reduced-calorie	(1 Tb)	41	4	1	5
Salad Dressing Mayo type	(1 Tb)	57	5	1	4
Tartar sauce	(1 Tb)	76	8	2	7
DAIRY PRODUCTS					
Cream, Non-dairy Creamers, and Toppings					
Half & half	(1 Tb)	19	2	1	6
Light cream	(1 Tb)	29	3	2	10
Medium cream	(1 Tb)	36	4	2	13
Heavy cream (whipping)	(1 Tb)	51	6	3	20
Sour cream, real	(1 Tb)	31	3	2	6
Aerosol whipped cream	(1 Tb)	10	1	1	3
Creamer, non-dairy, liquid	(1 Tb)	20	2	TR	0
Creamer, non-dairy, powder	(1 tsp)	11	TR	TR	0
Dessert topping, non-dairy, frozen	(1 Tb)	15	1	1	0
Eggs					
Whole, raw, large	(1)	75	5	2	213
Yolk, raw, large	(1)	59	5	2	213
White, raw, large	(1)	17	0	0	0
Egg substitute, liquid	(¼ cup)	53	2	TR	TR
frozen	(¼ cup)	96	7	1	1
Frozen Desserts					
Elan non-fat frozen yogurt N/A	(½ cup)				
Frozen yogurt	(½ cup)	113	TR	N/A	4

Food	Serving Size	Calories	Fat (g)	Sat. Fat (g)	Chol. (mg)
Ice cream, rich, 16% fat	(½ cup)	175	12	7	44
Ice cream, regular, 10% fat	(½ cup)	134	7	4	30
Ice milk, regular	(½ cup)	92	3	2	9
Ice milk, soft serve N/A	(½ cup)				
Sherbet, orange	(½ cup)	135	2	1	7
Milk					
Buttermilk, cultured (1%) N/A	(1 cup)				
Buttermilk, cultured	(1 cup)	98	2	1	10
Condensed, sweetened, canned	(½ cup)	491	13	8	52
Evaporated, skim, canned	(½ cup)	100	TR	TR	5
Evaporated, whole, canned	(½ cup)	169	10	6	37
Hot cocoa, w/whole milk	(1 cup)	218	9	6	33
Milk					
skim or non-fat	(1 cup)	86	TR	TR	5
1% fat	(1 cup)	102	3	2	10
2% fat	(1 cup)	122	5	3	20
whole	(1 cup)	149	8	5	34
Milkshake, vanilla, thick	(11 oz)	350	9	6	37
Milkshake, chocolate, thick	(11 oz)	356	8	5	32
Yogurt					
Non-fat, plain	(1 cup)	127	TR	TR	5
Low-fat, plain	(1 cup)	143	4	2	14
Whole, plain	(1 cup)	138	7	5	29
FAST FOODS					
Biscuit w/egg and bacon	(1 biscuit)	457	31	10	353
Burrito, w/beans and cheese	(2 burritos)	377	12	7	22
Boneless chicken pieces, w/barbecue sauce	(6 pcs.)	330	18	6	61
Chicken, drumstick, breaded, fried	(drum, thigh)	430	27	7	165
Chili con carne	(1 cup)	254	8	3	133
Enchilada, w/cheese	(1)	320	19	11	44
English muffin w/egg, cheese, sausage	(1)	487	31	12	274

Food	Serving Size	Calories	Fat (g)	Sat. Fat (g)	Chol. (mg)
Fish filet, breaded, fried	(1)	211	11	3	31
Fish sandwich, w/cheese	(1)	524	29	8	68
French-fried potatoes, in beef tallow	(3 oz)	265	14	6	15
Ham and cheese sandwich	(1)	353	15	6	58
Hamburger, single meat patty	(1)	275	12	4	36
Hamburger, double meat patty	(1)	544	28	10	99
Cheeseburger, 4 oz.	(1)	320	15	6	50
Hotdog	(1)	242	15	5	44
with chili	(1)	297	13	5	51
Hot fudge sundae	(1)	284	9	5	21
Onion rings, breaded, fried	(3 oz, 8–9 rings)	275	16	7	14
Pancake, butter, syrup	(3)	519	14	6	57
Potatoes, hashed brown	(½ cup)	151	9	4	9
Roast beef sandwich	(5 oz)	346	14	4	52
Submarine with cold cuts	(½ lb)	456	19	7	35
Taco	(1 small, 6 oz)	370	21	11	57
Vanilla shake	(10 oz)	314	8	5	32
FATS AND OILS					
Oil					
Canola	(1 tsp)	40	5	TR	0
Corn	(1 tsp)	40	5	TR	0
Olive	(1 tsp)	40	5	TR	0
Peanut	(1 tsp)	40	5	TR	0
Safflower	(1 tsp)	40	5	TR	0
Sesame	(1 tsp)	40	5	TR	0
Soybean	(1 tsp)	40	5	TR	0
Soybean/cottonseed (hydrogenated)	(1 tsp)	40	5	TR	0
Soybean, hydrogenated	(1 tsp)	40	5	TR	0
Sunflower	(1 tsp)	40	5	TR	0
Vegetable oil spray	1.25-second spray	7	1	N/A	0
Spreads					
Butter	(1 Tb)	102	12	7	31

Food	Serving Size	Calories	Fat (g)	Sat. Fat (g)	Chol. (mg)
Butter, whipped	(1 Tb)				
Margarine, stick, corn	(1 Tb)	102	11	2	0
Margarine, stick, safflower & soybean	(1 Tb)	102	11	2	0
Margarine, tub, corn	(1 Tb)	102	11	2	0
Margarine, tub, soybean	(1 Tb)	102	11	2	0
Other					
Bacon fat	(1 Tb)	92	10	3	9
Beef suet	(1 Tb)	117	1300	6	14
Chicken fat	(1 Tb)	115	13	4	11
Vegetable shortening	(1 Tb)	113	13	3	0
Lard	(1 Tb)	116	13	5	12
Butter Buds, prepared	(1 Tb)	6	0	0	TR
FISH AND SHELLFISH					
Bluefish, raw	(1 oz)	35	1	TR	17
Catfish, breaded and fried	(1 oz)	65	4	TR	23
Caviar, mixed	(1 oz)	71	5	N/A	167
Cod, Atlantic, cooked	(1 oz)	30	TR	TR	16
Eel, cooked	(1 oz)	67	4	TR	46
Fish sticks, frozen, reheated	(1 oz)	76	3	TR	31
Flounder, cooked	(1 oz)	33	TR	TR	19
Grouper, cooked	(1 oz)	33	TR	TR	13
Haddock, cooked	(1 oz)	32	TR	TR	21
Halibut, cooked	(1 oz)	40	TR	TR	12
Herring, pickled	(1 oz)	74	5	TR	4
Mackerel, Atlantic, cooked	(1 oz)	74	5	1	21
Pike, Northern, cooked	(1 oz)	32	TR	TR	14
Pompano, cooked	(1 oz)	60	3	1	18
Rockfish, cooked	(1 oz)	34	TR	TR	12
Salmon, Chinook, smoked	(1 oz)	33	1	TR	7
Salmon, Coho, cooked	(1 oz)	52	2	TR	14
Salmon, Sockeye, canned	(1 oz)	43	2	TR	12
Sardine, Atlantic, canned in oil	(1 oz)	59	3	TR	40
Seabass, cooked	(1 oz)	35	TR	TR	15
Snapper, cooked	(1 oz)	36	TR	TR	13
Sole (see Flounder)					
Swordfish, cooked	(1 oz)	44	1	TR	14
Tilefish, cooked	(1 oz)	42	1	TR	N/A

Food	Serving Size	Calories	Fat (g)	Sat. Fat (g)	Chol. (mg)
Trout, rainbow, cooked	(1 oz)	43	1	TR	21
Tuna, light, canned in oil	(1 oz)	56	2	TR	5
Tuna, light, canned in water	(1 oz)	37	TR	TR	12
Tuna, steak, cooked	(1 oz)	52	2	TR	14
Tuna salad: light tuna in oil, pickle relish, salad dressing, onion, celery	(½ cup)	192	9	2	14
Weakfish, cooked N/A	(1 oz)				
Yellowtail, raw	(1 oz)	41	1	N/A	N/A
Shellfish					
Clams, raw	(6)	40	TR	TR	18
Crab, Alaskan king, cooked	(1 oz)	28	TR	TR	15
Crab, blue, cooked	(1 oz)	29	TR	TR	28
Crab cakes, w/egg, fried in veg. oil	(1 cake)	93	5	TR	90
Crayfish, cooked	(1 oz)	32	TR	TR	50
Lobster, northern, steamed	(1 oz)	28	TR	TR	20
Mussels, steamed	(1 oz)	49	1	TR	16
Oyster, eastern, breaded, fried	(1 oz)	56	4	TR	23
Shrimp, cooked	(1 oz)	28	TR	TR	55
Shrimp, breaded, fried	(4 large)	73	4	TR	53
Scallops, fried	(1 oz)	61	3	TR	17
Squid, boiled	(3 oz)	149	6	2	221
FRUIT					
Apple, 2¾" across	(1)	81	TR	TR	0
Applesauce, canned, unsweetened	(½ cup)	52	TR	TR	0
Apricots, medium	(4)	68	TR	TR	0
Banana, 8¾" long (half)		52	TR	TR	0
Blueberries	(¾ cup)	56	TR	N/A	0
Cantaloupe	(1 cup, cubes)	56	TR	N/A	0
Cherries, sweet	(12)	59	TR	TR	0
Figs, medium	(2)	74	TR	TR	
Grapefruit	(half)	38	TR	TR	0
Grapes	(15)	53	TR	TR	0
Honeydew melon	1 cup cubes	60	TR	N/A	

Food	Serving Size	Calories	Fat (g)	Sat. Fat (g)	Chol. (mg)
Kiwi fruit	(1 large)	56	TR	N/A	0
Mango	(half)	67	TR	TR	0
Orange, 2½" across	(1)	69	TR	TR	0
Papaya	(1 cup, cubes)	55	TR	TR	0
Peach, 2½" across	(1)	56	TR	TR	0
Peaches, canned, juice pack	(2 halves)	68	TR	0	0
Pear, 2½" × 3½"	(1)	98	TR	TR	0
Pineapple	(¾ cup, cubes)	57	TR	TR	0
Plum, 2⅛" across	(2)	73	TR	TR	0
Raspberries	(1 cup)	60	TR	TR	0
Strawberries	(1¼ cup)	57	TR	TR	0
Watermelon	(1¼ cup, cubes)	64	TR	N/A	0
Dried Fruits					
Apples	(4 rings)	62	TR	TR	0
Apricots	(7 halves)	58	TR	TR	0
Dates	(2½)	57	TR	N/A	0
Figs	(1½)	72	TR	TR	0
Prunes	(3)	60	TR	TR	0
Raisins	(2 Tb)	54	TR	TR	0
Fruit Juices					
Apple juice	(½ cup)	58	TR	TR	0
Cranberry juice cocktail	(⅓ cup)	46	TR	N/A	0
Grapefruit juice, unsweetened	(½ cup)	47	TR	TR	0
Grape juice	(⅓ cup)	42	TR	TR	0
Orange juice	(½ cup)	56	TR	TR	0
Pineapple juice	(½ cup)	65	TR	0	0
Prune juice	(⅓ cup)	60	TR	0	0
GRAIN PRODUCTS					
Breads					
Bagel	(1)	150	1	N/A	N/A
Biscuit, made w/milk	(1)	92	3	TR	TR
Bread, white	(1 slice)	65	TR	TR	TR
Bun, hamburger, or hotdog	(1)	119	2	TR	2
Corn muffin	(1)	126	4	1	21
Croissant	(1)	170	9	N/A	N/A

Food	Serving Size	Calories	Fat (g)	Sat. Fat (g)	Chol. (mg)
English muffin, plain	(half)	65	TR	N/A	N/A
French baguette	(1 slice)	102	1	TR	1
French toast	(1 slice)	142	8	2	123
Muffin, bran	(1)	104	4	1	41
Pancake, w/egg, milk, 6"	(1)	169	5	1	39
Pita	(1)	174	TR	0	0
Popover	(1)	90	4	1	59
Roll, hard	(1)	156	2	TR	2
Rye bread	(1 slice)	61	TR	TR	TR
Sourdough bread	(1 slice)	68	TR	0	0
Stuffing mix	(½ cup)	130	1	TR	1
Waffle, homemade, 7"	(1)	209	7	2	94
Whole wheat	(1 slice)	56	TR	TR	TR
Cereal **Cooked**					
Hominy grits, regular	(1 cup)	145	TR	N/A	0
Cream of wheat, regular	(1 cup)	133	TR	N/A	0
Oatmeal, regular, quick, instant	(1 cup)	145	2	TR	0
Ready-to-Eat					
Cheerios	(1 oz)	110	2	N/A	0
40% bran flakes	(1 oz)	93	TR	N/A	N/A
Corn flakes, Kellogg's	(1 oz)	100	0	0	0
Granola, homemade N/A	(1 oz)				
Grapenuts	(1 oz)	110	0	0	0
Nutrigrain, wheat	(1 oz)	100	0	0	0
Puffed wheat, plain	(1 oz)	100	0	0	0
Quaker oat squares	(1 oz)	100	2	N/A	0
Shredded wheat	(1 large biscuit)	90	1	N/A	0
Swiss Familia Muesli		106	2	N/A	0
Wheat germ, plain, toasted	(1 oz)	108	3	TR	0
Crackers					
Bread sticks	(5)	96	TR	TR	TR
Cheese crackers, 1" square	(10)	52	2	TR	3
Graham crackers	(4 squares)	109	3	TR	0
Matzo	(1 board)	119	TR	N/A	0
Melba toast	(1)	16	TR	0	0
Oyster crackers	(1)	3	TR	TR	0

Food	Serving Size	Calories	Fat (g)	Sat. Fat (g)	Chol. (mg)
Ritz crackers	(1)	17	1.00	N/A	N/A
Saltine crackers	(10)	12	TR	TR	0
Wheat Thins	(1)	9	TR	N/A	N/A
Zwieback crackers	(4 pieces)	119	3	1	5.8
Pasta and Grains, Cooked					
Bulghur	(1 cup)	151	.4	TR	0
Couscous	(1 cup)	201	.2	TR	0
Noodles, chow mein, canned	(1 cup)	237	14	2	0
Noodles, egg	(1 cup)	213	2	TR	53
Rice, white	(1 cup)	265	TR	TR	0
Spaghetti	(1 cup)	197	TR	TR	0
MEATS					
Beef					
Eye of round, roasted	(1 oz)	48	3	.5	.5
Top round, roasted	(1 oz)	52	2	.7	.2
Flank steak, lean only, choice grade, broiled	(1 oz)	59	3	1	19
Round steak, lean only, broiled	(1 oz)	54	1	TR	22
Top loin steak, lean only, broiled	(1 oz)	55	2	1	22
Chuck roast or steak, blade, lean only, braised	(1 oz)	71	4	1	30
Tenderloin, lean only, broiled	(1 oz)	60	3	1	24
Arm roast or steak, lean only, braised	(1 oz)	61	2	1	29
Corned beef, cooked	(1 oz)	71	5	2	28
Ground beef, extra lean, broiled	(1 oz)	73	5	2	25
lean, broiled	(1 oz)	77	5	2	25
regular, broiled	(1 oz)	82	6	2	26
Short ribs, lean only, braised	(1 oz)	84	5	2	26
Lamb					
Leg, shank portion, roasted LN	(1 oz)	51	2	TR	25
Leg, lean, roasted	(1 oz)	54	2	.8	25
Loin chops, broiled LN	(1 oz)	61	3	TR	27
Rack, rib, roasted LN	(1 oz)	66	4	1	25

Food	Serving Size	Calories	Fat (g)	Sat. Fat (g)	Chol. (mg)
Pork					
Bacon, fried	(2 slices)	73	6	2	11
Canadian bacon, grilled	(1 oz)	52	2	TR	16
Chitterlings, simmered	(1 oz)	86	8	3	41
Fresh pork, lean only					
center loin, fresh, broiled	(1 oz)	65	3	1	28
shoulder, arm picnic, roasted	(1 oz)	65	4	1	27
shoulder, Boston blade, roasted	(1 oz)	73	5	2	28
sirloin, fresh, broiled	(1 oz)	69	4	1	28
tenderloin, roasted	(1 oz)	47	1	TR	26
whole leg, roasted	(1 oz)	62	3	1	27
Ham, boneless					
extra lean, roasted	(1 oz)	41	2	TR	15
canned, extra lean, baked	(1 oz)	39	1	TR	9
canned, regular, baked	(1 oz)	64	4	1	18
Liver, braised	(1 oz)	47	1	TR	101
Spareribs, lean and fat, braised	(1 oz)	113	9	3	34
Veal					
Leg, stew meat, cooked	(1 oz)	53	1	TR	41
Leg cutlet, cooked unbreaded, roasted	(1 oz)	43	TR	TR	29
Boneless loin, roasted	(1 oz)	50	2	TR	30
Rib chop, roasted	(1 oz)	50	2	TR	33
Organ Meats					
Brains, beef, simmered	(1 oz)	45	4	TR	582
Brains, veal, braised	(1 oz)	41	3	TR	579
Kidneys, veal, braised	(1 oz)	46	2	TR	224
Liver, veal, braised	(1 oz)	47	2	TR	159
Sweetbreads, veal, braised	(1 oz)	49	1	N/A	133
Tongue, beef, braised	(1 oz)	80	6	3	30
Tongue, beef, smoked N/A	(1 oz)				
Tripe (raw)	(1 oz)	28	1	TR	27
Luncheon Meat and Sausage					
Bologna, beef, pork	(1 oz)	90	8	3	16

Food	Serving Size	Calories	Fat (g)	Sat. Fat (g)	Chol. (mg)
Braunschweiger, pork	(1 oz)	102	9	3	44
Chicken spread, canned	(2 Tb)				
Frankfurter					
beef and pork	(1 oz)	91	8	3	14
chicken	(1 oz)	73	6	2	29
Pepperoni, pork, beef	(1 oz)	141	12	5	22
Salami, dry, pork, beef	(1 oz)	119	10	3	22
Sausage					
chorizo, beef, pork	(1 oz)	125	11	4	N/A
Italian, pork, cooked	(1 oz)	92	7	3	22
knockwurst, pork, beef	(1 oz)	87	8	3	16
pork, fresh, cooked	(1 oz)	105	9	3	24
liverwurst, pork	(1 oz)	92	8	3	45
Polish, pork	(1 oz)	92	8	3	20
Vienna, beef, pork, canned, 24g	(1½ links)	67	6	2	12
NUTS AND SEEDS					
Almonds	(1 oz)	167	15	1	0
Brazil nuts	(1 oz)	186	19	5	0
Cashews, dry-roasted	(1 oz)	163	13	3	0
Coconut, dried, shredded sweetened	(2 Tb)	44	3	3	0
Filberts (hazelnuts)	(1 oz)	179	18	1	0
Macadamia nuts, oil-roasted	(1 oz)	204	22	3	0
Mixed nuts, dry-roasted	(1 oz)	168	15	2	0
Peanut butter	(1 Tb)	95	8	1	0
Peanuts, dry-roasted (Nabisco)	(1 oz)	170	15	2	0
Peanuts, oil-roasted	(1 oz)	165	14	2	0
Pecans	(1 oz)	189	19	2	0
Pine Nuts	(2 Tb)	93	9	1	0
Pistachios	(1 oz)	164	14	2	0
Pumpkin seeds, whole	(1 oz)	126	6	1	0
Sesame seeds	(1 Tb)	52	4	TR	0
Sunflower seed kernels, toasted	(1 oz)	175	16	2	0
Walnuts, black	(1 oz)	172	16	1	0
Walnuts, English	(1 oz)	182	18	2	0

Food	Serving Size	Calories	Fat (g)	Sat. Fat (g)	Chol. (mg)
POULTRY					
Chicken, Cooked					
Light meat, w/o skin	(1 oz)	49	1	TR	24
w/skin	(1 oz)	63	3	TR	24
Dark meat, w/o skin	(1 oz)	58	3	TR	26
w/skin	(1 oz)	72	4	1	26
Breast, meat only	(1 oz)	47	1	TR	24
meat and skin	(1 oz)	56	2	TR	24
Wing	(1 oz)	82	6	2	24
fried w/batter, meat and skin	(1 oz)	92	6	2	22
Gizzard	(1 oz)	43	1	TR	55
Heart	(1 oz)	52	2	TR	69
Livers	(1 oz)	45	2	TR	179
Roll, chicken, light	(1 oz)	45	2	TR	14
Game					
Duck w/skin, roasted	(1 oz)	96	8	3	24
Duck w/o skin, roasted	(1 oz)	57	3	1	25
Goose w/o skin, roasted	(1 oz)	67	4	1	27
Pheasant w/o skin, raw	(1 oz)	38	TR	TR	N/A
Quail w/o skin, raw	(1 oz)	38	1	TR	N/A
Squab w/o skin, raw	(1 oz)	40	2	TR	N/A
Turkey, Cooked					
Light meat					
meat only, roasted	(1 oz)	44	TR	TR	20
meat w/skin, roasted	(1 oz)	54	2	TR	21
Dark Meat					
meat only, roasted	(1 oz)	52	2	TR	25
meat w/skin, roasted	(1 oz)	61	3	TR	26
Turkey ham, cured thigh meat	(1 oz)	36	1	TR	N/A
pastrami	(1 oz)	40	2	TR	N/A
roll, light and dark meat	(1 oz)	42	2	TR	16
SALAD DRESSINGS					
Blue cheese	(1 Tb)	77	8	2	3
French	(1 Tb)	67	6	1	N/A

Food	Serving Size	Calories	Fat (g)	Sat. Fat (g)	Chol. (mg)
Italian	(1 Tb)	69	7	1	0
Mayonnaise	(1 Tb)	99	11	2	8
Mayonnaise-type	(1 Tb)	57	5	TR	4
Russian	(1 Tb)	76	8	1	N/A
Thousand Island	(1 Tb)	59	6	TR	N/A
Vinegar and oil, Kraft	(1 Tb)	70	7	1	N/A
SOUPS, CANNED					
Bean w/bacon, prepared w/water	(1 cup)	172	6	2	3
Beef broth or bouillon, ready-to-serve	(1 cup)	16	TR	TR	TR
Beef, chunky-style, ready-to-serve	(1 cup)	171	5	3	14
Chicken broth, prepared w/water	(1 cup)	39	1	TR	1
Chicken, chunky-style, ready-to-serve	(1 cup)	178	7	2	30
Chicken noodle, prepared w/water	(1 cup)	75	2	TR	7
Chicken rice, prepared w/water	(1 cup)	60	2	TR	7
Cream of chicken, prepared w/water	(1 cup)	116	7	2	10
Cream of mushroom, prepared w/water	(1 cup)	129	9	2	2
Gazpacho, ready-to-serve N/A	(1 cup)				
Minestrone, prepared w/water	(1 cup)	83	3	TR	2
Oyster stew, prepared w/water	(1 cup)	59	4	3	14
Split pea w/ham, prepared w/water	(1 cup)	189	4	2	8
Tomato, prepared w/water	(1 cup)	86	2	TR	0
Tomato rice, prepared w/water	(1 cup)	120	3	TR	0
Vegetarian vegetable, prepared w/water	(1 cup)	72	2	TR	0
SWEETS AND DESSERTS					
Banana bread N/A	(1 slice)				
Brownies, w/nuts 3″ × 1″ × ⅞″	(1 slice)	97	6	1	TR

Food	Serving Size	Calories	Fat (g)	Sat. Fat (g)	Chol. (mg)
Cake, w/o frosting					
angel food 1/16 of 9¾" tube	(1 slice)	117	TR	N/A	0
devil's food 2" × 2" × 2"	(1 slice)	143	7	2	2
white, 2-layer 1/8 of 8" cake	(1 slice)	311	13	3	2
Boston cream pie, 2-layer 1/12 of 8" cake	(1 slice)	208	6	2	59
fruit cake dark, ¼" × 2" × 1½" w/butter	(1 slice)	54	2	TR	10
pound cake 3½" × 3" × ½"	(1 slice)	142	9	2	44
sponge cake 1/16 of 9¾" tube	(1 slice)	146	3	TR	12
yellow, 2-layer 1/8 of 8" cake	(1 slice)	309	11	3	46
Cake frosting					
chocolate, prepared w/milk and fat	(1 Tb)	65	2	1	3
coconut w/boiled frosting	(1 Tb)	38	TR	TR	0
fudge made w/water, from mix w/butter	(1 Tb)	59	2	1	4
white boiled	(1 Tb)	19	0	0	0
Cookies, sandwich 1¾" × 3/8"	(1)	50	2	TR	4
chocolate chip 1¾" × ½"	(1)	30	2	TR	3
fig bars 1½" × 1¾" × ½"	(1)	50	TR	TR	5
gingersnaps 2" × ¼"	(1)	29	TR	TR	3
macaroons 2¾" × ¼"	(1)	90	4	3	21
oatmeal w/raisin 2⅝" × ¼"	(1)	59	2	TR	5
sugar w/butter 1 oz	(1)	126	5	1	11
Doughnut, plain 3¼" × 1"	(1)	164	8	2	25
Pastry, Danish, plain 4¼" × 1"	(1)	274	15	5	42
Pie, apple, 2 crust 1/8 of 9" pie	(1 slice)	302	13	3	0
cherry, 2 crust 1/8 of 9" pie	(1 slice)	308	13	4	0
custard 1/8 of 8" pie	(1 slice)	249	13	4	12

Food	Serving Size	Calories	Fat (g)	Sat. Fat (g)	Chol. (mg)
lemon meringue ⅛ of 9″ pie	(1 slice)	268	11	3	9
pumpkin ⅛ of 9″ pie	(1 slice)	241	13	5	7
pecan ⅛ of 9″ pie	(1 slice)	431	24	3	6
Pie crust, baked (⅛ of 9″ diameter)		113	8	2	0
Candy					
Caramels, plain or chocolate	(1 oz)	113	3	2	TR
Chocolate Dark, plain	(1 oz)	156	9	N/A	N/A
Milk, plain	(1 oz)	147	9	5	6
Milk, w/almonds	(1 oz)	151	10	5	5
Chocolate coated peanuts	(8 to 16)	159	12	3	TR
Chocolate kisses	(6)	147	9	N/A	N/A
Fudge, plain	(1 oz)	113	3	1	TR
Gumdrops	(1 oz)	98	TR	N/A	0
Hard candy	(1 oz)	109	TR	N/A	0
Marshmallow	(1 oz)	90	0	0	TR
Mints, uncoated	(1 oz)	116	3	TR	TR

VEGETABLES

For all-fat-budgeting purposes, vegetables are virtually fat free and have no cholesterol, with the exception of avocado, which is cholesterol-free but contains 31 grams of fat per avocado.

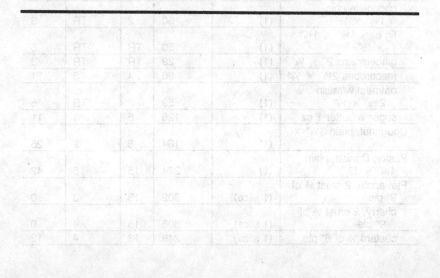

APPENDIX B

Your Fat Gram Allowance:
How It's Figured

The average American diet derives 40 percent of its calories from fat. Everyone agrees that's too high. While experts recommend a 30 percent fat level as a goal, many also point out that a 25 percent or 20 percent diet may be more protective or even necessary for protection where certain cancers are concerned.

The chart on page 30 will give you fat figures based on one's average calorie consumption. Here's how the figures are arrived at:

Calories are units of food energy. For a man who consumes 2500 calories daily of the average American diet, 40 percent of that energy, or 1000 calories, is supplied by fat.

There are 9 calories in a gram of fat, so by dividing 1000 by 9 (1000 ÷ 9) we learn he is presently eating 111 grams of fat daily. If no more than 30 percent of his calories are to derive from fat, he must take 30 percent of his daily 2500, which is 750 calories. Divide that number by 9 (750 ÷ 9) and you get 83. Thus, his 30 percent allowance will allow him 83 grams of fat daily.

This calculation remains the same for any calorie intake level and can be used to determine any fat percentage desired.

APPENDIX C

The Bottom Line: Q. & A.

Here are some food questions people frequently ask me, with answers that may be useful in meal planning.

Q. *You say fatty fishes are now desirable. But I've read that striped bass and bluefish are not safe because of high mercury levels.*

A. Two indicators of contamination from environmental pollution are a fish's habitat and its fat content.

Bottom line: Stripers and blues, because they are near-shore fish, are more likely to be contaminated than farther offshore or deep-water fish, like yellowfin tuna and haddock. Fatty fish such as salmon and swordfish also tend to accumulate contaminants. All can be eaten in limited quantities. You're safe with a variety.

Q. *If I'm trying to eat in a healthy way, shouldn't I pay attention to beta-carotenes?*

A. Many vegetables and fruits contain carotenes, a family of orange pigments that the body converts to Vitamin A. They are found in sweet potatoes, red peppers, the winter squashes, and carrots; they are also in kale, collards, spinach, and turnip, beet, mustard, and dandelion greens, where the chlorophyll drowns out the color. The "cruciferous" vegetables also contain them: broccoli, brussels sprouts, and the cabbages. Ditto fruits like mango, papaya, cantaloupe, dried apricots, nectarines, tangerines, and oranges.

No one knows for sure how beta-carotenes operate. One theory is that they sop up free radicals and singlet oxygen, substances thought to damage DNA and perhaps lead to tumors. Another theory is that beta-carotenes might act by stimulating the immune system. Smokers especially should make a point of eating more fruits and vegetables rich in carotene, since some evidence links these foods to a reduced risk of lung cancer and tobacco-related mouth cancers. At the very least they will give you some additional fiber and help you to eat fewer calories as fat. Better still: Stop smoking.

Bottom line: The National Cancer Institute has urged the public to eat more fruits and vegetables rich in carotenes, but until a ten-year study and other trials are completed, no one will know for sure that beta-carotenes work—or how. In the meantime, vitamin supplements that contain beta-carotenes aren't recommended to anyone other than smokers.

As long as we don't know which carotene or carotenes confer protection, however, it is a good idea for everyone to try and eat a full complement of carotenes from natural sources.

Q. *If fat is so bad for you, aren't the new synthetic fats a good idea?*
A. Many people believe that products like NutraSweet's Simplesse, made from the protein of egg whites or milk whey and P & G's Olestra, a compound of sugar and fatty acids generically known as sucrose polyester, are the answer to this fat-loving country's health problems. Whether these products will have a significant impact on our health is another issue. After all, artificial sweeteners have been around for 20 years, and the population is not getting any thinner (in fact, people are heavier). And there is the danger that when foods made with these products become available to the public they are used as an excuse for binging on other high-fat foods.

Bottom line: Artificial fats are not a substitute for a lifestyle change that combines healthful foods with continual, moderate exercise. Furthermore, the first ice creams to be made with synthetic fats were on the whole poorly received by food critics.

Q. *What's all the fuss about tropical oils? How can vegetable oils be bad for you?*
Bottom line: Coconut, palm, and palm kernel oils, collectively called tropical oils, are widely used in the food industry because they stay fresh longer than other oils, are less likely to give off-flavor to food products, and are more economical. However, while not of animal origin, they are highly saturated and thus have a strong potential to raise serum or blood cholesterol. Palm kernel oil and coconut oil are about three times as saturated as lard. Palm oil, about as saturated as butterfat and so slightly less saturated than the other two, is, in addition, rich in palmitic acid, one of the most potent cholesterol-raising saturated fats.

Consumer groups have led the fight to alter the use of these oils because those highly at risk for a heart attack know the potential danger of tropical oils. As of this writing, 13 major food manufacturers have announced they will be reformulating many products to use less saturated fat.

Q. *I have high cholesterol. Will psyllium help reduce it?*
A. Psyllium, the husk of a grain grown in India, is best known as the main ingredient in Metamucil, a laxative. Like oat bran, it is high in soluble fiber, so any of the benefits implicit in adding soluble fiber to your diet might possibly apply.

Bottom line: Not enough is known at present about psyllium's use as a food, and, like other food fads, it should not replace a healthy diversity of foods containing soluble fiber. In any case, no *one* food will solve a high cholesterol problem, which should be discussed with your physician.

Q. *What about low-fat diets for children and adolescents?*
A. Strict low-fat diets can be dangerous for young children, particularly during the first two years of life; they can interfere with normal growth and should not be started without consulting a physician. (This is especially true for children who have moderately high or elevated cholesterol levels, as there are, at the moment, no fixed guidelines for managing high cholesterol in children.)

While adults are wise to use low-fat or skim milk, this source of readily absorbed calcium is an important part of a very young child's diet. Therefore, low-fat or skim milk should not be introduced before the age of two. In general, a moderately low-fat diet that features a variety of foods will not harm a child over the age of two years. The basic elements are much the same as for their parents—fish, poultry, lean meats, egg consumption limited to three or four a week, whole-grain breads and cereals, fruits and vegetables.

As far as snack or junk food is concerned: Try to provide interesting, non-junk snacks and low-fat, vitamin-rich dinners and turn a blind eye to the occasional fast-food binge. Kids require a tremendous amount of energy to grow, so snacking isn't that awful. Much worse would be to turn them off of healthy eating entirely by constant carping.

Bottom line: In the best of all possible worlds, your children will embrace your new way of eating with enthusiasm. The fact is, that depending on their ages, you may be faced with anything from complete acquiescence to downright rebellion. Be prepared for anything and don't be deterred from your chosen course. If you're having fish, and they turn up their noses, you can always give them pasta, which most kids seem to thrive on and adore.

Furthermore, remember that temporary preferences for single foods are very common among younger children. Don't withhold the favored food while this is going on; just offer a small portion of it along with other foods.

Do push for organized physical activity for youngsters of all ages, which helps reduce body fat stores and raise the level of protective HDL cholesterol.

Q. *I love chocolate. I read that it doesn't raise cholesterol. Does that mean I can indulge when I feel like it?*

Bottom line: The good news about chocolate is that cocoa butter, its fat component, has been shown not to cause the increase in blood cholesterol that might be expected based on its saturated fat content. This is because more than half the saturated fat is stearic acid, which does not raise cholesterol levels. However, it's still fat (44 grams in a 4-ounce candy bar), so prudence is indicated.

APPENDIX D

Glossary

Butter granules: These are low-fat, low-calorie, low-sodium instant natural butter-flavored granules (like Butter Buds) containing no cholesterol, made by blending spray-dried butter with other natural ingredients. They add a melted butter flavor to foods. They may be turned into a liquid by adding water or may be sprinkled in dry form directly on hot, moist foods such as potatoes, vegetables, fish, and hot cereals. They may also be used dry on spaghetti and popcorn. The liquid can be used with baked potatoes, green beans, corn on the cob, noodles, rice, and pancakes, and in gravies, sauces, and soups. They are available in a box of eight ½-ounce packets or a 2.5-ounce jar.

- ½ teaspoon of Butter Buds sprinkles = the taste of 2 teaspoons (10 grams) butter
- 1 packet (8 teaspoons) mixed with ½ cup (4 ounces) hot tap water yields 4 ounces liquid "butter"

Foods containing Butter Buds liquid may be simmered or boiled. Any leftover liquid should be refrigerated and used within three days. Because this product is practically fat-free, it cannot be used for frying.

Canola oil: This is a variety of rapeseed (mustard family) oil, a polyunsaturate originally developed and grown in Canada, hence the acronym "Canada oil." Of the cooking oils, it is lowest in saturated fat and second only to olive oil in monounsaturates.

Cocoa: Because of its fat content, chocolate is high in fat and saturated fat. Many recipes calling for hard chocolate can be made lower in fat by substituting cocoa powder. The standard equivalent is 3 tablespoons for every 1 ounce of chocolate, plus 1 tablespoon of some shortening (to replace the fat). I've found this is usually not necessary, especially if you use a really terrific cocoa. One I highly recommend and use myself is the rich and intense Pernigotti cocoa, imported from Italy and sold through the Williams-Sonoma chain. It is available in 13.5-ounce tins at all their stores, and may be ordered by writing or calling their mail order department. Williams-Sonoma, 100 North Point Street, San Francisco, CA 94133; tel: 415-421-4242.

Egg substitutes: Two alternatives to using high-fat, high-cholesterol eggs are: Use only the whites, which contain all the protein and no fat or cholesterol, or use an egg substitute, such as Egg Beaters, which is fat-free. A third possibility is to combine an egg white with ¼ cup Egg Beaters if, say, you are making scrambled eggs. This gives you some real egg flavor.

Note that ¼ cup Egg Beaters is equivalent nutritionally to one medium egg; if you are making a substitution in a recipe calling for large or extra-large eggs, use the same amount for each egg.

Evaporated skim milk: This is canned, heat-sterilized concentrated skim milk (about half the water has been removed). Once the can is opened, the contents should be refrigerated (tightly sealed) and used within about five days.

Legumes: A legume is any vegetable that is the seed of a plant having pods. Beans, peas (fresh and dried), lima beans, soy beans, and lentils are among the legumes we eat. A peanut is a legume as well. Because all legumes absorb nitrogen from the air (a second characteristic that distinguishes them from other vegetables) they are a rich source of protein.

Olive oil, extra-virgin: This is olive oil made from the first pressing. It is golden if made from ripe olives and greenish if partly ripe fruit is used. It has a pronounced, fruity olive oil flavor and is best in salads and pastas where this is desirable. Extra-virgin olive oil is also slightly less acidic than regular olive oil.

Olive oil, virgin: This also comes directly from the fruit but may result from a second pressing. It has a nutty overtone.

Peanut oil: This is a polyunsaturate, for limited use in stir-frying. It doesn't burn until it has reached 440°. Chinese peanut oil has more flavor than Planter's, the kind found in most supermarkets.

Reduced-sodium soy sauce: This has from 33⅓ to 40 percent less sodium than regular soy sauce, depending on the brand. Read the label.

Sesame oil: Dark-brown Chinese sesame oil is frequently called for as a seasoning and in salads. Do not confuse it with the odorless pale-yellow sesame oil often found in health food stores. Because dark sesame oil has a low burning point (420°), it is never used for frying.

Sun-dried tomatoes: Available at specialty food stores, sun-dried tomatoes give interesting depth of flavor to many dishes, especially those calling for regular tomatoes. Sun-dried tomatoes can also be used in assorted antipasti, with thin slices of mozzarella and in salads. Two kinds are available: dry-packed and those cured in olive oil. The former are much less expensive, and, for our purposes, more desirable. If you can find only those in olive oil, rinse the oil off briefly with boiling water. Five sun-dried tomatoes weigh about 1 ounce, or ¼ cup chopped.

APPENDIX E

Special Products

Bamboo steamers: These are available in 4- to 16-inch diameters and are now found in many housewares stores. My 10-inch bamboo steamer is just right for my needs and fits nicely in my wok. Always use it with either the wok lid or the steamer's own bamboo lid on. Do not clean it with harsh detergents and dry it thoroughly after using it.

Calphalon griddle: Of heavy-gauge anodized aluminum, this 20½- × 12½-inch griddle fits across two burners on a gas or electric stove for almost fat-free contact cooking of eggs and pancakes. The other side is ridged, great for quickly grilling flattened chicken breasts, hamburgers, and so forth.

Gravy Strain (®): This is a fat separator cup with a cunning long spout, used to remove fat from soups, stocks, sauces, and gravies. I try to keep gadgets at a minimum, but this one I find indispensable. Made of FDA-approved Lexan, it comes in 1-cup and 4-cup sizes, and is found in better housewares stores.

Kitchen scale: This is useful for weighing food portions (both cooked and raw) until you train your eye, as well as for weighing nuts, grains, pasta, and other foods whose measurements are often given in weight rather than volume. Check the accuracy of the scale by weighing a small item of known weight, like a 4-ounce stick of margarine.

Non-stick pans: These are indispensable for low-fat cooking. A T-Fal pan is quite adequate for quick sautéing and the one I grab most frequently. Wearever's Silverstone and top-of-the-line Supra are heavy commercial-gauge aluminum pans with non-stick interiors and removable handles so the pan can be popped into the oven or under the broiler if required. Sizes range from 7- to 14-inch diameters in the Silverstone line, 8 to 12 inches in the Supra line. Lids are available.

BIBLIOGRAPHY AND REFERENCE MATERIAL

BIBLIOGRAPHY

Gorbach, Sherwood, David Zimmerman, and Margo Woods. *The Doctors' Anti-Breast Cancer Diet*. New York: Simon & Schuster, 1984.

Ornish, Dean. *Stress, Diet & Your Heart*. New York: Holt, Rinehart & Winston, 1982.

Pritikin, Nathan. *The Pritikin Promise: 28 Days to a Longer, Healthier Life*. New York: Simon & Schuster, 1983.

Saltman, Paul, Ph.D., Joel Gurin, and Ira Motherer. *California Nutrition Book*. Boston: Little, Brown & Co., 1987.

REFERENCES

Tannenbaum, A., "The Genesis and Growth of Tumors. III. Effects of a High Fat Diet." *Cancer Research* (1942), 2:468–475.

Karmali, R.A., J. Marsh, and C. Fuchs, "Effect of Omega-3 Fatty Acids on Growth of a Rat Mammary Tumor." *Journal of National Cancer Institute* (1984), 73 (2): 457–61.

Toniolo, Paolo, *et al.*, "Calorie-Providing Nutrients and Risk of Breast Cancer." *Journal of National Cancer Institute* (Feb. 15, 1989).

National Academy of Sciences, Committee on Diet, Nutrition and Cancer. *Diet, Nutrition and Cancer*. Washington, D.C.: National Academy Press, 1982.

The Surgeon General's Report on Nutrition and Health. Washington, D.C.: U.S.
  Department of Health and Human Services (Oct. 1988).
Tufts University Diet and Nutrition Letter, II, 10 (Dec. 1989).
Stone, Sally and Martin. *The Brilliant Bean.* New York: Bantam 1988.

REFERENCES FOR APPENDIX A

USDA AGRICULTURE HANDBOOK No 8 SERIES

Series #	Food Group	Year
8–1	Dairy and Egg Products	1976
8–4	Fats and Oils	1979
8–5	Poultry Products	1979
8–6	Soups, Sauces and Gravies	1980
8–7	Sausages and Luncheon Meats	1980
8–8	Breakfast Cereals	1982
8–10	Pork Products	1983
8–11	Vegetables and Vegetable Products	1984
8–12	Nut and Seed Products	1984
8–13	Beef	1986
8–14	Beverages	1987
8–15	Finfish and Shellfish Products	1987
8–16	Legumes	1986
8–17	Lamb, Veal and Game	1989
8–20	Cereals, Grains and Pasta	1989
8–21	Fast Foods	1988

USDA Nutritive Value of American Foods in Common Units, Agricultural Handbook No. 456, 1975 (plus 1989 updates).

USDA Provisional Table on the Fatty Acids and Cholesterol Content of Selected Foods, 1984.

Nutrient Values of Muscle Foods, 1st Edition, National Meat and Livestock Board, Chicago, 1988 (based on USDA data).

Manufacturer's Data.

INDEX

Italicized words are recipe titles.